RESOURCES

FOR THE

TEACHING OF

ANTHROPOLOGY

RESOURCES FOR THE TEACHING OF ANTHROPOLOGY

EDITED BY

David G. Mandelbaum,
Gabriel W. Lasker,
Ethel M. Albert

Including "A Basic List of Books and Periodicals
for College Libraries," compiled by Rexford S. Beckham
with the assistance of Marie P. Beckham

Memoir 95
AMERICAN ANTHROPOLOGICAL ASSOCIATION

*This volume is also published in a trade
edition by the University of California Press*

©*1963 by David G. Mandelbaum*
Library of Congress Catalog Card Number: 63-9935
Designed by John B. Goetz
Printed in the United States of America

Memoirs Editor: Fred Eggan

Contents

GABRIEL W. LASKER

Introduction

THERE IS A DEARTH of information on anthropology courses and teachers and on books and visual aids helpful in teaching anthropology. The present volume gives some information on these matters. The material is of several sorts, and different chapters will prove of interest to different individuals. Thus, a person responsible for classroom teaching may be interested in teaching aids (Chapter V) and how to use them (Chapter IV) and in lists of books relating to the subjects he teaches which the college library should have (Chapter VII). Those responsible for development of the department of anthropology, whether they are experienced members of the department or college administrators, may well be interested in the status and trends in anthropology teaching (Chapters I and II), as well as in the building of a library (Chapter VI) and personnel problems (Chapter III). Finally, those concerned about the profession more generally, whether officers of professional societies or ordinary members, may find reasons to consult all the chapters, for the prospects for jobs in anthropology, the status of teaching of the subject, and the availability of books and teaching aids are all pertinent to the development of the discipline and its institutions.

The survey of college catalogs (Chapter I) provided an opportunity to enumerate changes in courses during the decade since Erminie Wheeler-Voegelin (1950) made her study. Few government publications give separate statistics for anthropology, but data from the U.S. Department of Education on earned degrees in anthropology are included and analyzed in Chapter I.

Chapter II deals with enrollments and staff in anthropology courses in the State of California. Comparable data for the rest of the country would be very valuable but is difficult and expensive to obtain. A study within a local region enabled us to locate all institutions where anthropology is taught and to find out something about the teaching of anthropology in almost all of them. By repeated letters, telephone calls, and personal visits, we were able to fill in most items of information (in the questionnaire on which the survey is based) for over 90 per cent of all California institutions and to include every institution with a large program in anthropology. The colleges for which it was most difficult to get completed questionnaires were, in general, small institutions in which one or two courses in anthropology are taught by a nonanthropologist. Therefore, if one attempted a study of a national sample but had a lower percentage of returns, in extrapolating one would do well to assume that the institutions missed have many fewer students of anthropology and more nonanthropologist teachers of the subject than the schools which respond. One type of information lacking in the analysis in Chapter II which should be made good in a future survey is on actual size of classes in various types of institutions and courses. It would be interesting to know to what extent the increases in enrollments are met by new classes and added sections and to what extent by large lecture sections, with or without discussion sections.

In Chapter III Ralph Beals anticipates a probable shortage of teachers of anthropology in the next ten years and discusses the need to train students to fill the potential vacancies. He also calls for better exchange of information on new openings and applicants.

Women with training in anthropology could be utilized better than they now are in teaching. In his paper on the anthropology curriculum, David Mandelbaum mentions the possible use as readers and teaching assistants of women who cannot take a full time job. California statistics suggest that women anthropologists may be more highly trained than male teachers in comparable jobs (Chapter II). Beatrice Miller, in a letter to *Current Anthropology* (1961), notes that university rules concerning nepotism create a special problem in a field such as anthropology where husband-wife fieldwork teams are deemed desirable. Full use of the capacities of all trained anthropologists would not meet the whole problem of anticipated needs for teachers. As Eggan says in his paper on graduate training, we need a realistic appraisal of our various needs and should shape our graduate programs in part to their measure.

Chapters IV and V deal with audio-visual resources. In the former, Birdwhistell considers how and where to use them and, equally important, how and where not to use them. Some of the presently available materials of this type for use in courses in physical anthropology are listed in Chapter V. The exact method of use of specific materials in particular types of courses is lacking from Chapter V, but in the papers on the introductory and advanced courses in physical anthropology a few films, slides, and other materials are singled out as particularly appropriate. Baerreis does the same for archaeology in his paper on teaching techniques in that subject.

There are many motion pictures which show life in various parts of the world, but exceedingly few have been made specifically for the teaching of anthropological concepts. In 1960, Mr. Robert G. Gardner, of the Film Study Center of the Peabody Museum at Harvard, prepared the following list of twenty films as examples of those useful in teaching anthropology:

All My Babies	*Nanook of the North*
Bathing Babies in Three Cultures	*Nomads of the Jungle*
Farrebique	*On the Bowery*
Four Families	*Pather Panchali*
Grass	*Primitive People*
The Hunters	*The Quiet One*
Lascaux, Cradle of Man't Art	*Social Behavior of Rhesus Monkeys*
Loon's Necklace	*Song of Ceylon*
Man of Aran	*Trance and Dance in Bali*
Moana	*Walkabout*

I would add *Baboon Behavior, Angotee,* and *North Indian Village* to any general list of films for teaching anthropology. Two catalogs of anthropological films (Audio-visual Center, Indiana University, 1960; and Audio-visual Aids Library, Pennsylvania State University, 1960) each list over 350 films, but both omit many worthwhile items. One includes only five of Gardner's selected list of twenty films and the other only eight.

New ethnographic films suitable for classroom use are constantly appearing. For instance, American Indian Films (Kroeber Hall, University of California, Berkeley), has released three: *The Sinew-Backed Bow and Its Arrow, Pine Nuts—a Food of the Paiute and Washo Indians of California and Nevada,* and *Buckeyes—a Food of the California Indians.* There is a need not only to encourage the production of films for class use but also to list them on a continuing basis. Although some moving pictures such as *Grass* and *Nanook* remain valuable teaching aids decades after they are produced, many films become obsolete at least as rapidly as textbooks, and there is no opportunity for revised editions of films. This, and the fact that most films were not planned specifically for teaching, necessitates selecting parts of films and carefully setting them in the context of other materials of the course, as Birdwhistell notes.

No comprehensive lists of colored slides for the purpose of teaching anthropology is available. Since needs vary so greatly and slides are produced in such number and diversity, cataloguing is impractical. Many museums sell color slides. Thus, the American Museum of Natural History in New York, sells slides on ancient man, Mexican archaeology, Melanesia, Micronesia, and the art of Africa and Peru. The University of Wisconsin Anthropological Slide Project offers for sale two large sets on fossil man and twelve sets of slides on archaeological excavations and objects found in them from selected sites in Guatemala, the Greater Antilles, Venezuela, and various areas and prehistoric periods in the United States. Professor Jack R. Conrad of the Department of Sociology and Anthropology, Southwestern University, Memphis, Tennessee, has available for sale a set of slides on symbol systems, technology, social organization, religion, and the arts.

In general, slides and movies serve best for presenting anthropological concepts in the framework of one or a few cultures. Sets on single cultures, fully described and keyed to textual material, help most in teaching anthropology. After all, students have seen many good pictures of native life in magazines and elsewhere. For such images to be useful in learning anthropology, they have to be related to each other and to the anthropological interpretation of whatever is shown.

In cultural anthropology and linguistics, records and tape recordings have a proper place. Thus, in demonstrating cultural continuity and change, African music may be compared with Latin American music and North American jazz. Folkway Records (117 West 46th Street, New York) has issued much authentic "ethnic" music collected by anthropologists. For cultural anthropology, the "Ways of Mankind" records are useful (made under the direction of Walter Goldschmidt of the University of California at Los Angeles and available from the National Association of Educational Broadcasting, University of Illinois, Urbana). Although taken from a radio program and hence presented for the general public rather than the college student, these records present anthropological concepts in connection with concrete episodes and are especially useful in stimulating the interest of beginning students.

Television as a teaching resource in anthropology is not dealt with in the present volume, although a number of anthropology courses have been given on television (for instance at Chicago City Junior College, Wayne State University, and the University of Kentucky). At the 1960 meeting of the American Association of Physical Anthropologists, Dr. Charles E. Snow of the University of Kentucky described his experience with an open-circuit television course in physical anthropology. One point which he emphasized is that instructional television can bring the student magnified images in great detail. Visual aids can be blown up so that every student can see them properly. In discussing a closed-circuit television course in social science at Michigan State University in which he taught, J. C. Messenger, Jr. (1960), notes that television teaching presents distinct challenges and opportunities, but that students miss a great deal by not having face-to-face relationships with their instructors in the classroom.

Chapters VI and VII are intended to aid in the building of an anthropology library. John Rowe's paper treats some principles of acquisition. The library list assembled by Rex Beckham is arranged so as to facilitate locating some of the salient books in a particular subject. The increased enrollments in anthropology put a heavy burden on the library, since the librarian is unable to increase the number of copies of out-of-print books and may be unwilling to purchase adequate numbers of those in print to meet what he thinks may be only a temporary need.

The discussion of resources might well have been extended to deal more fully with books about anthropology. It seemed, however, that textbooks are best discussed in connection with specific types of courses. Many of the papers (Hymes, Pike, Lasker, Washburn, Leslie, Paul, among others) give just such kinds of bibliographic information. Furthermore, there is at present a rapid rate of publication of new books of readings, textbooks, and reprints, so any list is soon obsolete. Morris Opler (1961) briefly discusses some fifty books on cultural anthropology available as paperbacks.

Another publishing development important for the teaching of anthropology is the availabity of reprints of articles in quantity for student use. Review articles appearing in *Current Anthropology* are available in this form at cost. The *Scientific American* issues its "Readings in Life Sciences," which include reprints of several articles on evolution and genetics. The Bobbs-Merrill Company issues reprints of sociological articles (including a number from anthropological journals) and is planning a similar service for anthropology. The difficulty with using journal articles and reprints in teaching is that many of the articles were originally written for a different audience—either fellow researchers or the general public. There is still a great need for materials prepared specifically to fit the student's needs. Commercial publishers to some extent meet this in respect to textbooks, but if there is to be a development of new courses and the preparation of readings, textual material, visual aids, and exercises to go with them, interested anthropologists and foundations will have to collaborate to produce them. The present inventory of resources for the teaching of anthropology may provide a starting point for such enterprises.

REFERENCES CITED

AUDIO-VISUAL AIDS LIBRARY, Pennsylvania State University
    1960   Films for Sociology and Anthropology available from the Pennsyl-
            vania State University Audio-Visual Aids Library, University Park,
            Pa.
AUDIO-VISUAL CENTER, Indiana University
    1960   Films for Anthropology. Bulletin of the Audio-Visual Center, Divi-
            sion of University Extension, Indiana University vol. 5, no. 6. Bloom-
            ington, Indiana.
MESSENGER, JOHN C., JR.
    1960   The teaching of anthropology in a general education program. *In*
            teaching anthropology, A. H. Whiteford, ed. Beloit College, Beloit,
            Wisconsin.
MILLER, BEATRICE
    1961   Current Anthropology 2:299.
OPLER, MORRIS E.
    1961   Cultures and customs throughout history. New York Herald Tribune
            Book Review, January 15, 1961, section 11, pp. 10, 12, 38.
VOEGELIN, ERMINIE W.
    1950   Anthropology in American universities. American Anthropologist
            52:350-391.

GABRIEL W. LASKER
*with the assistance of Zenon Pohorecky
and Lewis Klein*

I. *A Survey of Catalog Listings in Anthropology*

T HIS STUDY is based on data that have been compiled from catalogs of 66 of the United States colleges and universities which offer a degree with a major in anthropology. The catalogs were those available in 1960, and the data will be referred to that year even though the dates of the catalogs vary (Table 1). The survey also shows changes in course offerings in the past decade, using as a base line information taken from a survey done by Dr. Erminie Voegelin (1950), who used catalogs of the 1948-1950 period current in 1950. She found that anthropology was being taught in 305 of the 600 institutions whose catalogs she examined.

THE SAMPLE

It was not feasible for us to survey all anthropology courses offered in United States institutions of higher learning. Even the extensive Voegelin survey of 1950 omitted all junior colleges, and it did not include summer sessions, extension courses, or offerings at several hundred four-year colleges. A total survey now would be an even greater task. The data for this survey were gathered from the catalogs of all the colleges and universities which are listed as having awarded degrees with

7

TABLE 1

State	Name of Institution	Dates of Catalogs Used
I. Independent Department of Anthropology: total, 33		
Arizona	University of Arizona	1959–60, 1960–61
California	Stanford University	1960–61
	University of California, Berkeley	1960–61
	University of Southern California	1960–61
Colorado	University of Colorado	1958–60
	University of Denver	1960–61
Connecticut	Yale University	1959–60, 1960–61 (College and Graduate School)
District of Columbia	Catholic University of America	1958–59
Hawaii	University of Hawaii	1960–61
Illinois	Northwestern University	1960–61
	Southern Illinois University	1960–61
	University of Chicago	1960–61
	University of Illinois	1960–61
Indiana	Indiana University	1961–62
Kentucky	University of Kentucky	1958–59
Louisiana	Tulane University	1960–61
Massachusetts	Brandeis University	1959–60
	Harvard University	1959–60, 1960–61 (Including Radcliffe)
Michigan	University of Michigan	1960–61
Minnesota	University of Minnesota	1960–62
Nebraska	University of Nebraska	1959–60
New Mexico	University of New Mexico	1959–60
New York	Columbia University	1960–61 (Including Barnard, Columbia College, Fac. Pol. Sci.)
	Hamilton College	1958–59
Oklahoma	University of Oklahoma	1958–59
Oregon	University of Oregon	1960–61, 1961–62
Pennsylvania	University of Pennsylvania	1958–59, 1959–60, 1960–61, 1961–62 (Including College and Graduate School, Coll. Lib. Arts Women, Coll. Collateral Courses)
Texas	University of Texas	1959–61
Utah	University of Utah	1960–61
Washington	Washington State University	1960–61, 1961–62
	University of Washington	1959–61
Wisconsin	Beloit College	1959–60
	University of Wisconsin	1960–62

TABLE 1 (*Continued*)

State	Name of Institution	Dates of Catalogs Used
II. Programs of Anthropology: total, 4		
California	University of California, Riverside (Division of Social Sciences)	1960–61
	Sacramento State College	1960–61
	San Francisco State College (Division of Social Sciences)	1960–61
Oregon	Reed College (Division of History and Social Sciences)	1959–60
III. Combined Departments: total, 27		
Arkansas	University of Arkansas (Sociology and Anthropology)	1958–59
California	University of California, Los Angeles (Anthropology and Sociology)	1960–61
	University of California, Davis (Anthropology and Geography)	1960–61
	University of California, Santa Barbara (Sociology-Anthropology)	1956–59
District of Columbia	American University (Sociology and Anthropology)	1956–59
Florida	Florida State University	1957–58, 1959–60 (Undergraduate, Graduate)
	University of Florida (Sociology and Anthropology)	1960–61
Illinois	Wheaton College (Sociology and Anthropology)	1960–61
Kansas	University of Kansas (Sociology and Anthropology)	1959–60, 1960–61
Michigan	Michigan State University (Sociology and Anthropology)	1960–61
	Wayne State University (Sociology and Anthropology)	1958–59
Missouri	University of Missouri (Sociology and Anthropology)	1960
Montana	Montana State University (Sociology and Anthropology)	1959–60
New York	Brooklyn College (Sociology and Anthropology)	1960–62
	City College, City of New York (Sociology and Anthropology)	1960–61
	Cornell University (Sociology and Anthropology)	1961–62
	Hunter College, City of New York (Sociology and Anthropology)	1960–61
	New York University (Sociology and Anthropology)	1960–61
	Queens College, City of New York (Anthropology and Sociology)	1960–61

TABLE 1 *(Continued)*

State	Name of Institution	Dates of Catalogs Used
	Syracuse University (Sociology and Anthropology)	1959–61
	Vassar College (Economics, Sociology and Anthropology)	1960–61
North Carolina	University of North Carolina (Sociology and Anthropology)	1960–61
Ohio	Ohio State University (Sociology and Anthropology)	1960–61
Pennsylvania	Bryn Mawr	1960–61, 1959–60 Grad.
Texas	Texas Technological Institute (History, Anthropology and Sociology)	1958–59
Virginia	University of Virginia (Sociology and Anthropology)	1960–61, 1961–62 Grad.
Wisconsin	Lawrence College (Anthropology and Sociology)	1958–59

Host Departments: total, 2

Maryland	Goucher College (Sociology)	1960
New York	Fordham University (Political Philosophy and Social Science)	1959–61

a major in anthropology in the academic year 1957-58 (Gertler 1959). This list was somewhat revised, in that two institutions were added, and the several campuses of the University of California, grouped together in the Gertler list, are considered separately. Colleges which to a considerable extent share the same faculty and offer the same courses (Harvard and Radcliffe, Columbia and Barnard, three schools of New York University, and three of the University of Pennsylvania) are lumped together in our study. The compilation of the data from the catalogs of the 66 institutions was done by Mr. Lewis Klein and Mr. Zenon Pohorecky, who also abstracted from Voegelin's (1950) survey the comparable data for those of the institutions which offered anthropology courses at that time.

The 66 institutions covered by this study are not all those which gave degrees in anthropology during the 12 years for which relevant statistics are now available (1947-48 through 1958-59, see references in Table 4). Twenty-five additional institutions gave anthropology degrees in that period, but they conferred only 2.65 per cent of all anthropology degrees granted in that period. Hence, the 66 institutions covered in this survey gave over 97 per cent of all anthropology degrees awarded in the United States during the 12 year period considered.

Of these 66 institutions, 60 also offered anthropology courses in 1950,

TABLE 2

TEACHING STAFF IN ANTHROPOLOGY IN THE INSTITUTIONS SURVEYED[1]

| | 1950 | | | | 1960 | | | |
| | regular staff | | affiliated staff | | regular staff | | affiliated staff | |
	PH.D.	NOT PH.D.	PH.D.	NOT PH.D.	PH.D.	NOT PH.D.	PH.D.	NOT PH.D.
Professors	60	4	13	0	149	1	22	0
Associate Professors	38	0	9	0	72	1	7	1
Assistant Professors	45	13	6	3	93	6	8	1
Instructors	13	19	1	2	14	11	2	1
Other	12	14	1	1	19	14	2	1
Subtotal[2]	168	50	30	6	347	33	41	4
Total	218		36		380		45	

[1] Data are lacking for one institution (Texas Technical College) in both years and are possibly incomplete for one other, Washington State University, for 1960.
[2] Excluding four individuals whose rank is not given for 1950 and 32 individuals whose rank is not given for 1960.

and direct comparisons can be made using the Voegelin tabulations. Comparisons of total course and staff as between 1950 and 1960 thus consist of data for these 60 institutions for 1950 and the same for 1960, plus six additional ones (American University, Brandeis, Sacramento State, and the University of California campuses at Davis, Riverside, and Santa Barbara). These additional six, which did not offer courses in anthropology during the period covered by the 1950 tabulation, account for 5.5 per cent of the staff and 4.9 per cent of the courses in the 1960 sample.

SHIFTS IN DEPARTMENTAL ORGANIZATION

The departmental organization for anthropology as of 1960 is shown in the list of institutions included in this survey (Table 1). Of the 60 in which anthropology was taught in 1950, 44 retain the same departmental framework for anthropology. When there has been a change, in every case but one it has been toward more departmental independence for anthropology. In six institutions in which anthropology was part of a combined department in 1950, it was set up as an independent department by 1960. Two other independent departments appear where formerly some anthropology courses were given under the aegis of another department. One independent department replaces a program in anthropology. Of the six institutions not in the 1950 survey, one has an independent department, three have combined departments, and two have programs in anthropology. One college which had an independent department in 1950 had a combined department by 1960.

TABLE 3

NUMBER OF COURSES LISTED IN 1950 (60 INSTITUTIONS)
AND IN 1960 (66 INSTITUTIONS)

	1950	1960	Change in Per Cent
Introductory			
1. General	38	47	24
2. Physical Anthropology	18	33	83
3. Cultural Anthropology	24	44	83
Fields and their Methods			
4. Cultural Anthropology[1]	44	107	143
5. Archaeology[2]	47	104	121
6. Linguistics[3]	62	122	97
7. Physical Anthropology[4]	74	162	119
Regional			
8. North America[5]			
a. Ethnology and General[6]	96	137	43
b. Archaeology	48	68	42
9. South and Central America[7]			
a. Ethnology and General[8]	55	90	64
b. Archaeology	32	49	53
10. Africa[9]			
a. Ethnology and General[10]	29	63	117
b. Archaeology	3	1	−67
11. Europe			
a. Ethnology and General[11]	11	8	−27
b. Archaeology	13	9	−31
12. Asia[12]			
a. Ethnology and General[13]	79	161	104
b. Archaeology	15	10	−33

[1] These figures exclude 299 courses in regional ethnology in 1950 and 492 in 1960. They also exclude 14 courses in 1950 and 25 in 1960 which deal with both the ethnology and archaeology of a particular region. The total of all ethnology courses including regional ones has increased 75 per cent from 357 to 624.

[2] These figures exclude 111 courses in regional archaeology in 1950 and 138 in 1960. They also exclude the 14 courses in 1950 and 25 in 1960 which deal with archaeology and ethnology of a particular region. The inclusive total of archaeology courses including these regional courses has increased 55 per cent, from 172 to 267.

[3] Eight courses in the linguistics of a particular region are included for 1950 and 18 for 1960, but the figures exclude five courses in Language and Culture in 1950 and 25 in 1960. If these are included the total has increased 96 per cent, from 75 to 147.

[4] The total of introductory and other physical anthropology courses has increased 112 per cent, from 92 to 195.

[5] Excluding 15 courses in 1950 and 10 in 1960 which deal with American Indians but are listed under linguistics or other aspects.

[6] Includes two courses in 1950 and seven in 1960 devoted to American society or the American Negro. Includes six courses in 1950 and eight in 1960 which are listed as ethnology and archaeology.

[7] Excludes two courses in the physical anthropology and one in art of the region from 1950 and one in folk culture and one in folklore in the region from 1960.

[8] Includes two courses in 1950 and five in 1960 on ethnology and archaeology in the region.

[9] Excludes two courses in 1950 and seven in 1960 which deal with linguistics or other aspects in the region.

[10] Includes one course in 1950 and three in 1960 which deal with ethnology and archaeology.

[11] Includes two courses in 1950 and in 1960 which deal with ethnology and archaeology.

[12] Excludes two courses on social organization in Asia and one on Indoeuropean linguistics from 1960.

[13] Includes two courses in 1950 and seven in 1960 that deal with ethnology and archaeology.

TABLE 3 (*Continued*)

	1950	1960	Change in Per Cent
13. Oceania[14]			
a. Ethnology and General[15]	43	58	35
b. Archaeology	0	1	
14. World Ethnography	17	40	135
15. Prehistory	26	55	112
Subjects			
16. Aspects: Social Organization[16]	47	95	102
17. Aspects: Religion	25	46	84
18. Aspects: Other[17]	74	131	77
19. Dynamics[18]	41	105	156
20. Topics: Culture and Personality	33	73	121
21. Topics: Language and Culture	5	25	400
22. Topics: Other	10	25	150
23. Types	11	15	36
24. Service and Social Problems	14	32	129
25. Museum Methods	21	15	−29
26. History and Theory	45	115	156
27. Advanced	110	241	119
Total	1210	2287	89

[14] Excludes one course in an aspect from 1950 and two courses in linguistics from 1960.
[15] Includes one course in each year which deals with ethnology and archaeology.
[16] Includes one course in 1950 and four in 1960 which deal with social organization of a particular region.
[17] Includes courses on arts and crafts, inventions, technology, or material culture (1950:18, 1960:27); art (1950:16, 1960:18); music (1950:6, 1960:6); folklore or mythology (1950:13, 1960:25); philosophy (1950:2, 1960:1); government, law or politics (1950:5, 1960:21); and economics (1950:11, 1960:24). In 1960 there was also one course each on folk music and literature, primitive art and music, and music and poetry.
[18] Includes 10 courses in 1950 and 25 in 1960 which deal with applied anthropology. Includes two courses on the Negro in 1950 and six in 1960. One other course in 1950 and two in 1960 have been counted as North American regional courses.

STAFF

Table 2 compiles figures on teaching staff in anthropology from 59 institutions of the 1950 list and from 65 institutions of the 1960 sample (relevant data were not available for Texas Technical College in either period and may be incomplete for Washington State University in the 1960 sample). For the 59 institutions for which there are data in both periods, the total regular and affiliated staff increased from 258 to 457, an increase of 77 per cent. The proportion of individuals with the Ph.D. on the regular teaching staff in anthropology increased from 168 out of 218, or 77 per cent, in 1950, to 347 out of 380, or 91 per cent, in 1960. This does not include teaching assistants.

The proportions of regular staff in various ranks shifted. In 1950, 29 per cent were full professors (64 of 218), by 1960, 39 per cent were

TABLE 4

EARNED DEGREES, BY LEVEL, IN ANTHROPOLOGY AND ALL SUBJECTS IN
INSTITUTIONS OF HIGHER EDUCATION IN THE UNITED STATES*

ACADEMIC YEAR	Bachelor's and First Professional Degrees			Master's except First Professional Degrees			Doctor's Degrees		
	ALL SUBJECTS No.	ANTHRO-POLOGY No.	PER CENT	ALL SUBJECTS No.	ANTHRO-POLOGY No.	PER CENT	ALL SUBJECTS No.	ANTHRO-POLOGY No.	PER CENT
1947–48	272,311	168	.062	42,449	43	.101	3,989	16	.401
1948–49	366,698	299	.082	50,763	61	.120	5,050	19	.376
1949–50	433,734	324	.075	58,219	82	.141	6,633	34	.513
1950–51	384,352	255	.066	65,132	67	.103	7,338	51	.695
1951–52	331,924	257	.077	63,587	76	.120	7,683	37	.482
1952–53	304,857	214	.070	61,023	85	.139	8,309	33	.397
1953–54	292,880	265	.090	56,823	94	.165	8,996	46	.511
1954–55	287,401	280	.097	58,204	87	.149	8,840	44	.498
1955–56	311,298	308	.099	59,294	78	.132	8,903	47	.528
1956–57	340,347	350	.103	61,955	77	.124	8,756	49	.560
1957–58	365,748	359	.098	65,614	118	.180	8,942	51	.570
1958–59	385,151	433	.112	69,497	115	.165	9,360	55	.588

* Data from: Story, 1948, 1949, 1950, 1951, 1952; Rice and Carlson, 1953, 1954, 1955; Rice and Poole, 1957; Gertler and Keith, 1958; Gertler, 1959; Tolliver, 1961.

full professors (150 of 380). The proportion of associate and assistant professors remained about the same, 19 per cent and 20 per cent, for associate professors, 26 per cent and 25 per cent for assistant professors. Instructors made up 14 per cent in 1950, 7 per cent in 1960. Other designations, such as lecturer, fell from 11 per cent to 8 per cent.

COURSES IN ANTHROPOLOGY

We can compare the total number of courses (undergraduate and graduate; one-semester or one-quarter) listed in 60 institutions in 1950 with the number listed by them ten years later. The total rises from 1,210 courses to 2,175, an increase of 82 per cent. The total for all 66 in our sample is 2,287. More courses in anthropology were listed in these 66 catalogs for 1960 than were listed in the whole survey of 305 catalogs covered in 1950.

In order to show the present distribution of course offerings and the trends since 1950, we have classified all courses listed in our sample into 27 categories. This is a different classification from that used in Voegelin's survey, which entailed 12 main categories and numerous subcategories. The 1950 survey gives an abbreviated title for each course listed, and these were used to reclassify the courses according to our present system.

The classification in Table 3 follows, in general, the distinctions made by David G. Mandelbaum in his paper on the curriculum in anthropology (Mandelbaum *et al., The Teaching of Anthropology*). Some courses were difficult to classify, and a few might well have been listed in more than one category. In order to simplify the analysis, however, each course is listed only once in the category which seems to fit the major emphasis or content of the course.

Introductory Courses

We have ordinarily listed as "introductory" only courses open to freshmen or sophomores. However, one course offered to upper division students who have had no prior work in anthropology in 1950 and 10 such courses in 1960 could not be classified reasonably in any other way, and they are classified as introductory. We have distinguished (1) general courses introductory to all of anthropology, (2) courses introductory to physical anthropology (often including some prehistory in their treatment of human origins), and (3) introductory courses specifically on cultural anthropology. This method of classifying excludes "introductory" courses on special fields of anthropology such as archaeology or linguistics even if they are open to freshman students. Although introductory courses were offered in most of the institutions of the 1950 sample, it is noteworthy that there has been an increase in the number of introductory courses, during the decade, from 84 to 111 (32 per cent).

Courses in the Major Fields of Anthropology and Their Methods

Four fields are distinguished under this heading and in Table 3. Category 4 comprises courses dealing with the concepts, methods, and techniques of ethnology and cultural anthropology, e.g., Problems in Cultural Anthropology, Ethnological Field Techniques, The Nature of Culture, Cross-cultural Analysis. Category 5 comprises courses dealing with concepts, methods, and techniques of archaeology, e.g., Theory and Methods of Archaeology, Geochronology. Category 6 comprises courses on concepts, methods, and techniques of linguistics, e.g., Linguistic Field Methods, Phonetics, and Phonemics, and on languages of a particular region or stock, e.g., Athapascan Languages. Category 7 comprises courses dealing with the methods, concepts, and materials of physical anthropology, e.g., Problems of Physical Anthropology, Human Dentition, Human Evolution, Biometric Anthropology.

All these fields have shared in the increase in number of courses. Furthermore, courses in the various anthropological fields seem to be increasingly focused on world-wide questions of process rather than local questions of history.

Although general courses in cultural anthropology have increased by 143 per cent from 44 to 107 courses, regional ethnological courses have increased at a slower rate, 65 per cent, from 313 to 517 courses. In category 4 "cultural anthropology," there are only 107 courses in the 1960 sample, as against 122 courses in linguistics and 162 in physical anthropology, but most of the courses in all of the subsequent categories are mainly ethnological. Hence there is a great preponderance of courses in cultural anthropology and ethnology, but they have been divided into subcategories by region, aspect, topic, etc. in the present classification.

The increase in general archaeology courses (121 per cent) from 47 to 104 courses) is even more striking relative to the increase in archaeological courses with regional focus (24 per cent, from 111 to 138 courses). The full measure of interest in anthropological linguistics is not reflected in our data, since several universities offer such courses in separate linguistics departments. There has been a decline in the number of regional courses in linguistics in anthropology departments.

Regional Courses

Courses on regions and areas, whether dealing with whole continents or smaller divisions, are listed as: 8. North America, north of Mexico, 9. Central and South America, 10. Africa, 11. Europe, 12. Asia, and 13. Oceania. In Table 3 each of these categories is subdivided into those which deal with ethnology and with general anthropology, on the one hand, and those which deal only with archaeology, on the other. It is difficult to classify some regional courses, since they cross continental boundaries and deal with such subjects as Eurasia, the circumpolar region, the New World, North and Central America, and Africa and Asia. These courses are classified with the region which seems to be most emphasized. Thus, New World courses were listed with North America, most circumpolar courses were listed with Asia, and courses on the peoples of the U.S.S.R. were listed with Asia except in the case of a course on "Peoples of Eastern Europe and the U.S.S.R.," which was listed under Europe. The Philippines and Indonesia are classed with Asia. The "regional" category includes courses on civilization areas. Courses dealing with the whole world or multiple areas in the Old World have been separately classified as 14, "world ethnography." Similarly, courses listed under category 15, "prehistory," deal with the whole world or major areas of the Old World.

Regional courses have not increased in number to the same extent as most other courses. In respect to ethnology, North America remains a popular region in terms of number of courses, 137, but is now exceeded by those on Asia, 161. Courses on the ethnology of Africa have shown the most rapid increase during the decade, and those on Asia and its various subzones have grown almost as rapidly. At the other extreme, courses on the ethnology of Europe were few to begin with and have in fact decreased.

In respect to archaeology, regional courses are, with few exceptions, confined to the Americas, and a few courses on American archaeology have been added during the 1950-1960 decade. For the other areas of the world, very few regional archaeology (or archaeology and ethnology) courses were taught in 1950, and in the 10 years surveyed there had been no increase.

Courses on Aspects of Culture

The term "aspect" refers to such subcategories of culture as social organization, religion, music, art, folklore, political organization, law, economics, and technology. Courses dealing with such aspects of culture have increased 86 per cent, about the same rate as for all courses.

Category 16, "social organization," comprises courses on social structure, e.g., Social Stratification, kinship analysis, e.g., Analysis of Kinship Systems and social organization of wider scope, e.g., Comparative Social Organization, as well as courses called simply Primitive Society or Social Anthropology. In addition, a few courses dealing with the social organization of a particular area, e.g., Social Anthropology of Contemporary America, are included, when the primary emphasis seems to be on the social rather than on the regional material.

Category 17, "religion," includes courses entitled Primitive Religion or Comparative Religion and a number judged to be dealing with similar subject matter, e.g., Magic and Religion and Primitive Society and Religion.

Category 18, "other aspects," comprises courses on all aspects of culture not included in the two preceding categories. A large increase in the number of offerings dealing with government, political organization, and law is noteworthy, whereas courses on material culture and the technology of specific regions have decreased in number.

Courses on Cultural and Social Dynamics

Included in category 19, "dynamics," are all courses judged to be concerned with the processes of culture change, either in the perspective of long term growth or in the close analysis of an applied situation. Included also were some courses in race relations when they were judged to be concerned more with the processes of assimilation, syncretism, or acculturation than with social problems. Some examples of the latter are Culture in Conflict and the Negro in the New World. Voegelin (1950) notes that no applied anthropology courses had been listed in a survey covering 1940-41 but that 35 such courses were taught a decade later. Ten of these 35 courses on "applied anthropology" were given in institutions of our 1950 sample; in institutions of the present survey the number of such courses has risen from 10 to 27. Taken together with applied anthropology, all courses on cultural change and processes of change have increased in number. The increase of 156 per cent for the decade is among the greatest of any of the principal categories.

Courses on Topics

These are mainly courses which deal with the interrelation of aspects or with special points of view. The most frequently offered is a course in culture and personality, Category 20. Voegelin (1950) reported an increase from two to 58 such courses in the decade before 1950. We have listed under this rubric courses dealing with culture from a psychological approach; besides those titled Culture and Personality we include those on the socialization process, cross-cultural studies of childhood, and on national character. In the decade since 1950 courses in this category have more than doubled, from 33 to 73.

Courses in "language and culture," Category 21, rare in 1950, have increased 400 per cent. Such courses are offered at 23 of the 66 institutions of the 1960 sample. It may be that courses of similar content have been classified under "linguistics" if the title did not include the word culture.

Category 22, "other topics," includes all courses on topics other than those included in Categories 20 and 21. They vary widely in subject matter and include such titles as: Communication Theory and Culture; Biology, Society and Culture; Habitat, Economy and Society. These also show a large increase.

Courses on Culture Types

Courses in Category 23 deal with certain types of cultures and societies without firm regional anchoring. Most concern peasant communities, but hunter, plantation, and nomadic types are the subject matter of a few courses. The increase in the number of courses from 11 to 15 in this category reflects an increase in the number of courses on contemporary folk societies.

Service and Social Problems Courses

Three types of courses have been included under Catetory 24: first, courses in anthropology designed for members or students of some profession other than anthropology, e.g., Anthropology and Education, and Indian Administration and Indian Affairs; second, courses directed to some widespread social problems for an audience of nonanthropologists, e.g., Sociology of Minority Relations and Proseminar in International Affairs; third, courses designed to aid the anthropologist in presenting his material or representing his profession in a more interesting light to a nonprofessional audience, e.g., Representational Methods in Anthropology and Scientific Illustration. Courses in this category have increased by a large percentage in this decade but in 1960 are still given in only 23 of the 66 institutions sampled. Similar courses on social problems are often taught in other departments. The increase of such courses in anthropology departments may indicate that anthropology is thought to have something specifically helpful to offer in the resolution of such problems.

Museum Methods

Courses dealing with the work of museums, Category 25, decreased in number during the decade. It may be that growth in museums themselves has been slow, since public support for research in anthropology has been primarily channeled through universities rather than museums.

Courses on History and Theory of Anthropology

Category 26 has been conceived so as to include a wide range of integrative courses. History of Anthropology courses have been viewed as integrating anthropology with its past, Theory of Anthropology courses as integrating the study of culture with some of the other behavioral sciences. Included perforce in this category have been a few courses in statistics applicable to two or more of anthropology's major fields. Courses on the history and methods of a particular field, whether social-cultural anthropology or some other, are listed under the respective fields. The increase in history and theory courses cannot be ascribed solely to the lengthening shadow of anthropology's past (for disciplines like anatomy with deep traditions do not indoctrinate their students in history). Rather the growth in courses in history and theory must be a reflection of interest in the leading ideas of the field and the course of their development.

Advanced Courses

Category 27 comprises courses seemingly designed to fit the student's individual interests. There is a large number of such courses. Examples include Directed Research, Independent Reading, Field Work, Graduate Seminar. This category has shown a 119 per cent increase during the 1950-1960 decade. Listings of this sort are not necessarily a clear reflection of practice—since, on the one hand, such a listing may be published although there are no students who sign up for the course, and on the other hand, many teachers offer personal instruction for which students do not formally enroll.

DEGREES

A survey of degree listings shows that anthropology has had an increasing proportion of all degrees awarded (Table 4). In the postwar years the proportion of bachelor's and doctor's degrees in anthropology to the total for all subjects was highest in the last year for which data are available (1958-59). The ratio for master's degrees was higher in that year than in any year except the previous one. The proportion of anthropology degrees to all degrees is higher for master's than for bachelor's degrees and far higher for doctor's than for either bachelor's or master's degrees in every year. Thus, in the years from the end of World War II through 1958-59, anthropology teaching has been far more occupied with preparing doctor's degree candidates than the higher educational institutions as a whole. In the last year for which data are available, 1958-59, the proportion of master's to bachelor's degrees was nearly one and one-half times as high for anthropology as for all subjects and of doctor's to bachelor's degrees over five times as high.

For the 12 years under consideration, women have earned 48 per cent, 31 per cent, and 18 per cent respectively of bachelor's, master's, and doctor's degrees with a major in anthropology. For all subjects the corresponding percentages of degrees awarded to females are 32 per cent, 32 per cent, and 10 per cent for the three levels.

COMPARISON WITH SURVEY DATA FOR CALIFORNIA

The fact that additional types of data are available relative to teaching of anthropology in California (Lasker and Nelson, elsewhere in this volume) permits of some comparisons and, if due caution is observed, possibly some extrapolation. Thus the frequency with which different kinds of courses are offered in degree-granting institutions can be compared with the number of students enrolled in courses of these types in California in 1960. Introductory courses represent only 5.4 per cent of all courses in degree-granting institutions but 60 per cent of enrollments in all types of institutions in California. An introduction to physical anthropology is offered less often than one in either cultural anthropology or general anthropology in degree-granting institutions across the country, but in California 35.5 per cent of all anthropology enrollments are in an introduction to physical anthropology, and this is more than all other introductory courses combined. Among the remaining kinds of courses, the proportion of enrollments in cultural anthropology in California is greater than the proportion of courses in cultural anthropology and world ethnography in the national sample. On the other hand, enrollments in advanced and integrative courses in California occur less frequently relative to other categories than in the survey sample. Most other types of courses show small differences in emphasis in the two studies.

By separately calculating the data for the nine California institutions in the survey of 66 degree-granting institutions in the United States, it is seen that California accounts for 71 of 457 (15.5 per cent) of the listed anthropology staffs, 279 of 2,287 (12.2 per cent) of the listed anthropology courses, and 105 of 603 (17.4 per cent) of anthropology degrees granted in 1958-59. For those who wish to attempt some sort of extrapolation, these data can be considered in relation to the fact that California had at least 160 teachers and 28,007 course enrollments in anthropology in 1960.

CONCLUSIONS

The teaching of anthropology has greatly increased in the decade 1950-1960. In the institutions sampled, staff in anthropology increased by 77 per cent, courses offered by 89 per cent, and degrees granted by 49 per cent. The number of bachelor's degrees awarded in 1958-59 was greater by 34 per cent, master's degrees by 89 per cent and doctor's degrees by 189 per cent than those of 1948-49, respectively. Even if allowance is made for the fact that during the base year of 1948-49 few doctor's degrees and many bachelor's degrees were granted in all subjects, it is clear, both in degree statistics and in course offerings, that anthropology at the undergraduate level is largely a service department offering broadening experience to those specializing in other disciplines. This is seen in the ratio of graduate students to undergraduate majors.

REFERENCES CITED

GERTLER, DIANE B.
    1959   Earned degrees conferred by higher educational institutions, 1957-58. Washington, D.C., U.S. Department of Health, Education, and Welfare (formerly, Federal Security Agency), Office of Education, Circular No. 570.
GERTLER, DIANE B., AND VIRGINIA W. KEITH
    1958   *Ibid.* for 1956-57, Circular No. 527.
RICE, MABEL C., AND NEVA CARLSON
    1953   *Ibid.* for 1952-53, Circular No. 380.
    1954   *Ibid.* for 1953-54, Circular No. 418.
    1955   *Ibid.* for 1954-55, Circular No. 461.
RICE, MABEL C., AND HAZEL POOLE
    1957   *Ibid.* for 1955-56, Circular No. 499.
STORY, R. C.
    1948   *Ibid.* for 1947-48, Circular No. 247.
    1949   *Ibid.* for 1948-49, Circular No. 262.
    1950   *Ibid.* for 1949-50, Circular No. 282.
    1951   *Ibid.* for 1950-51, Circular No. 333.
    1952   *Ibid.* for 1951-52, Circular No. 360.
TOLLIVER, W. E.
    1961   Earned degrees conferred 1958-59, Bachelor's and higher degrees. Washington, D.C., U.S. Department of Health, Education, and Welfare, Office of Education, Circular No. 636.
VOEGELIN, ERMINIE
    1950   Anthropology in American universities. American Anthropologist 52:350-391.

GABRIEL W. LASKER
AND HAROLD NELSON

II. *Student Enrollments and Teachers of Anthropology in California*

THIS SURVEY COVERS accredited junior colleges, colleges, and universities in the state of California. The rate of increase in new colleges and in college population in California has been more rapid than in most of the United States, but the rapid rate of growth is becoming more general throughout the country. The purposes of this survey were to obtain data on enrollments in anthropology courses of various types and on the educational background of the teachers of these courses in all types of institutions of higher learning. Until an intensive nation-wide survey becomes possible, such a survey as this should prove of value in charting plans for departments and for the profession. By obtaining nearly complete coverage of one large state, we have the advantage of full data within the area studied.

One hundred and twenty-five institutions of higher education were surveyed. In tables, data for these has been grouped according to the classification given in the appendix. Seventy-three of the 125 institutions offer courses in anthropology, 46 do not (but of these 10 plan to do so), and six probably do not. Questionnaires were returned from 66 of the 73 institutions in which anthropology is taught; these include all the large and medium size institutions in the state. We estimate that the survey covers 90 per cent of institutions which teach anthro-

TABLE 1

Enrollments in Anthropology in California*

	1958–59 Spring		1959 Summer	1959–60 Fall		1959–60 Spring		1960 Summer	1960–61 Fall	
	day	exten-sion		day	exten-sion	day	exten-sion		day	exten-sion
Universities with graduate programs	3,340	294	752	3,885	338	3,983	353	793	4,556	401
State colleges	2,485	169	354	2,528	207	3,099	252	441	3,141	469
Private colleges	377	40	30	185	28	428	85	77	371	97
Junior colleges	2,828	927	445	2,993	1,104	3,201	1,186	371	3,331	1,332
Total	9,030	1,430	1,581	9,591	1,677	10,711	1,876	1,682	11,399	2,299

* In the case of two institutions on the quarter system, Winter quarter enrollments are reported by evenly dividing them between Fall and Spring.

pology, 96 per cent of the teachers of anthropology, and 98 per cent or 99 per cent of the enrollments.[1]

The list of institutions covered and the two questionnaires distributed are given in the appendix to this chapter. As in all questionnaire returns, discrepancies appeared. In some cases a form was returned with data for more than one course, or more than one form was received for the same course. In a few cases incidental data on qualifications for teaching were substituted for the answers to the specific questions posed. Enrollment figures from individual teachers did not always add up to totals supplied by administrative officials. A few individuals teach at more than one institution, but they have been tabulated only with one. All of the discrepancies were resolved by accepting what appeared to be the more reliable set of data or, where there was no basis for such choice, the more conservative version, or else by omitting the doubtful information.

ENROLLMENTS

The course enrollments for 1960 in anthropology in the 66 responding institutions totalled 27,969. This figure is for the calendar year and includes spring, summer, and fall enrollments. Except for two institutions on the quarter system, these represent semester courses, usually of three hours per week. Graduate enrollments, a small fraction of the total, are included. There are more enrollments at Berkeley and Los Angeles than in the other state university campuses and state colleges combined, or in the junior colleges combined; private colleges have comparatively few students in anthropology (Table 1).

The overall increase from 1959 to 1960 was 20 per cent. Enrollments increased from the spring semester of 1958-59 to that of 1959-60 by 20 per cent and from the fall of 1959-60 to that 1960-61 by 22 per cent.

TABLE 2

ENROLLMENTS IN ANTHROPOLOGY IN CALIFORNIA 1959 AND 1960 BY TYPES OF COURSE

Courses	Universities with Graduate Programs		State Colleges		Private Colleges		Junior Colleges		TOTALS	
	1960	1959	1960	1959	1960	1959	1960	1959	1960	1959
Introductory										
General	655	653	0	0	283	211	508	371	1,446	1,235
Physical Anthropology	2,878	2,429	1,264	880	140	140	4,929	4,989	9,211	8,438
Cultural Anthropology	1,330	1,148	2,432	1,578	303	88	3,702	2,825	7,767	5,639
Fields and Their Methods										
Ethnology and Cultural Anthropology	952	725	637	594	123	88	0	0	1,712	1,407
Archaeology	298	118	192	90	0	0	106	33	596	241
Linguistics	165	57	63	32	7	2	0	0	235	91
Physical Anthropology	280	194	145	112	0	0	0	0	425	306
Regional										
North America	309	332	390	360	139	96	0	0	838	788
Central and South America	352	303	156	118	20	8	0	0	528	429
Africa	286	160	81	114	0	0	0	0	367	274
Asia	57	176	73	109	0	0	0	0	130	285
Europe	35	0	0	0	17	0	0	0	52	0
Oceania	152	126	65	67	0	0	0	0	217	193
Concepts and Comparisons										
Aspects										
Social Organization	328	374	134	164	0	0	0	0	462	538
Religion	470	448	149	191	9	0	0	0	628	639
Other	267	131	10	11	0	0	0	0	277	142
Dynamics	333	214	32	20	0	0	0	0	365	234
Topics										
Culture-Personality	201	203	339	269	0	0	0	0	540	472
Language-Culture	147	118	60	3	0	0	0	0	207	121
Types	38	17	0	30	17	27	0	0	55	74
Service	24	40	21	0	0	0	0	0	45	40
Advanced	504	510	77	33	0	0	0	0	581	543
Not Classified	25	113	1,082	968	0	0	176	79	1,283	1,180
Totals	10,086	8,609	7,402	5,743	1,058	660	9,421	8,297	27,967	23,309

Summer school enrollments listed for 1959 and 1960 were essentially the same. All types of institutions have shared in this trend, and partial data for the spring semester of 1961 from 15 institutions indicate that it is continuing.

The increase in enrollments in anthropology courses has far outstripped the increase in the college population. According to *Opening Fall Enrollments in Higher Education, 1959,* the increase in degree-credit students in the United States from the fall of 1958 to the fall of 1959 was 4.4 per cent. For the State of California this increase was from 386,520 to 408,465 students, an increase of 5.7 per cent. In California, in 1959, there was approximately one enrollment in an anthropology course for every 18 students. If the number of students in the

state increased another 5.7 per cent by 1960, there was approximately
one enrollment in an anthropology course for every 15 students on the
campuses in California that year. The increase occurred in all types
of colleges and in virtually all types of courses.

CLASSIFICATION OF COURSES

In Table 2 enrollments are listed according to type of course. Each
course is listed only once, under the rubric which seems to represent
the main emphasis. Under "introductory," we have listed three kinds
of courses open to students in their first two years of college: those
which deal with elementary cultural anthropology, with elementary
physical anthropology, or with both. We have included in the "not
classified" category at the bottom of the column 572 enrollments in
1959 and 636 in 1960 known to be in lower division courses but for
which the kind of introductory courses was not specified. Thus in 1959
and 1960, 68 per cent of all enrollments are in introductory courses:
15,884 in 1959 and 19,060 in 1960, an increase of 20 per cent. Approximately half of these enrollments are in junior colleges.

The second category on Table 2, "fields and their methods," includes courses on one of the general fields within anthropology—ethnology, archaeology, linguistics, physical anthropology—given mainly for
students who have had an introductory course. The "regional" courses
deal with cultures within a geographically defined area. The internal
classification of "regional" courses is somewhat arbitrary. A course on
Circumpolar Peoples has been grouped within North America since
that is where its primary concern seems to lie, and one on Peoples of
the U.S.S.R. is included under Asia for the same reason. Under the
general classifications of "concepts and comparisons," we have distinguished four groupings—"aspects," "dynamics," "topics," "types." The
"aspects" courses have been further classified as "social organization,"
"religion," and "other." The "other aspects" category includes courses
on art, technology, music, mythology, folklore, economics, politics, and
law. Under "dynamics," we have included courses on culture change,
including applied anthropology. Courses concerning long-time change,
as studied by archaeological methods only, have been listed under
"archaeology" rather than "dynamics." "Topics" include courses on culture and personality and language and culture, in which a set of problems is discussed from the approach of different methods and theories.
"Types" refer to courses which deal with social and cultural categories,
such as folk societies and nomadic cultures.

"Service" courses are those given for special purposes. In this compilation, the category comprises courses on museum techniques and on
anthropology and education. "Advanced" courses comprise reading

courses, honors courses and similar special courses for undergraduates (in which there were 151 enrollments in 1959 and 200 in 1960) and otherwise unclassified graduate courses.

The preponderant image one gets from the enrollment data is of a rising interest in all of anthropology. After the introductory courses, the fields and methods courses have the most enrollments. This reflects the large number of enrollments in courses in ethnology and cultural anthropology. In the regional courses, the largest number of students are in courses on North America. Next in descending order of frequency come Central and South America, Africa, Oceania and Asia, and lastly, Europe. Of the various "Concepts and Comparisons" courses, Religion, Culture and Personality, Social Organization, and Cultural Dynamics attract more student enrollments than courses on other aspects, other topics, or types. Only a few courses in this survey were identified as belonging to the service category. Since much advanced and graduate instruction is outside registered courses, the advanced course category gives an inadequate picture of teaching on this level.

EDUCATIONAL BACKGROUND AND TEACHING EXPERIENCE

Personnel information was submitted by 137 teachers of anthropology in 63 institutions. In addition, respondents and catalogs gave some information on ten other teachers in five of these institutions, and data from catalogs on seven other teachers at four additional colleges have been included. There are six other institutions in California which are known to offer courses in anthropology but for which none of these

TABLE 3

RELATION BETWEEN THE DATE WHEN TEACHERS BEGAN TO TEACH ANTHROPOLOGY AND THE DATE WHEN THEY BEGAN TO TEACH AT THEIR PRESENT INSTITUTION

	Universities with Graduate Programs	University Extension	State Colleges	Private Colleges	Junior Colleges
Taught anthropology in a year prior to that in which he came to present institution	27	4	8	1	5
Came to present institution and started to teach anthropology in the same year	14	4	15	5	21
Came to present institution in a year prior to that in which he started to teach anthropology	1	0	0	5	26

sources yielded data. Added into the total, they show that there are at least 160 teachers of the subject in the state.

As crude measures of teaching experience, we have tabulated the year when the respondent started teaching at the present institution and the year when he started teaching anthropology (Table 3), the degrees held by anthropology teachers (Table 4), and the subjects in which they earned their degrees (Table 5).

The amount of prior experience in teaching of anthropology varies greatly according to type of institution. A majority of the teachers in universities with graduate departments commenced teaching anthropology prior to 1951. But in every other category of institution, a majority began teaching anthropology in 1957 or later. Nevertheless, the two most experienced anthropology teachers in point of years—both retired from other posts—are now teaching in junior colleges. As shown in Table 3, only in universities with graduate departments are a majority of teaching appointments in anthropology given to persons with a record of performance in teaching the subject elsewhere. In every other type of institution the majority came to their present post in the same year or a previous year to that in which they started to teach anthropology.

This seems to imply that most teachers in state institutions with four-year programs in anthropology and many individuals in every other type of institution were hired to teach anthropology without having taught it elsewhere and that a majority of junior college teachers and an appreciable number of the teachers of anthropology in private colleges were hired primarily to teach other subjects, since they did

TABLE 4

HIGHEST DEGREE EARNED BY 152 TEACHERS OF ANTHROPOLOGY IN THE STATE OF CALIFORNIA AND THE STATUS OF FEMALE TEACHERS

	Universities with Graduate Programs	University Extension	State 4-Year Colleges	Private Colleges	Junior Colleges
Ph.D. or other earned doctorate	38	2**	28	7**	8‡
Master's degree or qualified for Ph.D.	5*	5*	5	3	44**
Bachelor's degree	0	3	2†	1	4
Total	43	10	35	11	56

* Includes one female.
** Includes two females.
† Includes one female who teaches in extension.
‡ Includes one female who teaches in extension and one who teaches in regular session.

TABLE 5

SUBJECT IN WHICH HIGHEST DEGREE WAS EARNED BY TEACHERS OF
ANTHROPOLOGY IN THE STATE OF CALIFORNIA

	Universities with Graduate Programs	University Extension	State Colleges	Private Colleges	Junior Colleges	TOTAL
Ph.D.:						
Anthropology	30	2	23	2	4	61
Anthropology plus another subject	4		1		1	6
Sociology or Social Science	1		1	4		6
Linguistics	2					2
History			1	1	1	3
Other*	1		2		2	5
Master's (or qualified for Ph.D.)						
Anthropology	4	5	3		5	17
Anthropology plus another subject	1		1	1		3
Sociology or Social Science				2	11	13
History					6	6
Geography			1		3	4
Education			1		5	6
Psychology					3	3
Other**					8	8
Bachelor's						
Anthropology		2	1	1		4
Other***		1	1		3	5

* One each in experimental medicine, librarianship, political economy, English, and two unknown.
** One each in philosophy, language, geology, educational psychology, botany, zoölogy, paleontology, and economics.
*** One each in psychology, botany, geography, general curriculum, and mathematics.

not teach anthropology in their first year in their present position. Thirty-two of 136 teachers (23.5 per cent) began to teach at their present post in a year prior to that in which they began to teach anthropology.

The majority of anthropology teachers in the state have earned the Ph.D. or other doctor's degree (Table 4). The proportion is highest in the universities with graduate programs, 88 per cent, and lowest in junior colleges, 14 per cent.

All but one of the eleven women teachers are employed in junior colleges, private colleges, or extension teaching. The five women teachers in extension teaching hold higher degrees (and have had more teaching experience) on the average than men who teach extension courses. Similarly two of the four women who teach anthropology in junior colleges hold the Ph.D. degree, whereas only six of 52 male junior college anthropology teachers have doctor's degrees.

The subjects in which anthropology teachers earned their highest degrees varies greatly (Table 5). Of university teachers, 91 per cent have their highest degree in anthropology or anthropology plus another subject; of junior college teachers, only 19 per cent have this background. The diversity of training is especially great in the junior colleges and private colleges, where the teaching of one or more courses in anthropology is often only a part time responsibility of a teacher with other duties. The fact that anthropology is frequently placed in a social science department may account for the fact that of those who do not have their highest degree in anthropology, over half have it in sociology, social science, psychology, or history.

The teaching of anthropology by persons without the Ph.D. can be accounted for only in small part as in-service training by those who will eventually earn the Ph.D. in the subject. Of 54 teachers with a Ph.D. degree in anthropology, 23 started teaching anthropology in a year prior to that in which the degree was awarded, 11 in the same year, and 20 in a subsequent year. On the average, those with Ph.D. degrees in anthropology started to teach the subject four months prior to getting their Ph.D. degrees.

From the remarks volunteered in the personnel questionnaires, it is clear that some respondents consider formal education in anthropology as only one part of the experience relevant to competence as a teacher. Field work, including weekend and summer archaeological digs and other excursions in anthropology, are repeatedly mentioned. Several teachers without past formal training in anthropology express an interest in forthcoming summer teacher's institutes, and some of the more experienced teachers look to field or laboratory or museum research to provide fresh concrete experiences for their teaching.

One should not minimize, however, the significance of the fact that there are teachers of anthropology who have little or no contact with current research and thinking in anthropology. A number of the junior college teachers of anthropology lack access to current anthropological publications: only 24 of the 68 junior colleges in the state subscribe to the *American Anthropologist,* although at least 41 junior colleges offer a course in anthropology. Nevertheless, on the whole, the level of enthusiasm, even among those with heavy teaching loads and responsibility for teaching other subjects, appears to be high, and this may be one reason that the enrollments in the anthropology courses they teach have been increasing so rapidly.

SOME NEEDS FELT BY TEACHERS OF ANTHROPOLOGY

In all but the first few course questionnaires distributed, we asked, "What specific kinds of materials could a project devoted to the teaching of anthropology assemble and publish that would be of assistance to you?" This question was not answered by every recipient nor in respect to every course. A few respondents answered that nothing additional is needed. Approximately 180 positive suggestions were made. These call for annotated bibliographies, new textbooks, lists of films, and other audio-visual aids. Also listed as desirable are translations, workbooks, abstracts, syllabi, survey data, and articles on what other teachers think and do. There is no sharp difference in the kinds of requests coming from the teachers in the junior colleges and those in other types of institutions. However, the junior college teachers more often request lists of available films and other audio-visual aids and bibliographies suitable for the courses they teach, whereas the teachers of upper division and graduate students more often call for the production of new materials. The respondents want help with audio-visual aids in the form of new materials and lists of carefully selected films and other audio-visual materials critically reviewed from the point of view of anthropology. They ask how, where, and for how much they may obtain these materials. There is general agreement that slides should be of the 2″ × 2″ size and in color. Film strips are mentioned only once.

Maps are also in demand, especially in connection with courses in world ethnology, archaeology, and introductory physical anthropology. Suitable ones are needed on prehistoric sites, racial types, human genetic traits, tribes, and linguistic groups.

Other types of visual aids frequently mentioned include models of tools, casts of remains of primitive man, and circulating collections of artifacts. Information is wanted on how to secure museum exhibits on loan and on how to use ethnological material in the classroom.

A considerable number of teachers would like to have information on courses taught by others. Junior college teachers, with their heavy teaching loads, would appreciate detailed course outlines for introductory courses in both physical and cultural anthropology. In respect to both they would also like to have prepared field and laboratory problems, course bibliographies (with abstracts), and lists of books and journals for purchase by their libraries. In universities and four-year colleges, too, there are teachers who would like to see the syllabi of other teachers, or an analysis of course content around the country. More often they request the basic materials—for instance, field notes and quotations from which to construct exercises in a course on religion, more laboratory problems, materials for courses in linguistics, and problem material on the nature of culture.

Although not strictly an answer to our question, meetings of various kinds were requested. Some junior college teachers would welcome an annual regional workshop and arrangements for participating in university or museum digs, and they would like to see increased availability of visiting lecturers.

One junior college teacher no doubt speaks for many others when he asks about funds available for research and information on how to get them. The relation of scholarship to research is probably so taken for granted by most teachers that they fail to mention it explicitly, but perhaps nothing is more on the minds of respondents than the need for balance between creative scholarship and transmission of anthropological knowledge.

CONCLUSION

Some of the needs mentioned in the questionnaires are being met at least partially by the publications of the Educational Resources in Anthropology Project. Intended as a first effort of profession-wide magnitude, the Project has perhaps revealed many more needs than it could have anticipated or met. The survey of the teaching of anthropology in California shows that between 1959 and 1960 the number of students enrolled in virtually all types of courses and in every type of institution increased sharply. The courses are in many cases taught by persons trained in other fields or short of the Ph.D. level in anthropology. Furthermore, these teachers feel the need for many types of aid in their teaching. It is hoped that this presentation of the status of the teaching of anthropology in one state will help in the planning for the solution of the problem.

ACKNOWLEDGMENTS

In February, 1960, John F. Goins of the University of California, Riverside, together with Harold Nelson (coauthor of this paper) circulated a questionnaire to 67 colleges in Southern California similar to that used in the present survey. Noel Korn, of Valley Junior College, assisted in approaching the respondents to the earlier questionnaires for up-to-date information. Mr. Joel Champion assisted in tabulating the results. We are grateful to them for their help and to all those who responded.

NOTE

[1] Subsequent to the completion of tabulations, a return was received from one additional junior college in which anthropology was introduced in 1960. The teacher, who has a B.A. in social science with a concentration in anthropology, began teaching at his present institution in 1960. He reports two courses, both in the evening division, with 20 students in the introductory course in cultural anthropology in the spring of 1960 and 20 students in the introductory physical

anthropology course in the fall. Hence the total of reported anthropology enrollments in 1960 is 28,007.

REFERENCES CITED

GOINS, JOHN F., AND HAROLD NELSON
    1960   Report of a survey of anthropological teaching in the Southern California region. Educational Resources in Anthropology Project, University of California, Berkeley. Mimeographed.
OPENING FALL ENROLLMENTS IN HIGHER EDUCATION: INSTITUTIONAL DATA
    1959   U.S. Department of Health, Education and Welfare, U.S. Government Printing Office.

APPENDIX

Institutions Surveyed and the Two Questionnaire Forms

The institutions of various types which returned questionnaires comprised:

Those with graduate programs which have given Ph.D. degrees in anthropology: four—Southern California; Stanford; University of California, Berkeley; University of California, Los Angeles.

State colleges (and other state university campuses which have not given a Ph.D. in anthropology): fourteen—Alameda; California Polytechnical College (Pomona); Chico; Fresno; Humboldt; Los Angeles; Sacramento; San Fernando Valley; San Diego; San Francisco; San Jose; University of California, Davis; University of California, Riverside; University of California, Santa Barbara.

Private colleges (and private universities which have not given a Ph.D. in anthropology): eleven—Biola, College of Holy Names, Immaculate Heart, Loyola University of Los Angeles, Mills, Mount Saint Mary's, Occidental, Pomona, University of the Pacific, University of San Francisco, Whittier.

Junior colleges: thirty-seven—American River, Bakersfield, Chaffey, City College of San Francisco, College of San Mateo, College of Sequoias, Contra Costa, East Los Angeles, Foothill, Fresno City, Fullerton, Glendale, Hartnell, Long Beach City, Los Angeles City, Los Angeles Harbor, Menlo, Modesto, Monterey Peninsula, Mount San Antonio, Napa, Oakland, Orange Coast, Palomar, Pasadena, Pierce, Sacramento City, San Bernardino Valley, San Diego City, San Jose City, Santa Barbara, Santa Monica, Santa Rosa, Taft, Vallejo, Valley, Ventura.

QUESTIONNAIRE 1

COURSE INFORMATION

Institution.

Course (number and name).

Department.

Name of Instructor (Mr., Miss, Mrs.).

How often given (every semester, once a year, etc.).

Class hours per week for (semester, quarter, year).

Lab or section meetings, hours per week.

Prerequisites.

Number registered at beginning of semester:

	Spring 1959	Fall 1959	Spring 1960	Fall 1960
Day Class				
Extended Day or Evening Class				
Summer School Class	1959		1960	

Is course included in a major curriculum or concentrated program, and, if so, what?

Textbooks used in course.

Special assignments or activities in connection with course (e.g., archaeological field work, interviewing or observation, lab problems).

If there is a dittoed or mimeographed course syllabus or outline of topics covered, we would appreciate it if you would enclose a copy.

What specific kinds of materials could a project devoted to the teaching of anthropology assemble and publish that would be of assistance to you?

Remarks or additions.

QUESTIONNAIRE 2

Institution.

Educational background of anthropology instructor.

   Name (Mr., Miss, Mrs.).

   Degree(s):

     Date(s)

     Subject(s)

     Institution(s)

Undergraduate work in anthropology (courses and institutions) (if undergraduate major in anthropology, please indicate).

Graduate study in anthropology (courses or major fields).

Graduate study in other subjects (courses or major fields).

Year when you started teaching at present institution.

Year when you started teaching anthropology.

If engaged in part-time teaching, please explain.

Remarks or additions.

RALPH L. BEALS

III. *Personnel Resources:*
Building the
Anthropology Department

Discussion of personnel problems and the building of the anthropology department can be delightfully uninhibited by facts. We cannot answer with any accuracy such simple questions as: How many anthropologists are needed? Are we training anthropologists in ways best suited to meet future needs? To answer these questions, such agencies as the National Science Foundation and the National Education Association should be encouraged to list anthropological data separately rather than include it under such general headings as "Social Science."

Data on problems of department building are even less abundant. Two-year colleges, four-year colleges, and universities have very different staffing problems. At the university level there may be significant distinctions between large and small institutions. Finally, in universities and in many colleges there are significant unresolved problems concerning the goals of undergraduate anthropology courses. (See papers by Mandelbaum, Du Bois, and others in Mandelbaum *et al., The Teaching of Anthropology* 1962.) Most institutions recognize the service and liberal arts functions of anthropology courses; these usually are the only basis on which anthropology is included in the curricula of two-year institutions. Nevertheless, as two-year institutions bear an increasing share of undergraduate education, the quality of instruction in them will assume ever more importance for the upper division pro-

grams and for the recruitment of students to the field of anthropology.
(See papers in this volume by Lasker and Lasker and Nelson; for the
two-year college in California see also California, 1958; University of
California, 1960; Liaison Committee, 1960.)

PERSONNEL NEEDS: PRESENT AND FUTURE

The ERA survey in this volume gives data regarding the number of
California institutions currently offering one or more courses in anthropology. The annual report of the U.S. Department of Health, Education, and Welfare on *Earned degrees conferred by Higher Educational Institutions* (1960) lists ninety institutions as conferring the
A.B. degree in anthropology in the period 1954-1955 to 1957-1958. The
numbers of A.B. degrees conferred annually were 280, 308, 309, and
359. The trend seems to be toward the offering of anthropology in an
increasing number of institutions and the expansion of programs in
institutions already offering anthropology. In addition, enrollments
and consequently the demand for teachers may be expected to increase
somewhat more rapidly than in a number of older disciplines.

Turning to the question of the present number of teachers and potential future demands for teachers, answers can be given only by sub-
mitting the few existing data to such techniques as scrying and scapuli-
mancy (sometimes known as extrapolation). Sturtevant (1959) estimates
there are 1,000 to 1,500 anthropologists in the United States and im-
plies that a large number are teaching. The National Education Association reports that anthropology teachers in degree-granting institutions in 1957-58 and 1958-59 constituted about 3 per cent of all new
full-time social science teachers. If we make the (precarious) assump-
tion that the same ratio holds for the present and will continue to hold
for the future, we can estimate that in 1960 there were around 800
full-time teachers of anthropology in the United States and that in the
eleven years from 1959-60 to 1969-70 inclusive, between 1,000 and
1,200 new anthropology teachers will be needed in degree-granting institutions (NEA 1959: 51, Table 30; 57, Table A). If we project the
1958-59 rate, we will produce only about 600 new Ph.D.'s in the current decade, but there is some indication that the number of graduate
students is increasing, and this will raise the production (NSF 1960).
Furthermore, the relatively new demand for M.A.'s suggests the desir-
ability of some intensive investigation of the market and the supply
at this level.

HOW TO MEET THE NEEDS

The graduate student situation clearly needs more analysis. The National Science Foundation Studies (1954, 1960) show that anthropology

graduate students received inadequate support and that anthropologists show the highest mean elapsed time between the A.B. and the Ph.D., 10.7 years. As of April 1, 1958, 664 anthropology graduate students were enrolled more than half time at all levels, and 198 students were enrolled at less than half time. Forty-five foreign students are not included in these figures.

Clearly a substantial increase in the number of Ph.D.'s needed will occur in the next decade. In part, the demand will be met by the increasing number of universities offering Ph.D. programs. Other universities are expanding their programs to attract and handle a larger number of students. Even more important, however, are devices to shorten the period of Ph.D. training. Improvement of the undergraduate preparation of students planning to enter advanced studies, without interfering with other functions of anthropology courses, would permit advancing the time when students begin actual involvement in research. This and other steps suggested in several papers in the companion to this volume (Mandelbaum *et al.* 1962) should shorten the interval between the A.B. and Ph.D. In California the annual increase in enrollments in anthropology courses in the past two years has been 20 per cent or better as compared with annual increases in total college and university enrollments of 5.7 per cent (Lasker and Nelson elsewhere in this volume).

In addition to curricular improvements, increased financial resources for graduate student training are needed. Teaching assistantships or other devices for some supervised teaching experience seem desirable. Funds are needed to provide earlier field research training, perhaps for very good students at the undergraduate level. Much more reliable funds should be available to guarantee students the opportunity not only for field research in connection with doctoral dissertations but also for support while they are engaged in the extended analysis required by anthropological field data and in writing the dissertation.

THE JUNIOR COLLEGE STAFFING PROBLEM

The junior college situation requires a word about the M.A. degree. During 1954-1958 the number of M.A. degrees awarded was slightly more than twice the number of Ph.D. degrees awarded (U.S. D.H.E.W. 1960). An increasing number of teaching staff is being employed without the Ph.D. degree, especially in the junior college where the M.A. is at best the most advanced degree required. Most M.A. programs in anthropology probably are not particularly suited to the needs of the prospective junior college teacher. Field research is normally deferred to the doctoral program. In anthropology, even for persons interested only in teaching, the field research experience is of great value. The increasing role to be played by two-year colleges will mean that half or more of the lower division teaching of anthropology in the United States may soon be done by persons without any field experience. The most critical point of our deliberations concerning the teaching of anthropology may be the kind of instructors to be prepared for the rapidly growing two-year colleges.

There is little indication of the extent to which anthropology is taught in junior colleges outside of California. In many states anthropology is not recognized for the junior college teaching credential (Mandelbaum 1960). Even in California a majority of junior college teachers of anthropology have had little or no formal training in the subject. Moreover, few individuals teaching anthropology in the junior colleges without degrees in anthropology have any significant training in biological sciences. This is the more deplorable where introductory courses in physical anthropology may have large enrollments. In not a few small four-year colleges throughout the country, the situation probably is little different.

Clearly many teachers in junior colleges do a very good job of instruction in anthropology, including some with no earned degrees in the subject (Mandelbaum 1960). Nevertheless, one may doubt that even the dedicated teacher ordinarily has an ample and balanced grasp of the discipline without some formal training in it. Indeed, one may doubt whether even instructors with the M.A. in the discipline ordinarily will have the empathy and understanding of other cultures which seem to come from field research, or will be well acquainted with the growing edges of the discipline. If improved standards can be developed in areas where the junior college establishment or growth is just beginning, it may save a good many future difficulties for universities and four-year colleges. Such improvement must come through outside pressures, for the selection of personnel and teaching assignments in junior colleges generally are made by administrative officials with highly varied educational backgrounds.

A number of helpful steps may be taken by the national association, by regional or local societies, and by universities and colleges.

1) Seek acceptance of anthropology toward general degree requirements in colleges and universities whether a major in anthropology is offered or not. Many institutions "have no social science requirement for bachelor's degrees toward the fulfillment of which anthropology might count" (U.S. D.H.E.W. 1959:4).

2) Seek acceptance of anthropology as a subject-matter field for junior college teachers.

3) Encourage discussion of teaching problems among university, col-

lege, and junior college teachers of anthropology. Each type of institution has special problems which often are not fully known or understood by teachers in other types. Wherever possible, the attendance of administrators from two-year colleges should be sought because of the large role they play in the selection of personnel and in teaching assignments.

4) Support summer institutes for college teachers of anthropology under the National Science Foundation program.

THE FOUR-YEAR COLLEGE

Four-year colleges present a wider variety of staffing problems. This is particularly true when work leading to the M.A. and the junior college credential may be offered. A substantial number of the undergraduate students enrolled in anthropology courses in four-year colleges will not be majors if, indeed, a major is offered. However, the number of larger institutions offering majors is increasing. In California, for example, at least four state colleges are offering majors, and three or four more will soon do so. Again, only a select few of the majors probably will continue into graduate work. In addition, an increasing number of four-year colleges may be expected to offer the master's degree.

In many smaller four-year colleges, and even in some larger ones, the initial introduction of anthropology is very similar to the situation in junior colleges. The first courses either are offered by someone with minimal training in the subject, or, if a trained anthropologist is appointed, he is expected to teach some other subject as well. Usually a major is not contemplated, at least initially. Offerings commonly include an introductory course in physical anthropology, a series of basic courses in cultural anthropology, and often some archaeology with an accompanying field course.

The usual pattern is the initial appointment of a single anthropologist. If his offerings are successful, one or more additional anthropologists are added in time. An undergraduate major may be attempted with two men but more often follows the appointment of a third man in the subject. In some cases the anthropologist in a four-year college has only the M.A. but often has or is far along toward the Ph.D.

So far as training is concerned there would seem to be no justification for special programs for teachers in the four-year college. It is true that the teaching demands call for a fairly broad background rather than intense specialization in one of the subfields of anthropology. Nevertheless, even those students interested primarily in a teaching career and with little concern with research after the Ph.D. will benefit from good research training and experience. For those four-year colleges offering, or planning to offer, the M.A., a quality research Ph.D. should be demanded for a majority of the faculty. In view of the fact that an increasing number of graduate students probably will be coming from the four-year colleges, the universities should encourage no less.

UNIVERSITY PROBLEMS

University problems are perhaps more varied than those of other institutions. One axis of variation is whether anthropology is being introduced for the first time or whether there is to be a strengthening of an existing offering in anthropology. Another is whether the program is planned to be purely for undergraduates or is to include the conferring of the M.A. or the Ph.D. Thirdly, these problems differ depending upon whether the institution is large or small and the amount of emphasis to be placed on varying parts of the program.

With respect to the first set of variables, the situation differs little from that in the four-year colleges. Perhaps the main difference is that a university which makes claim to over-all quality in its faculty and which has more selective entrance requirements than do many of the four-year colleges should place emphasis on attracting research-oriented faculty. To do so, however, I suspect will create built-in drives toward expanding graduate offerings.

Where anthropology is to play a significant role in the undergraduate colleges, these institutions should be staffed with high quality personnel with good Ph.D. training. To attract such people, however, there must be some research opportunity. Whether this can be done without ultimately developing more doctoral graduate programs than the field can sustain remains to be seen. There is an important opportunity for both colleges and universities to experiment with ways of providing faculty with good research opportunities without necessarily establishing a full degree program at the graduate level.

The establishment of new offerings in anthropology in an institution where the subject has not hitherto been taught may be done in two ways. One young and promising man may be hired to introduce the subject, and additional appointments, primarily at low academic ranks, may be made as the program gradually develops. The alternative is to hire several men at once, one or more of whom is a "name" appointment. In old, established and large institutions the latter method may be preferable, for it immediately establishes a status for the discipline among the older and entrenched social sciences. In a younger and rapidly growing institution, the first method allows a more organic growth and more integrated relationships with the growing institution. In either case, the first two or three appointments may still call for considerable teaching versatility.

In considering the variable of institutional size, early decisions on several points may clarify and simplify staffing problems. In general it seems to me wise for small universities not to try to train graduate students intensively in all branches of anthropology. It is true that graduate students especially need some familiarity with all the specialties of anthropology. This may be provided adequately by a broadly trained faculty. It is my personal opinion that unless a staff of more than six to eight is contemplated, concentration on training students in ethnology and social anthropology will permit a department to achieve distinction and to give intensive training at all levels. The faculty may include specialists in subfields, but they should be able to teach effectively in more than one role.

The large institution intending ultimately to offer a graduate program may perhaps be more flexible in its staffing. Nevertheless, as in smaller institutions, persons with primary interests in one of the subfields of the discipline must be prepared and qualified to teach a variety of courses outside their special interests if they are appointed at an early stage in the development of a department. As the department grows, of course, they are able to narrow the focus of their teaching to approximate more closely their research interests. Established departments, especially when making appointments at more advanced levels, may have more specific requirements.

I have spelled out some of the obvious aspects of staffing to emphasize two trends in current demand and their relation to graduate student training. Reviewing recent inquiries, on the one hand there is the continuing demand for individuals with quite broad training able to teach a wide variety of courses, often including introductory courses in one of the subfields of anthropology. Alternatively, the demand may be for a person well trained in one of the subfields of anthropology who is competent to teach a variety of standard introductory or areal courses. A straightforward inquiry for a man who is competent to begin and to develop a program of teaching and research in archaeology or physical anthropology or linguistics or some other areal or subject field is fairly rare.

The moral of these remarks, I think, is that we need to keep two goals in mind in Ph.D. training. One is the need to give as broad a background to students as is possible. This is particularly true of students preparing for careers primarily in teaching. The other objective, particularly for students planning research careers and who are most apt to wind up in a university setting, is laying adequate foundations for a rather specialized research program. In our training programs, particularly at the larger institutions, both these goals should be provided for, and it should be borne in mind that some students will be trained primarily in breadth and others rather narrowly in special fields. For the majority, however, I think some compromise between the two ends probably is necessary if we are not still further to prolong the interval between B.A. and Ph.D.

Here I wish to register my objection to proposals for two kinds of Ph.D.'s. The Ph.D. degree traditionally has been awarded primarily for demonstrated ability to design and carry through independent research after a man has demonstrated his general grasp of the discipline. To award the Ph.D. degree to men without research experience ultimately is to turn out teachers who are insufficiently aware of the sources and nature of scientific knowledge. I strongly believe that the profession should insist on the research Ph.D. degree even for men whose temperament and interests primarily are in teaching. Suggestions for the dual Ph.D. sound suspiciously like the voice of the professional educator who would like to see the Ph.D. brought to the level of most Doctorates of Education.

THE MARKET PLACE

The market place includes the ways by which persons and jobs are brought together, the relations between individual and institution, and the problems of mobility. Insofar as anthropologists conform to general academic patterns there seems no point in recapitulating the total picture of the academic market place given by Caplow and McGee (1958). But anthropologists do, I think, present qualitatively some differences from their academic peers. Moreover, Caplow and McGee are admittedly dealing with a rather selective sample drawn primarily from among universities belonging to what they call the "major league." Consequently it seems worthwhile to comment upon other types of institution, subjective though impressions may be.

Given the small size of the profession, it would appear that in the past anthropology relied even more heavily upon personal contact, meetings, and letters in searching for personnel for replacements or new appointments than do other disciplines. This still seems to be true of the major universities, but there is some evidence that advertising and the use of agencies is increasing in the smaller institutions, particularly where administrators usually make the selection.

Variations in recruitment procedures emphasize the currently haphazard practices by which the job and the man get together. Two things seem to be clear. If the finding and recruitment of anthropology personnel is in the hands of administrators, there should be more sense of responsibility and clearer definition of criteria for selection. Moreover, however unfortunately the social status position of registrants in placement agencies may be viewed, students would be well advised to place their credentials on file at such agencies.

Some conditioning also must be given our graduate students as to the realities of the academic market. Students with research interests —and I think the proportion in anthropology is perhaps high—must reconcile themselves to the possibility of taking early jobs in "Siberia." Siberias sometimes grow up to higher status institutions, and the determined research worker is not precluded from achieving substantial professional status and hence moving upward institutionally.

Caplow and McGee observe that basically faculty members are hired first of all to teach. However, in the higher status institutions most of their advancement depends not upon teaching but upon research and publications. However, in the few very top-flight institutions, Caplow and McGee claim, the teaching and research functions have been successfully integrated.

Caplow and McGee find that the emphasis upon research and publication increases professional standing and loyalties and reduces the institutional involvement of the individual. Consequently in general throughout the academic world the greatest mobility, particularly at the more advanced ages and ranks, is to be found precisely among the individuals in institutions of high status with the best salary scales.

In the past the mobility of high ranking faculty in anthropology in the best institutions does not appear to have been excessive. This is rather surprising for anthropology by its nature should tend even more to weaken institutional loyalties in favor of professional interests. Not only are a high proportion of anthropologists research oriented but also their research tends to take them away from the institution more than do other disciplines. Impressionistically there seems recently to have been an increase in mobility among anthropologists in high ranking institutions, and this trend may be expected to continue. Related to the foregoing is the increasing availability of research funds, creating more temporary vacancies which are increasingly difficult to fill.

This impressionistic survey suggests a number of important conclusions which merit further investigation.

1) We need more investigation of the number and kinds of jobs and the training requirements for each. A significant increase in jobs seems certain. We do not know the distribution of these potential jobs among different kinds of institutions—a pattern that may change significantly in the next decade or two—or what the job requirements will be.

2) We need much more information about the numbers of graduate students, the training they are receiving, and the extent to which we should tailor training to the job requirements. Thus far our training seems oriented primarily to preparing people for the universities with combined teaching and research requirements.

3) We need much better organization of the market place. In part this is a simple matter of communications machinery. Information

about jobs and their specifications needs to be much more widely circulated. Concomitantly we need to find ways for knowledge of persons wishing jobs to be circulated without loss of "face."

Certain points emerge clearly from this survey. In the next decade everything points to a relatively competitive sellers' market for jobs. Orderly recruitment to meet departmental personnel requirements will be difficult, while at the same time new Ph.D.'s may not find the jobs for which they are best qualified.

REFERENCES CITED

CALIFORNIA
   1958   A study of faculty demand and supply in California higher educa-
               tion, 1957-1970. Liaison Committee of The Regents of the Uni-
               versity of California and the California State Board of Education.
               Berkeley and Sacramento.
   1960   A master plan for higher education in California, 1960-1975. Sacra-
               mento.
CAPLOW, THEODORE, AND REECE J. McGEE
   1958   The academic marketplace. New York.
GOINS, JOHN F., AND HAROLD NELSON
   1960   Report of a survey of anthropological teaching in the Southern
               California Region (mimeographed). Riverside and Santa Monica,
               California.
LANZ, CHARLES C.
   1960   Digest of responses to anthropology-sociology questionnaire circulated
               to public junior colleges in Spring, 1958. In Report on the Con-
               ference on Anthropology, Appendix II, 1960. University of Cali-
               fornia.
MANDELBAUM, DAVID G.
   1960   The teaching of anthropology in the United States: a review of the
               symposia of the project for educational resources in anthropology.
               Wenner-Gren Foundation for Anthropological Research, New York.
               Privately circulated.
NATIONAL EDUCATION ASSOCIATION
   1959   Teacher supply and demand in universities, colleges, and junior
               colleges, 1957-1958 and 1958-1959. Washington, D.C.
NATIONAL RESEARCH COUNCIL
   1958   Census of graduate students in basic and applied natural sciences
               in the U.S. and possessions as of April 1, 1958. Washington, D.C.
NATIONAL SCIENCE FOUNDATION
   1954   Graduate enrollment and support in American universities and col-
               leges. Washington, D.C.
   1960   The science doctorates of 1958 and 1959: their numbers, character-
               istics and employment. Washington, D.C.
STURTEVANT, WILLIAM C.
   1959   Anthropology as a career. Smithsonian Institution Publication 4343,
               Washington, D.C.

UNITED STATES, DEPARTMENT OF HEALTH, EDUCATION AND WELFARE

1957   Biennial survey of education in the United States, 1954-1956. OE-
        10003, Washington, D.C.

1959   Social science requirements for Bachelor's Degrees. *In* Bulletin
        1959:8. Washington, D.C.

1960   Earned degrees conferred by higher educational institutions. Wash-
        ington, D.C.

UNIVERSITY OF CALIFORNIA, OFFICE OF RELATIONS WITH SCHOOLS

1960   Report of the conference on anthropology for California two-year
        and four-year collegiate institutions (jointly sponsored by the de-
        partment of anthropology and sociology at University of California,
        Los Angeles, and the Southwest Anthropological Association with
        Los Angeles State College as host institution) (mimeographed). Los
        Angeles.

RAY L. BIRDWHISTELL

IV. *The Use of Audio-Visual Teaching Aids*

A s I AM USING the phrase here, a "teaching aid" is any device utilized in the strategy of the curriculum to implement the transmission process integral to the special communication system of education. I shall outline several techniques and discuss some of the resistances to them. As a teacher and anthropologist, I am not sanguine about swift revision of teaching methods. Unless the new technological developments are utilized in a suitable environment, they will be little more than appendages and hardly worth the effort necessary for their acquisition and exploitation. Properly used, they greatly enrich and improve teaching and research.

INTRODUCTION

For the last century and a half, we have seen throughout the Western world a crescive recognition of the relationship between the concept of universal education and the dream of democracy. From labor unions and church groups and from political and military leaders we have seen a swelling demand for universal, if not better, educational facilities and practices. How can we best adapt our ideals to this wave of demand? We may put our present position into better perspective by examining certain trends in recent history.

Even the least penetrating analysis of the effects of war on social organization reveals its uneven impact on social process. Certain institutions respond by becoming more explicit, formal, and change-resistant. Others change at a velocity which makes them almost unrecognizable. In the modern Western world (and increasingly on a global scope), such changes are most easily seen in the technological area. Although propagandistic and indoctrinating practices are accelerated in wartime, education in the broadest sense tends to be little affected. In the United States, only in the last half century has literacy been considered necessary for the nonleadership military group. However, as military technology became increasingly complex and the number of complicated machines outstripped the number of mechanics, technicians, and technically skilled leaders, special literacies became increasingly necessary throughout the military structure. The demand for literate troops, the shock of disappointment at the rate of illiteracy and the patent inefficiency of traditional teaching methods led the military into experiments in education and indoctrination which approached in volume its accelerated programs in "hard" research.

Machines became more powerful and more complicated, and the velocity of their operations far exceeded the rate of human neural processes. Techniques for gaining acquaintance with them were needed. The high speed camera, new types of film and specialized developing methods, animation techniques, complex film strips and composite slides, in intricately engineered projection apparatus for visual demonstration were designed, machined and put into mass production. Sound engineering kept pace with these innovations. The compact and reliable tape recorder has become almost as common as the typewriter and the duplicating machine as standard equipment in training centers.

These techniques were born in or adopted by the entertainment industry. For thirty years Hollywood and the radio industry had given them a luxury stamp; thus, they were sparingly used in the American school system. The fact that the athletic and the art, music and dramatics departments were first to find use for them did little to modify the luxury image or to enhance their prestige as teaching devices. It remained for the military to demonstrate their "practicality." GI's returned to civilian life to do research, to teach, and to administer. Conversion to peace required a retooling for the school system comparable to that which confronted industry. The masses of students, the critical shortage of classrooms, teachers, and textbooks, and the volume of information accumulated from military research and not yet available in traditional forms combined to create a situation which made public school officials particularly ready for innovation. Not only were primary and secondary school boards now prepared to invest in equipment formerly regarded as window dressing but, in many school systems, special departments were set up to investigate, purchase, repair, and control these items. The education colleges were quick to respond to and take the lead in these developments.

ACQUISITION, SCHEDULING, USE, AND REPAIR OF EQUIPMENT

In spite of these propitious conditions, most college departments have not adapted their programs to the new developments. Why? In some colleges, departments of audio-visual education became a new speciality, and, all too often, were no more integrated into the college program than, say, a department of secretarial science or commercial art. In others, the audio-visual department was attached to the administrative or maintenance branch of the college. The faculty was largely unconvinced of the advantages of technical teaching aids. Central control of the limited equipment, the necessity of scheduling for class use, and the problems of transporting and utilizing the apparatus dampened the interest of all but the most enthusiastic departmental proponents of teaching aids. The faculty complained that they could not get equipment when they needed it and that what they received was seldom convenient for their purposes. A number of faculty members find the presence of the projectionist objectionable. In some cases this seems to be no more than the usual feeling about the disturbing presence of a stranger in the classroom. In others, the projectionist, usually a part-time employee and an undergraduate, evidences his own discomfort by awkward and obtrusive overactivity. Even more exasperating is the breakdown rate of the equipment; it always seems to break down during class time. As one instructor put it, "Of what use to me is film made for high school students, by cameramen and directors who couldn't make the grade, projected by juvenile delinquents on equipment which breaks down in the middle of class session?" There is little point in recommending technical aids to instructors in anthropology, unless we recognize the resistances, objectively based or otherwise, which hamper their adaptation and use. It will, perhaps, be useful to take a series of these objections and to make some suggestions for meeting them.

THE DIFFICULTIES OF CENTRAL CONTROL

A number of the leading experts in audio-visual education agree with the complaints of their academic colleagues about the difficulties of central control. All too often systems of equipment lending and control, while providing an efficient method for round-the-clock utilization of equipment and specialized employees, create situations which stultify the educational process. Certain disciplines, or certain courses within certain disciplines, can anticipate audio-visual needs for a particular hour. Physics, chemistry, and biology, particularly in their large introductory sections, can and do develop a scheduling system which, in an adequately supplied audio-visual situation, reduces friction to a minimum. However, even in such tightly planned courses, unless the department has a sink-or-swim philosophy, discussion sessions often reveal the need for relistening or reviewing. Scheduling from a college-wide or a division-wide pool becomes increasingly difficult in proportion as courses are more flexible.

Even if only presentation devices are used, e.g., tape recorders, record players, sound and silent projectors, audio-visual equipment is expensive. As one director of audio-visual education told me:

It is exceedingly difficult to budget the equipment needs of a college. Formulas based on use records are illusory. They often lead only to decreased use of the equipment, since the inconvenience created by shortage discourages old users and seldom recruits new ones. Few institutions are willing to budget an oversupply of equipment, since no honest audio-visual man will claim that equipment shortage or scheduling problems are the only or even the central detriments of its use.

Conversations with experienced men have led me to the conclusion that one answer to the equipment problem lies in more flexible arrangements than some institutions are presently willing to support.

Any large institution needs a central equipment depot, porters, and projectionist. Medium skilled technicians, at rates beyond those paid today in most institutions, should be employed as maintenance personnel. Reliable machinery is precision made. Even when most carefully purchased with an eye to durability and easy repair, it is delicate and complex. Clumsy repair can turn its clockwork into a destroyer of invaluable tape and film. Multiple or unusual uses of audio-visual equipment leads inevitably to breakdown. No institution should purchase equipment unless arrangements are made for its upkeep. One technician says that standard use at a university involves repair bills of roughly one-quarter to one-half of the original cost of the equipment.

In addition to a central depot of pooled equipment, most departments should have certain items of equipment of their own. A department of anthropology which makes more than the most routine presentations of audio-visual material should budget much of its own apparatus. Although a few institutions have a sufficiently large and well-trained repair staff, most departments will find it to their advantage to stock repair items like tubes and small tube testers, lamps, belts, and the like. Furthermore, after careful investigation of the reliability of dealers and repair shops, maintenance contracts should be purchased. I cannot overstress the need for careful investigation of repairmen. The rapid expansion of the tape recorder and the home movie industries is leading to a considerable repairman lag which may take several years to overcome.

OPERATION OF EQUIPMENT

The advantage of lecturer-operated equipment for social science lectures is clear. Not only does it eliminate the intrusive operator so often complained about, but it also serves to leave control with the teacher. The chalk and blackboard, the pointer and map are part of the teacher's traditional tool kit. All too often, even when the most careful signals are worked out between lecturer and a machine operator, there is a lag in response, if not a complete breakdown in communication. Or, if in the midst of a lecture I discover a new idea in the slides, film, or tape, I find it very difficult to give clear instructions to a projectionist or operator. As a result I, the operator, and the class are confused and disgruntled.

Modern technology makes the projectionist unnecessary, if the lecturer is willing to learn or assign the not too difficult task of threading film or tape. Generally, projection equipment and recorders can be modified for remote control operation by a hand-carried control box that weighs less than a textbook and can be attached by an extension cord to the projector or recorder. It is best to select a hand control with a hook on it, for temporary attachment to podium or blackboard. Such a hook may seem insignificant but it allows a great measure of freedom to the lecturer. Furthermore, light switches and outlets in most college classrooms should be conveniently placed. Maintenance departments are at least as stubborn as academicians in their resistance to innovation, but the utility of properly outlets and switches makes worthwhile the applied anthropological effort entailed.

To achieve compactness and maneuverability in projectors, tape recorders, closed television units, radios, and the like, manufacturers often install puny speakers which can defeat the most conscientious sound production engineer or most tolerant listener. Larger and attractively baffled speakers can be installed at relatively low cost. Mobile speakers, 12 inches or more in diameter, greatly increase the audibility and usefulness of most audio-visual equipment. The greater reliability of the sound results in a reduction of listening fatigue which more than justifies the cost of installation. For classes requiring more fine-grained listening, I recommend a listening table constructed to permit multiple listening through jacked-in earphones. For comfort's sake I urge padded earphones.

Despite my preference for lecturer-operated apparatus I recognize a central difficulty: many people cannot, so to speak, establish a sympathetic bond with machinery. For whatever psychological or cultural reasons, some are clearly "machinicidal"; others use the machine only as a tool of destruction. I have seen too many projectors and tape recorders jammed, jimmied, dropped, and knocked over by direct contact, or even apparently destroyed by telekinesis, to doubt this. When these depredations are added to the spoilage of slides, photos, tapes, and films by well-meaning but destructive manipulators, the results are not only prohibitively expensive but also psychologically unbearable. I have heard of but have never seen a mature individual overcome such destructive tendencies. Some of my psychiatric friends assure me that machinophobia can be overcome, but I remain unconvinced. The implicit caveat is even more applicable in the research than in the demonstration situation. Several of my colleagues have met this problem by having a member of the class with special or, at least, normal mechanical aptitudes take over the operation tasks, while another student takes carbon paper notes for the class assistant.

There has been some discussion recently about the advisability of adding a course or courses to the curriculum to train the potential college teacher in the use of cameras, still or movie, tape recorders and projectors, in film development, slide mounting, and the like. Although such courses may be found in certain of the colleges of education, I question their utility in the anthropological program. Except for the student who has already had considerable experience with recording or presenting sound and light recordings, a single course will do little more than increase his reading ability in one or two specialized areas and/or reduce his anxiety about handling the equipment. These are not negligible values but are hardly sufficient to warrant the inclusion of such technical courses in already packed curricula. More important, separation of the tool from the task it is to perform is the usual consequence. For the anthropological teacher or research worker these instruments provide special techniques for the selection, storage, and recovery of data. When the instrument as such takes precedence over implementation, it stands between the researcher and his data. At times the machinophobe is preferable to the machinophile. He can be persuaded to let the apparatus alone.

THE LOCATION OF AUDIO-VISUAL EQUIPMENT

It is one of the oddities of our time that five thousand dollars worth of precision equipment may be placed in a room guaranteed to reduce its effectiveness to below the level of performance of a hundred dollar mass production unit. Modern school construction often places the instructor in a sun-flooded, live-sound resonating chamber. The problems posed are not difficult to solve. Heavy draperies, round-hooked on a heavy pipe, can go a long way toward handling both problems.

They reduce light to a level suitable for projection (total darkness is neither needed nor recommended) and absorb sound bounce. Heavy blue uniform material (available at very low cost at federal surplus depots) is easily adaptable for this purpose. Some administrators object to the expense of cleaning draperies. However, if classrooms are constructed as concrete and glass sound chambers, some adaptation for seeing and listening must be made. The returns in listening comfort are such that I am not hesitant to recommend the addition of at least one carpeted classroom to any departmental budget. New carpet materials have been developed which are attractive and sturdy and are easier and less expensive to maintain than various other types of floors.

A final thought in this matter. Anthropology departments are growing. Many have waited a long time for adequate office and classroom space and look forward to leaving old buildings for new. However, it is often easier to remodel thick-walled, small-windowed old buildings than to deal with the new constructions, in which these features are almost impossible to achieve. The administrator offered a choice should get technical help. Good sound and light conditions are necessary for behavioral scientists but hard to find in new buildings.

SELECTION AND USE OF FILMS AND SLIDES

The best equipment, adapted for maximal convenience in the most carefully sound- and light-engineered class or work rooms, can be worthless if the teacher cannot make adequate and intelligent use of them. The lecturer wishing to exploit the latest in modern film and sound technology is often at the mercy of amateur movie-makers, whose crude products are scarcely worth projecting. He may feel even more distress when he reviews most of the so-called documentary films now available to him. No more than two or three out of a total of fifty minutes of a film may seem relevant to his purposes. Unless we can develop good films, better techniques for using existing records and devices, and maximize graduate student interest in such techniques, our discussion of equipment is in the worst sense academic.

I maintain that the only way for an anthropological student or teacher to learn to utilize these tools properly is to learn to employ them with reference to the materials, objects, and events he knows best. Only then can he comprehend the appropriate utilization of sound and visual technology. The field worker who concentrates so much on the technical excellence of his photography or recording that he ignores the patterned subject matter that he wants to study or to communicate about, often gives us a product which is aesthetically intriguing but which is frequently of even less research or teaching value than the poorly lighted, badly focused film taken by the man who appreciates his subject matter but misuses his data collection or presentation apparatus.

A teaching aid is not a crutch or a substitute for lectures and discussion or research, though some may employ a film or a tape as a thinly veiled substitute for class preparation. Adequate use of audio-visual materials does not save time in a literal sense, but, rather, it makes severe demands on the serious teacher if he is to prepare properly for the presentation of such materials. I estimate that I show no more than 200 feet of film in a given class session (others report both longer and shorter durations). I usually show the piece of film through its entirety and then go over sections of it in slow motion while discussing it. Often selection of a minute of filmed social interaction takes two to five hours of preview of the the total film. Because of my own special interests, I am sure that I spend more time on small stretches of film than is necessary or possible for most teachers. However, I do not believe that either film or tape can be adequately used without at least two previews. I am convinced, too, that an audience trained (as our students and faculties are) in viewing the commercial movie or television screen carries this training with it into the educational or scientific environment. Introduction to and discussions of the content of films or tape is necessary to overcome this. A single photograph discussed with sophistication and penetration is worth far more than a thousand feet of film presented without preparation, without selectivity, and without discussion.

Although it is uneconomical for anthropology departments to offer specialized courses in audio-visual techniques, just seeing good films or hearing good recordings, however skillful the lecturer may be, is insufficient training for the future teacher and researcher. Courses are needed in which students concerned with problems of pattern are encouraged to use the instruments appropriate to the collection or presentation of problem-centered data. In my experience, if the course has unity, the use of technical aids can be taught at the same time as other aspects of research.

For example, if I wish a class to give a patterned but personalized meaning to the concept of a dwelling unit, I may have the student select a home and explain how this particular home was selected in terms of general knowledge of the area in the light of present theoretical knowledge. I encourage the student to draw diagrams of the house and to select a room within the dwelling upon which to concentrate. I suggest that he map the room and, if possible, make a scale model, including walls, ceiling, and floors, and paying careful attention to colors, forms, and fabrics. I suggest, further, that with the use of a wide angle lens, he take at least two photos of the room from standard angles. After the student has fully familiarized himself with the room, he is urged to interview as many members of the family as possible concerning the use of the room, their feelings about it and its contents, and, when possible, the history of the objects and decorations in it. If more than one family in a neighborhood is being interviewed, informants from neighboring families are carefully led to the discussion of the house and room under study. Many students have simply constructed cameras, and with a little support some quickly learn how to make use of them. One of my students, for instance, took pictures at the eye level of each family member in his favorite sitting position. Another, quickly learned the trick of "hiding behind his camera" and took pictures at regular intervals which were tied in with a tape recording of family interaction. Still another urged various family members to pose in the room, in an endeavor to see whether he could find out anything about each family member's own photographic self-image.

I have, in some classes, used a single situation as the basis of investigation, in others, a range of instances. A group of seniors at the University of Louisville in a year's course with me worked on such diverse projects as a child's clothing, a mother's marketing habits and the activities surrounding the annual cycle of a given crop from the selection of a field for planting to the marketing of the crop. Both my students and I learned a great deal from these exercises, e.g. technically bad films soon become intolerable to the viewer, but technically excellent films which overemphasized a single member of the family or even a succession of individual members could be confusing, because it overstressed the relationship between the ethnocentric cameraman and his subject.

In general, the proposition governing courses which emphasize the appropriate use of technical aids is a familiar one: anthropology rests upon the comprehension of the event in context. Only through the intensive examination of some event, however dramatic or trivial, can the average student internalize the full meaning of this principle. Insofar as time conditions allowed, the presentation of data was taught as a task as important as its recording. The selection, recording, and communication of data are equivalent activities in science. It is my prejudice that they should be taught as such.

SPECIAL PURPOSE EQUIPMENT

Teaching these courses has given me an appreciation of a projector with a reliable reverse switch, which makes repetitive reviewing possible. An instrument like the Bell and Howell slow motion 16 milli-

meter projector is thus a necessary piece of anthropological teaching
equipment. The pace of viewing varies considerably from spectator
to spectator. On slow motion viewing, many students became aware of
things which the lecturer took for granted. As the student learns to appreciate the recelerated pattern, he often accelerates his viewing
speed and becomes a more sensitive observer. Not only does he become a better spectator, but he often becomes aware of the relativ-
ity of time in patterned social interaction. One of the unexpected re-
wards of multiple reëxamination of films is that many students for the
first time get the idea that "natives" are human. In a film in which the
cameraman inadvertently included a view of the audience to a native
dance, replaying even a small strip of this scene revealed that such audiences may argue, applaud, scoff, make love, or engage in any of the
other everyday details of spectatorship. They were not merely ceremonial personages. No less important is the fact that for many students,
it indicated that American audiences, who are often seemingly inat-
tentive to our own ceremonials, are not without culture.

Since I have so emphasized the importance of slow motion projection, I will be more specific here. A number of students have found film
readers (inexpensive editing devices) useful for the review of their
film data. The small image on the viewing plate of the reader makes
it ineffective as a teaching tool. A very useful instrument, the Bell
and Howell Slow Motion Analyser, retailing at slightly under $500.00[1]
is reliable, sturdy, and easy to operate. Resistance to the purchase of
this relatively expensive instrument evaporated when it was demonstrated as a research and teaching tool. Also, the fact that school and
college football coaches already possess such equipment may be used
as a lever for its purchase.

A much more effective but much more expensive projection unit is
the *PerceptoScope.* Designed for military use, it is gaining popularity
in the United States as an aid in reading acceleration and for the production and projection of radiological movies. Designed for the complete time control of in-focus images, the machine enables the projectionist to present 16 millimeter films at speeds from still to 24 frames
per second (conventional sound film speed) from a remote control
panel. The PerceptoScope costs $2,000.00 and takes some time to learn
to operate. However, as far as I know, it has no equal as a research or ex-
hibition device. Not the least of its attributes is the fact that one can
code the film so that the machine will stop and hold a given image for
examination for a predetermined period of time before proceeding to
the next examination point.

There are a number of good sound projectors on the market, but
they should be modified to take a frame counter. Not only does the

frame counter make it easier to find a particular stretch of material, but also it makes possible the absolute timing of behavior under examination. To repeat, the purchaser should be careful to order a projector which can be made to reverse, to avoid having to rewind in order to review a particularly interesting stretch. There is, further, justification for investing in the more expensive sound projector equipped for both optical and magnetic tracks. (The projector normally purchased has an optical sound track.) The addition of a magnetic track and recorder (obtainable in the Bell and Howell's model no. 302EYR at approximately $800.00) enables the lecturer to add his own comments to silent film which has been printed on magnetic film. He can erase and change these comments to fit the particular viewing situation. For one who is concerned with music and language analysis, the magnetic projector equipped with a frame counter is highly useful. He can take his tape recordings, transfer the sound to magnetic film and take timing readings. This has proved to be better for linguistic and musical clocking than the footage counter on the tape recorder. The magnetic sprocketed film does not stretch the way recorder-run tape does, and readings can be much finer.

No projection instrument, however skillfully tooled, can overcome the disadvantages inherent in shoddy, badly planned, or inappropriately edited film or tape. Again, if properly utilized, such films may be made into useful teaching material through the selection and time control provided by good instrumentation. The student may be shown the importance of what was otherwise ignored or avoided. It is usually possible to use the film to derive data unforeseen by the cameraman. That is, just as some of our best field material is hidden in notes we didn't know we took, so also do films contain material which was taken without the awareness of the cameraman.

Information about camera and recording equipment and suggestions for use change as new devices become available. Readers will nevertheless profit from the excellent article by Hitchcock and Hitchcock.[2] I find little to quarrel with in their selections, and it could well be made required reading for would-be field workers and their interested seniors. In addition, the results of a Wenner-Gren conference on anthropological films and movie-making, when they become available, will no doubt be very useful.

Here, however, I am more concerned with the general context of equipment than with equipment itself. The need for teaching techniques which are part of an over-all plan of teaching cannot be overemphasized. It has been my experience that one of the greatest handicaps to the systematic use of teaching aids is the inclination on the part of the teacher to think of the piece of equipment and then to plan pos-

sible uses for it. One should, rather, examine the problems in teaching
and research and then search for methods for their solution.

One of the immediate practical results of relating equipment needs
to actual problems is the likelihood of favorable action on requests for
grants to purchase audio-visual equipment. Some administrators, for-
tunately rare in anthropology, regard such equipment as a ceremonial
accoutrement of office rather than as tools integral to teaching or research. Requests which are clearly understood by the applicant and simply and lucidly justified in terms of this understanding are in general
sympathetically regarded by the reviewing officers of federal government agencies and foundations. Many institutions were and are too
poor to purchase even minimal recording and projection equipment.
With federal and foundation funds now available, it is possible, with
planning, to get good equipment, but grant requests are more likely
to succeed if they reveal clearly the close connection between the equipment requested and the specific teaching or research functions it is
to perform.

CONCLUSION

Teaching aids are not alien to the teaching tradition of anthropology.
we have always encouraged students to handle artifacts, bones, and
art objects. Maps, globes, and photographs have been the *sine qua non*
of ethnological and archaeological course work. The slide projector is
as customary a piece of basic equipment as the blackboard. More important, most anthropological teachers are devoted to the proposition
that field work—regardless of the anthropological specialty—is our primary learning situation. The field context in itself can be a fully
equipped laboratory for learning anthropological techniques.

Although archaeology, physical anthropology, and linguistics have
characteristically tied their teaching to their field tools, with a very few
notable exceptions, the novice in ethnology or social and cultural anthropology is thrown tool-less into the field. Those who have survived
the experience are testaments to the effectiveness of the method, but in
a world that demands hundreds of anthropologists where tens were
once required, the experience of these survivors does not necessarily
prepare them to teach in the situation occasioned by the new recognition and demand.

Exceptional students can be prepared for field work by the sink-or-
swim method, and we need not sacrifice in mass production our com-
mitment to field research as prerequisite training for the professional
anthropologist. By making appropriate use of tape, film, and still photography in our classes we can not only acquaint more students with
basic field data storage techniques but we can also prepare more stu-

dents for observation in a way heretofore impossible. Used carefully, such methods give to the student from other disciplines more dramatic and convincing insight into the dynamics of culture, and our own students are sensitized to their future operations.

Throughout the discussion above, *carefully* selected equipment, *systematically* studied film and tape, and the *appropriate* utilization of these have been stressed. The educational milieu is shifting; good equipment is becoming available. More and more American students have gained at least amateur control of the camera and the recorder. However, just any film with Bantus or Hopi in it, run through by an indifferent projectionist, in a class taught by a lecturer who feels "it can't do any harm and they might learn from it" can do more harm than good. The impact of these media is so demonstrably important that they must be used with acumen and caution. No department should undertake an expanded audio-visual program without self-confrontation concerning disciplinary directions and curricular ideals. Technical aids are too expensive and time-consuming for casual or careless insertion into the teaching program.

In the final analysis, it is not the expense involved in the purchase or maintenance of equipment nor even the precious hours of class time that weigh against lackadaisical appending of these devices to a teaching program. Disrespectful or fearful manipulation of instrumentation on the part of the teacher perpetuates or accentuates this attitude on the part of the student. There is no excuse for field work which does not make the best possible utilization of modern tools. The history of science can often be written in terms of its instrumentation. Preoccupation with toolmaking can arrest the development of a science; antiquated instrumentation can lead to its extinction.

NOTES AND REFERENCES

[1] This and other prices quoted are as of 1961.
[2] See John T. and Patricia J. Hitchcock. August, 1960. Some considerations for the prospective ethnographic cinematographer. American Anthropologist 62:656-674.

GABRIEL W. LASKER

V. *Teaching Aids*
in Physical Anthropology

(With a listing prepared by Kenneth A. R. Kennedy)

A SURVEY of the teaching of anthropology in the State of California (Lasker and Nelson, elsewhere in this volume) reveals that one
of the chief needs expressed by teachers of anthropology is for audio-
visual aids and for annotated lists of these, together with sources of
supply. As Professor Charles E. Snow of the University of Kentucky
shows in a discussion of his introductory course in physical anthropology which is given on television, there is ample opportunity to use visual aids and to devise new ones for courses in this subject. A moderate
variety of such aids for the teaching of physical anthropology is now
available, and the catalogs of the suppliers provide lists, illustrations
and prices.

Mr. Kenneth A. R. Kennedy, in the listing below, deals with slides,
casts, models, charts, and primate materials for dissection that are
available from biological supply companies. His report is supple-
mented with notes on sources and a few data about maps, films, and
anthropometric instruments. Kennedy considers separately teaching
aids for lower division (mainly introductory courses open to freshmen and sophomores), for upper division, and for graduate courses,
although he believes that in practice many of the aids will be useful
at all levels. In the following excerpt from his report and elsewhere, I
have added references to some suppliers of the type of materials mentioned. There is no implication that the sources listed in the notes offer

63

products superior to those of unlisted sources. In fact, comparable materials can sometimes be purchased more conveniently from local supply houses.

SKELETONS, CASTS, AND OTHER MATERIALS
AVAILABLE FROM BIOLOGICAL SUPPLY COMPANIES

I. LOWER DIVISION LEVEL

Teaching aids are most abundant for the purposes of a general course of instruction in human evolution, fossil man, races, genetics, and basic human anatomy.

A. *Human Evolution:* Sets of plaster casts are available to illustrate the changes in the cranium from Eocene primate fossil forms to living primates.[1,2,3] These are of two kinds: endocasts and casts of complete crania. These may be purchased individually or as mounted sets.[1]

B. *Living Primates:* In addition to plaster casts of ape and monkey crania,[1] actual skeletons of contemporary primates are available.[1,2,3] These may be bought completely articulated, or particular skeletal parts may be purchased separately. Skeletons of apes are difficult to acquire and should be ordered in advance, since supply houses do not always have them on hand. Photographic slides in color of wild and captive primates supplement the skeletal material.[2]

C. *Fossil Man:* The plaster casts include individual life-size reproductions of skulls and endocasts of fossil hominids from Java, China, Europe, and America.[1,4] Also available are plaster casts of other bones (Pithecanthropus femur, etc.). Models of both bony and reconstructed soft parts of particular fossil crania supplement the casts. Photographic slides of original fossil specimens are also available.[5,6] The paintings by Knight for the American Museum of Natural History show the ecological conditions of Pleistocene hominids.[2,6]

D. *Human Genetics:* The basic concepts of human genetics may be illustrated by charts, models, and photographic slides. One chart contains ten drawings of mitosis [sic] in the sex cell of a whitefish.[2] These same drawings are reproduced in painted high-relief models which are mounted on pedestals.[2] A panel of painted and high-relief models showing changes both in mitosis and meiosis and a set of color slides of these same models give a complete picture of these basic genetic processes.[1] For a practical demonstration of the familial distribution of a hereditary trait, the instructor may wish to distribute PTC leaflets to the class.[7]

E. *Human Anatomy:* The use to which the instructor may put the following aids, many of which are bulky and non-portable, will depend in large measure upon (a) the size of the class, (b) the appointments of the classroom, i.e., whether it is equipped as a laboratory with permanent fixtures, (c) the presence or absence of "quiz sections," where the student may receive additional material to that presented in the lecture hall. Some of the material described in this section of the paper may best be applied to upper division instruction which presupposes smaller classes and properly equipped laboratories.

Skeletons may be purchased either completely articulated or in boxes of non-articulated bones.[1, 2, 3, 8] Crania are complete or dissected into sagittal or horizontal halves. Plastic casts of a Homo sapiens skeleton and crania (male, female, child)[3, 8] may substitute for actual crania. A wide selection of charts is available on the skeletal system, various aspects of the skull, sections of human skin showing histological features, and human dentition.[1, 2, 8, 9] A large colored and high-relief model of a section of human skin with glands, hair follicles, and muscular features is useful in a description of skin and hair pigmentation.[2]

If an opaque projector is employed, key cards are useful.[2] These are sets of binder-size cards with biological drawings. Their opaque finish makes them suitable for this type of projection. If desired, the key cards may be used with examination cards, identical save for the omission of the labels. An enlarged edition of these cards is suitable for use as charts.[2] The subjects are the skeletal system, muscular system, joints, brain, dentition, skin and hair, and regional anatomical sections. Both cards and charts are in black and white.

II. Upper Division Level

A. *Evolution:* A set of 10 plaster casts showing changes in osseous features of vertebrate crania from Crossopterygians to man may be useful in illustrating the concept of morphological changes through time. This set is based upon the exhibit of W. K. Gregory at the American Museum of Natural History.[1]

B. *Living Primates:* Articulated or non-articulated skeletons of primates other than man may be purchased. Also particular parts of the skeleton of a desired species may be procured. Juvenile specimens are in stock in most supply houses from time to time. If requested, these companies will dissect a specimen to show the structure of particular regions (alveolar area, epiphyses of long bones, etc.).[1, 2] Microscopic slides of sections of monkey and human scalps showing histological features could be included in a study of primatology.[1, 2]

C. *Human Anatomy:* Human skeletons useful for a laboratory class include specimens upon which areas of muscle attachment have been painted.[1, 2, 3, 8] Sets of human bones with or without crania may be used for student identification. "Beauchene" mounts which display the individual bones as well as articulated crania of adults and juveniles are available.[1, 2, 3, 8] Some crania have painted upon them the locations of muscles, nerves, and blood vessels.[2, 8] For a study of the dentition, dissected mandibles of juveniles and adults may be of use.[2, 3, 8]

Complementing this skeletal material are charts illustrating the joint system and its structure; the muscular system (gross and regional); the skeletal system and the formation of bone; the eye and brain, the integumental system of the scalp and palm; the head and neck; the male and female pelvis and perineum, and the dentition.[1, 2, 8, 9, 10]

Models of human anatomical parts include the head and neck with the location of muscles, blood vessels, nerves, and areas of the brain indicated in color.[1, 2, 3, 8] Life-size and enlarged models are available. A good aid for instruction on the brain is one in which a model brain rests within the base of a model cranium[1, 2, 3] This brain may be lifted out and "dissected" into its various parts. Another model illustrates the skin viewed in three dimensions.[2] Models of juvenile and adult dentitions in dissected mandibles may be included in a study of how to tell the age of individuals from remains.[1,3,8] For the study of the pelvic region, a set of 16 models of pelves from the collection of T. Wingate Todd is available.[8] This set illustrates the four pelvic types described by Caldwell, Moloy, and D'Esopo.

Microscopic slides of transverse sections of skin from Caucasians and Negroes show the deposits of melanin and the form of the hair follicles.[1,2,3,11] There are also slides of periosteum, bone, and marrow and slides showing insertion of tendon and muscle with bone.[1,2,3,8]

III. GRADUATE LEVEL

Suggestions for teaching aids on this level are limited to anatomical specimens. Human and monkey brains prepared for dissection are available from biological supply houses.[2] Complete human cadavers present different problems of acquisition for study, since their possession demands legal recognition and licensing. To most students in physical anthropology, this privilege is available only through departments of human anatomy.

SOME PREFERRED TEACHING AIDS

Of all teaching aids, casts of fossil man are perhaps the most commonly used. Almost all the available molds have now been concentrated at one place, the University Museum at the University of Pennsylvania.[4] Although recently made casts may not be as carefully prepared as the specimens made by the late F. O. Barlow, most are adequate for classroom use. The most useful illustrations of fossil man are the colored 2″ × 2″ slides prepared by W. W. Howells[5] and the wall chart of skulls of fossil and living man and the living great apes.[9]

Good human skeletal material (usually specimens from India) and plastic skeletons (also cast from that of a small Indian) are available and, for many student uses, are superior to most archaeological skeletal remains. The Frohse anatomical charts, painted by Max Broedel, especially those on the skeleton, muscles, ear, and eye,[8,10] and the charts by Pauline Larivière[9] are excellent for pointing out features of human anatomy and for permanent display and use in the classroom. Some of the colored stereoscopic slides of dissections and specimens prepared by Dr. David L. Bassett of Stanford University are useful if the teaching involves much anatomical detail.[12] The serial dilution method of testing PTC sensitivity is preferable to use of paper leaflets for this purpose; the reagent (phenylthiourea) is readily available,[13] and a glass kitchen measuring cup and plastic picnic cups and spoons are the only other equipment necessary.

Maps

Maps are another visual aid; important because, as Ehrich (1960) has shown, many college students have very little knowledge of places. Wall maps,[9,10,14,15] outline maps,[9,10,14,15,16] flat maps,[14,15,16] plastic relief maps,[14,17] globes,[10,15,16] and topographical maps[18] are all valuable. The maps of the atlas of anthropology by Spencer and Johnson (1960) are useful but would be more so if political boundaries were shown.

Films

Relatively few motion pictures are suitable for showing in courses in physical anthropology. Two recent films on primates, *Baboon Behavior, Howler Monkeys of Barro Colorado Island,* and an earlier one, *Social Behavior of Rhesus Monkeys,* are often shown in such courses, and a film on the evolution of man intended for high school audiences is being prepared by the American Institute of Biological Sciences.

Anthropometric Instruments

One teaching device in physical anthropology, at least at the intermediate level, is to introduce the student to the concepts of variability and to statistical methods through exercises in anthropometry. Standard Martin instruments are available from a Swiss manufacturer[19] and inexpensive anthropometers, sliding and spreading calipers, and the lightweight Seabeck balance are made in the United States.[20] Because of the importance of measurements of body form and composition, a skinfold caliper,[21,22] and ordinary steel tapes and a physician's scale are useful. Access to a calculating machine[23] and computing machines is a legitimate equipment need of advanced students of physical anthropology.

General

At the advanced level any teaching aid which helps train in professional procedure is, of course, useful. Thus, materials collected by physical anthropologists, archaeologists, and ethnologists—community census data, protocols of experiments and tests, field notes, and photographs are useful for presenting unsolved problems to students. With these materials, students can work on such problems. The instructors can show what professional anthropologists do with their raw data. By saving series of his own manuscripts and proofs of his publications, the teacher can also show students the nature of professional criticism by editors. Such criticisms, from substantive questions down to details of writing style will show Ph.D. candidates what standards are expected when they present their research. Finally, for anthropology the subject is man, and this "audio-visual aid" to anthropological study is so ubiquitous that every student of the subject can have some firsthand experience observing, interviewing, measuring and evaluating him in many situations and ways.

NOTES

[1] Ward's Natural Science Establishment, Inc., P.O. Box 1712, Rochester 3, New York (skeletons, models, charts, slides).

[2] Turtox Products, General Biological Supply House, Inc., 8200 So. Hoyne Avenue, Chicago 20, Illinois (key cards, lantern slides, skeletons, charts, models).

[3] Carolina Biological Supply Co., Elon College, North Carolina (skeletons, histological slides, models, monkeys for dissection).

[4] The University Museum, 33d and Spruce Streets, Philadephia 4, Pennsylvania (casts of fossil man).

[5] Bureau of Audio-visual Instruction. Attention: Mr. Andrew E. Holmes, University of Wisconsin, 1312 W. Johnson Street, Madison 6, Wisconsin (color slides of fossil man).

[6] American Museum of Natural History, Central Park West at 77th Street, New York 24, New York (color slides of ancient man).

[7] American Genetics Association, 1507 M Street, N.W., Washington 5, D.C. (paper impregnated with phenylthiocarbamide-PTC).

[8] Clay Adams, Inc., 141 East 25th Street, New York 10, New York (skeletons, models, charts, slides).

[9] Denoyer-Geppert Co., 5235-59 Ravenswood Avenue, Chicago 40, Illinois (charts, maps, models, globes).

[10] A. J. Nystrom and Co., 3333 Elston Avenue, Chicago 18, Illinois (maps, charts, models, globes).

[11] Cambosco Scientific Co., 37 Antwerp Street, Boston, Massachusetts (models, slides, charts).

[12] Sawyers, Inc., Portland, Oregon (stereoscopic slides of human gross anatomy).

[13] Eastman Organic Chemical Co., Rochester 3, New York (Phenylthiourea-PTC).

[14] Weber Costello, Chicago Heights, Illinois (maps, globes).

[15] Rand McNally & Co., P.O. Box 7600, Chicago 80, Illinois (maps, globes).

[16] C. S. Hammond & Co., Maplewood, New Jersey (maps, globes).

[17] Aero Service Corporation, 210 East Cortland Street, Philadelphia 20, Pennsylvania (plastic relief maps).

[18] United States Geological Survey, Washington 25, D.C. (topographical maps).

[19] Siber, Hegner & Co., 183 Madison Avenue, New York 16, New York (anthropometric instruments).

[20] Swan Tool and Manufacturing Co., 30 Bartholomew Avenue, Hartford 6, Connecticut (anthropometric instruments).

[21] K. O. Lange, Wenner-Gren Aeronautical Research Laboratories, University of Kentucky, Lexington, Kentucky (skin-fold calipers, sliding calipers).

[22] British Indicators Ltd., Sutton Road, St. Albans, Herts, England (skin-fold calipers).

[23] There are agents for Facit, Friden, Marchant, Monroe, Olivetti, and Remington Rand in most cities (calculators).

REFERENCES CITED

EHRICH, R. W.
    1960   Ignorance of elementary geography among college students and student teachers. School and Society 88:65-66.
SPENCER, R. F., AND ELDEN JOHNSON
    1960   Atlas of anthropology. Dubuque, Iowa, Wm. C. Brown Co.

JOHN HOWLAND ROWE

VI. *Library Problems
in the Teaching
of Anthropology*

THE NUMBER OF VOLUMES in a college or university library system
may be limited by the availability of funds, but the value of the collection for teaching purposes reflects the willingness of the teaching
staff to devote time and thought to the problems of library organization and to the selection of materials to be acquired. Librarians ex-
pect faculty guidance in such matters and need it if they are to provide
the kind of service which will contribute effectively to the teaching program. A discussion of library problems in anthropology from the teacher's standpoint may prove helpful to college and university teachers
who have to deal with such problems.

Each subject has its own peculiar library problems, and anthropology has some especially serious ones. In the first place, the systems
of organization used in most general libraries in the United States
make it exceptionally difficult for anthropologists to find the literature of their field. Library materials are organized for the reader's
use in two ways: by call numbers and by subject headings in the catalog. The call numbers reflect a classification by subject and area which
is used in shelving the books. The subject headings provide cross-refer-
ences in the catalog when the cataloguer considers that a book contains
material pertinent to more than one subject.

The systems of call numbers now used in most general libraries
were devised and put into practice many years ago when anthropology

was generally visualized as a very small subject, and its point of view
was familiar to few readers. The result is that traditionally and in
current practice books which are written from the comparative point
of view of anthropology are catalogued and shelved with books which
are not, because of some similarity in the subject matter discussed. In
most general libraries the literature of anthropology is scattered from
religion and philosophy to warfare and marine transportation. This
situation may have the advantage of calling the attention of an occasional reader from another field to anthropological contributions related to his interest, but it creates undeniable difficulties for anthropology students.

Most libraries which maintain a subject catalog use the subject
headings of the Library of Congress, because these headings are
printed on the Library of Congress catalog cards and are also available
in a bulky manual. Unfortunately, the Library of Congress subject
headings are designed to help the "general reader" who knows no
anthropology, and the categories which are familiar to students of anthropology are either not represented at all or appear under unfamil-
iar names.

A further difficulty arises from the fact that anthropology includes
a concern for remote, obscure peoples who are often not numerous and
who speak languages which are seldom studied in American universities. A certain proportion of the literature on such peoples consists
of local publications issued in small editions by firms not used to dealing on an international market and which are seldom reviewed in
standard journals or listed in the more widely circulated book catalogs. Unless a special effort is made, backed by some personal knowledge of the area, most of this local literature goes out of print before the
anthropologists who want to use it can find out that it exists and request that it be ordered.

Some ways of meeting these special problems will be discussed in
the sections which follow.

GENERAL AND SPECIAL LIBRARIES

Anthropology books are handled in one of two ways in colleges and
universities in the United States. They either form part of a general
collection housed in a central library or they constitute a special collection housed in its own quarters convenient to the teaching and research facilities of the department. Each of these arrangements has certain advantages, and the balance of advantage varies according to the
nature of the teaching program and the size of the institution.

The central library arrangement is more economical and provides
better library service in smaller institutions in which the emphasis

is on undergraduate teaching. For this reason, most colleges and universities begin with a single central library. Any subsequent proposal to establish a specialized library for anthropology or any other subject then represents an expensive and difficult administrative reorganization. We should consider what the advantages of such a change might be, and under what circumstances these advantages outweigh the original expense.

Specialized libraries are always more attractive to readers than general libraries, because the specialized ones are small. It is easier for a reader to find the books on his subject in a small library and to learn to use its reference facilities. The service can also be more personal and informal, and the librarian who handles reference questions is more likely to know the books under his care. These advantages must be balanced against the disadvantages that the reader is less likely to happen on books in other fields which might interest him, and that a small library cannot afford to maintain extensive collections of general periodicals and reference works which may contain important material on its special subject. Readers who prefer to use a specialized library must still go to the central library for certain purposes, and extra travel is involved if the two libraries are in different buildings.

A specialized anthropology library has the advantage that it brings together the anthropology books which are scattered by the cataloguing systems used in general libraries. The effect is nearly the same whether the call number system of the central library is maintained or whether a special system using anthropological categories is instituted.

Something can be done about improving the subject entries in the catalog of a specialized library. Depending on the availability of cataloguers the improvement may consist merely of adding a few additional headings or of instituting an entirely new system. One of the few anthropology libraries in the United States which has its own system of subject headings is the Peabody Museum Library at Harvard. The Peabody Museum system is by no means the best which could be devised for the purpose, but at least it uses anthropological categories.

The catalog of the Peabody Museum Library illustrates another potential advantage of the specialized library. The Peabody Museum Library catalog includes cards for articles in journals as well as for books and monographs. This type of cataloguing is technically called "analytical cataloguing," and it is so expensive that general libraries can afford to do very little of it. Analytical cataloguing is such a valuable aid to research, however, that any specialized library should do as much of it as funds permit.

General libraries usually do not collect reprints as a matter of policy, but specialized libraries can increase their resources considerably by doing so. The most valuable reprints, of course, are those from general journals which the specialized library does not have. It should be remembered, however, that there is little point in collecting reprints unless the library can afford to catalog them.

As we noted earlier, the system of keeping all books in a central library is most appropriate for a relatively small institution concentrating on undergraduate instruction. When an anthropology department develops a graduate program to the point where it is handling more than about twenty students, however, the problem of meeting staff and student research needs requires better facilities than a central library can offer, and the establishment of a separate anthropology library is a great help to the teaching program.

If an anthropology department has a museum associated with it the combined needs of the department and the museum may justify the establishment of a separate anthropology library even without a major graduate program. The research value of museum collections is greatly increased if they can be used in close connection with the relevant literature, and it is not the same thing to have the books in another building where they are hard to find.

If there is a reasonable likelihood that a small anthropology department will develop a large graduate program or build up substantial museum collections, every effort should be made to start a specialized library before the need for it becomes acute. Even with substantial funds available it takes about ten years' work to build up a collection of anthropology books to the point where it is really useful for research, and the faster the collection has to be put together the more expensive it becomes.

On the other hand, there is no point in establishing a new specialized library unless reasonably adequate quarters can be provided for it and a qualified librarian put in charge. At the least, provision should be made for a well lighted room large enough to provide reading space for students and work space for the librarian. Many small specialized libraries are operated with volunteer help or under the supervision of a department secretary, but such arrangements rapidly get out ot hand if the collection of books grows much over 500 volumes.

COLLECTING POLICY

The problems of collecting books and other library materials in anthropology are much the same whether the materials collected are housed in a central library or in a smaller specialized one. Collecting involves two different kinds of operations: selection, or the decision as to what materials should be collected, and acquisition, or securing these materials after the decision that they are needed has been made. Acquisition is usually handled by specialists, either in the library system or in a purchasing department, but selection is a responsibility of the teaching staff.

The ideal selection policy, and the simplest to administer, would be to order every title in anthropology which becomes available and which is not already in the collection. However, there are few colleges and universities which can afford the cost of such a program. The volume of publication in anthropology is now so great that it would require an appropriation of at least $3,500.00 for book purchases to acquire the new materials available in 1960 which cannot be secured on exchange. The amount which could be spent on out of print materials offered by dealers would be difficult to estimate meaningfully, because the effective limit is the amount of searching through book catalogs which the staff finds time for. It would certainly not be difficult to spend more on out of print books than on new ones, unless the library already had a remarkably complete collection. It should be kept in mind also that it now costs anywhere from $3.50 to $6.00, mostly in labor, to accession a book, catalog it, and get it onto the shelf after it is acquired. A library with a high rate of acquisition must maintain a large staff of cataloguers. The expense of binding is another serious consideration which adds significantly to the cost of journals, monographs, and many foreign books.

In the more common situation in which unlimited funds are not available, priorities must be established and followed. Where the library supports a teaching program the first priority should naturally go to materials needed for instruction purposes, including lecture preparation by the teaching staff. A second priority should go to library materials needed for faculty research. Naturally, only the teacher involved can decide whether he needs this or that book for his teaching or research, and it is for this reason that book selection has to be a responsibility of the teaching staff. If it is shirked, both teaching and research suffer accordingly.

The selection of materials to be purchased has to be made from the materials which are known to be on the market. The more information available on the book market the better the selection which can be made. Information on new books can be obtained from reviews and lists of current publicatons in the standard journals and from those dealers' catalogs which list new as well as second hand materials. Information on the availability of out of print books comes entirely from dealers' catalogs. Anthropologists concerned with selecting or buying books should get their names on the mailing lists of some of the principal dealers who handle books on anthropology. There are dealers of this kind in New York, Mexico City, Lima, London, Edinburgh, Paris,

Leiden, Amsterdam, Bonn, Berlin, and a number of other cities, and the addresses of such dealers can be secured from the Order Department of any large library. At colleges and universities with established anthropology programs the central library usually receives many catalogs listing anthropological books and is glad to make them available to members of the teaching staff for selection purposes.

There is no easy solution to the problem of securing the more obscure local publications that rarely appear in the regular catalogs. The problem can only be handled by paying close attention to the citations in local works of scholarship and by corresponding with dealers in the area involved. Even so, much will be missed unless the anthropologists concerned can make periodic visits to the area with commissions to buy local publications for their library.

One of the best ways to stretch a limited library budget is through exchanges. Many monograph series and some journals are available on exchange; books rarely are, unless currency restrictions make a kind of international barter necessary. In order to arrange exchanges, of course, the institution must have a research series of its own to offer. Since the distribution of a series of research publications brings prestige to the institution which publishes it, anthropologists at many institutions find that it is easier to raise money to support a publication program than it is to raise funds to buy books. If a publication program can be established, however, it provides a very valuable supplement to the book budget as well as stimulating research output.

Another way to supplement an inadequate book budget is to encourage gifts and bequests to the library. Even without personal solicitation, public expressions of gratitude provide much encouragement for further gifts. All books received as gifts or purchased on gift funds should be marked conspicuously with the name of the donor, and for a large gift a special bookplate should be provided. Some publicity in the campus newspaper may also be helpful. If someone connected with the department retires or dies, a fund in his name to provide books for the anthropology collection is an excellent way to perpetuate his memory, the memorial being expressed in an appropriate book plate.

Care should be taken not to accept any gifts which carry with them a stipulation that the books given must be kept together, or that they may not be disposed of, or that they must not be allowed to circulate. A restricted gift is a permanent burden.

If the regulations of the institution permit the sale of duplicates, this practice will provide a small but valuable supplement to purchasing funds, while at the same time making more anthropological publications available to students and stimulating their interest in books. Duplicates can also be used in barter arrangements with other institutions, though such arrangements have the disadvantage that they require extensive correspondence.

SPECIAL PROBLEMS OF ANTHROPOLOGY LIBRARIES

The satisfactory operation of any library requires extensive technical knowledge which is usually transmitted in library schools but is also available in reference books and manuals. The technical knowledge of library problems now available, however, refers in large part to the problems of general libraries, and most published systems of call numbers and subject headings are designed for general library use. A beginning has been made toward studying the problems of specialized libraries in certain other fields, and a few special cataloguing systems have been devised, George L. Trager's classification system for linguistics being a pertinent example (Trager, 1948). Virtually no work of this kind has been done for other fields of anthropology, however. The number of anthropology libraries in the United States is now increasing rapidly, and the need for work on their problems is becoming urgent. The following projects would be particularly helpful:

a. A survey of existing anthropology libraries in the United States and abroad to collect information on the experience of different libraries in handling problems of organization, design of library quarters, acquisition, binding, cataloguing, reference, and circulation. The experience of older libraries in these respects would be very useful to newer ones, and information on such matters might prevent some repetition of earlier errors.

b. A call number classification for the literature of anthropology which would group the books in categories familiar to anthropologists. I know of only two published efforts in this direction, an antiquated one by Juul Dieserud and one published by me in Spanish (Dieserud 1908, Rowe 1947). Mine provides a relatively small number of categories, and it would be desirable to have also as an alternative a system with more and smaller subject divisions.

c. A manual of subject headings for anthropology libraries, the headings reflecting anthropological terminology and based on anthropological categories.

The suggestion has been made on a number of occasions that the problem on analytical cataloguing might be solved by making reproductions of the Peabody Museum Library catalog. I had occasion to check the Peabody Museum Library catalog with this suggestion in mind a few years ago and came to the conclusion that reproducing it would not solve the problem. The quality of the cataloguing and the quality of the subject coding is very variable, and the reliability of the coverage is deceptive. It would be better to explore the possibility of organizing a cooperative project supported by a group of anthropology libraries, each of which would undertake to do the analytical cataloguing of certain journals to uniform standards. The cards could be duplicated by offset at some institution which has the facilities for this process and distributed to the participating libraries, the expense of the reproduction being shared by the participants.

An exchange of information among anthropology libraries on problems of acquisition might also be useful, especially in dealing with the problem of local publications. A series of leaflets on acquiring foreign anthropology materials written by librarians who have dealt with such problems would have real value in this regard.

Perhaps what is most needed, however, is a more general realization on the part of anthropologists that they have an important stake in library problems, both as teachers and as research scholars.

REFERENCES CITED

DIESERUD, JUUL
    1908   The scope and content of the science of anthropology; historical review, library classification, and select, annotated bibliography; with a list of the chief publications of leading anthropological societies and museums. Chicago, The Open Court Publishing Co.
ROWE, JOHN HOWLAND
    1947   La organización de bibliotecas antropológicas. Boletín Bibliográfico, año XX, vol. XVII, diciembre. Lima, Nos. 3-4:158-178.
TRAGER, GEORGE LEONARD
    1948   A bibliographical classification system for linguistics and languages. Reprinted from Studies in Linguistics 3:54-108 (1945), 4:1-50 (1946). Washington (also Revisions 1-2, 1948-51).

ACKNOWLEDGMENTS

This paper has profited from suggestions by Robert E. Pfeiffer and Arthur B. Waugh of the staff of the University of California Library, Berkeley, to whom grateful acknowledgment is made. The estimate of the cost of acquiring current publications is based on research by Rexford S. Beckham done in 1959. The specific figure given for 1960 is my own calculation, however, and Mr. Beckham should not be held responsible for it.

COMPILED BY
REXFORD S. BECKHAM
with the assistance of Marie P. Beckham

VII. *A Basic List of Books and Periodicals for College Libraries*

THIS BIBLIOGRAPHY is a basic list of books and periodicals suitable for the undergraduate teaching of anthropology. It is intended primarily as a tool for the improvement of library resources, especially in institutions where course offerings in anthropology are relatively new. Since the list is mainly for library purchasing for undergraduate use, the emphasis is on titles in English and in print. Titles in foreign languages or titles not readily available for purchase have been included if their intrinsic importance warrants. No limit was set on the number of titles to be included. The list includes as many titles as a number of consultants on each section considered suitable and of more than immediate importance. It is our hope that the list will continue to be helpful for five or ten years and that most of the items listed will have lasting value.

It is assumed that any library using this list as a buying guide will reserve funds for more intensive acquisition in areas of special interest to members of the teaching staff.

The list began as an attempt to form a working collection for a new branch library at the University of California, Berkeley, where I was Art-Anthropology Librarian from 1956 to 1960. With the assistance of the faculty I compiled, along topical and areal lines, a number of basic lists of materials to be included in the new branch collection. Since no general bibliography of anthropology exists, there was considerable interest in these basic lists on the part of the faculty and students and, as word of their existence spread, on the part of anthropologists at other colleges and universities. A need for a general bibliography of the field definitely exists. The preliminary edition of this list has already been used to strengthen at least four library collections. It is our hope that this list will also partially fill the need for a general bibliography of anthropology for a few years to come.

The form of entry for each item in the bibliography is a combination of the forms used by the American Anthropological Association and by the Library of Congress. Each item is listed as found in the Library of Congress printed catalog, except that joint authors are listed on line with the main author for brevity of entry. Each item is listed in full only once. A title which could appropriately be listed in more than one section of the bibliography is listed in full in one section and referred to in a second section.

I should like to thank the following persons for aid in compiling the basic lists from which this list was partially formed or for comments on a preliminary edition circulated for criticism (help in both cases from many): Professor Emil W. Haury, University of Arizona; Professor Irwin T. Sanders, Boston University; Professor Elizabeth Colson, Brandeis University; Professor Frederica de Laguna, Bryn Mawr College; Professors Richard Adams, William Bascom, Gerald Berreman, George M. Foster, Robert F. Heizer, Theodore D. McCown, David G. Mandelbaum, Rene F. Millon, Robert F. Murphy, John H. Rowe, Richard F. Salisbury, and Sherwood Washburn, University of California, Berkeley; Professor David L. Olmsted, University of California, Davis; Professors Ralph L. Beals, Pedro Carrasco, Joel M. Halpern, and Harry Hoijer, University of California, Los Angeles; Professors Frederick Eggan, Lloyd A. Fallers, Clifford Geertz, McKim Marriott, David M. Schneider, and Sol Tax, University of Chicago; Professor Conrad M. Arensberg, Columbia University; Professors Cora Du Bois, Beatrice B. Whiting, and John W. M. Whiting, Harvard University; Professors John Brohm and Leonard Kasden, Harpur College, State University of New York; Dr. Raphael Patai, Theodore Herzl Institute, New York, New York; Professors Joseph B. Casagrande and Oscar Lewis, University of Illinois; Professor Harold E. Driver, Indiana University; Professor Richard K. Beardsley, University of Michigan; Professor Robert F. Spencer, University of Minnesota; Professor Melville J. Herskovits, Northwestern University; Professor Ward H. Goodenough, University of Pennsylvania; Professor George P. Murdock, University of Pittsburgh; Professor Edward Norbeck, Rice Institute; Professor Felix M. Keesing, Stanford University; Professors Douglas G. Haring and Donn V. Hart, Syracuse University; Professor Gabriel Lasker, Wayne State University; Professor Chester Chard, University of Wisconsin; and Professors Floyd G. Lounsbury and Irving Rouse, Yale University. I owe a special debt of gratitude to Professor David Mandelbaum, Director of the Educational Resources in Anthropology Project, who originally suggested this compilation, and to Professor Gabriel Lasker, a member of the Project staff, both of whom have been most helpful with their advice and encouragement for many months. Mrs. Cecily North and Mrs. Beatrice Germano, Interlibrary Loan librarians of the University of Nebraska and University of California libraries respectively, and Robert Pfeiffer, presently Art-Anthropology Librarian of the University of California, have saved me considerable last minute anguish in supplying bibliographic information on a number of elusive items.

Prices are listed for convenience in estimating the cost of book orders, but they are subject to change—almost invariably upward. Among the dealers with large stocks of anthropological works are the following:

B. H. Blackwell's
48-52 Broad Street
Oxford, England
(all areas of anthropology)

Explorers' Book Service
16 Columbia Terrace
Weehawken, New Jersey
(all areas of anthropology)

W. Heffer & Sons Ltd.
Petty Curry
Cambridge, England
(especially for African
    materials)

Hillary House Inc.
303 Park Avenue South
New York 10, New York
(all areas of anthropology)

Interart-Buchversand Klaus
    Renner
Grossfriedrichsburgerstrasse 32
München 59, Germany
(all areas of anthropology)

Kegan Paul, Trench,
    Trubner & Co.
43 Great Russell Street
London, W. C. 1
(especially for African
    materials)

Paragon Book Gallery
140 East 59th Street
New York 22, New York
(especially for Asian
    materials)

E. Scheuer
112 East 17th Street
New York 3, New York
(all areas of anthropology)

University Place Book Shop
69 University Place
New York 3, New York
(especially for African
    materials)

Categories

IV. Archaeology and culture history

    A. General   379-405

    B. Methods, theory, and techniques   406-437

V. Language and writing   438-476

VI. Physical anthropology

    A. General (texts, readings, essays)   477-495

    B. Human evolution   496-543

    C. Human genetics   544-553

    D. Somatology   554-561

VII. Applied anthropology

VIII. Publications dealing with peoples of specific areas, including archaeology, culture history, and contemporary ethnology

    A. Europe
        1. Archaeology
            a. General   581-586
            b. West and British Isles   587-598
            c. North   599-606
            d. Central   607-608
            e. South   609-614
            f. East   615-618
        2. Contemporary
            a. General   619
            b. West and British Isles   620-637
            c. North   638-644
            d. Central   645-647
            e. South   648-654
            f. East   655-666

    B. Middle East (including North Africa)   667-776

    C. Africa sub-Sahara
            a. General   777-800
            b. West   801-836
            c. East   837-900
            d. Central   901-923
            e. South   924-952

A Basic List
of Books and Periodicals
for College Libraries

I. SERIAL PUBLICATIONS

JOURNALS AND
MONOGRAPHIC SERIES

1. Africa. v. 1-   1928-
   Oxford University Press, Amen House, Warwick Square, London
   E. C. 4, for the International African Institute. Quarterly; subscription by membership at $7.25 per year to libraries.

2. American anthropologist. v. 1-   1888-
   Stephen T. Boggs, Exec. Sec., American Anthropological Association, 1530 P Street, N. W., Washington 5. Six times a year; subscription by membership at $15.00 a year to libraries. Subscription includes supplementary Memoirs.

3. American antiquity. v. 1-   1935-
   Society for American Archaeology, University of Utah Press, Salt Lake City 12, Utah. Quarterly; subscription by membership at $8.00 per year. Subscription includes supplementary Memoirs of the Society.

4. American journal of physical anthropology. v. 1-   1918-
   Wistar Institute of Anatomy and Biology, Woodland Ave., and 36th St., Philadelphia 4. Quarterly; $7.50 per year.

5. Anthropological linguistics. v. 1-   1959-
   Editor: Dr. Florence M. Voegelin, Anthropology Department, Indiana University, Bloomington, Ind. Nine times a year; $3.50 per year.

6. Anthropological quarterly. v. 1-   1928-
   Dept. of Anthropology, Catholic University of America, Washington 17, D. C., for the Catholic anthropological conference. Quarterly; $3.00 per year.

7.   L'Anthropologie. v. 1-   1890-
      Librairie Masson et Cie, 120 boul. Saint-Germain, Paris 6^e.
      Bi-monthly; 5000 fr. per year.

8.   Anthropos; revue internationale d'ethnologie et de linguistique.
      v. 1-   1906-
      Imprimerie St-Paul, Fribourg, Switzerland. Three times a year;
      60 Swiss fr.

9.   Antiquity; a quarterly review of archaeology. v. 1-   1927-
      Ashmore Green, Newbury, Berkshire, England. Quarterly; 30/-
      per year.

10.   Antiquity and survival; an international review of traditional art and
      culture. v. 1-   1955-
      N. V. Electrische DrukKerij "Luctor et Emergo," Laakweg 26,
      The Hague, Netherlands. Bi-monthly; f. 20 ($5.50).

11.   Archaeology; a magazine dealing with the antiquity of the world.
      v. 1-   1948-
      Archaeological Institute of America, Library Bldg., University
      of Cincinnati Library, Cincinnati 21. Quarterly; $5.00 per year.

12.   Current anthropology. v. 1-   1960-
      University of Chicago, 1126 East 59th St., Chicago 37, Ill. Five
      times a year; $10.00.

13.   Eastern anthropologist; a record of ethnography and folk culture.
      v. 1-   1947-
      Anthropology Dept., Lucknow University, Lucknow, India, for
      the Ethnographic and Folk Culture Society. Quarterly; Rs. 10 per
      year.

14.   Ethnohistory; devoted to the original research in the documentary
      history of the culture and movements of primitive peoples and re-
      lated problems of broader scope. v. 1-   1954-
      Indiana University, Rayl House, Bloomington, Ind., for the
      American Indian ethnohistoric conference. Quarterly; $3.50 per
      year.

15.   Ethnos. v. 1-   1936-
      Statens Etnografiska Museum, Stockholm. Quarterly; 15 Kr. per
      year.

16.   Human biology; record of research. v. 1-   1929-
      Wayne University Press, Detroit 1. Quarterly; $5.00 per year.

17.   Human organization. v. 1-   1941-
      Society for Applied Anthropology, New York State School of Indus-
      trial and Labor Relations, Cornell University, Ithaca, New York.
      Quarterly; subscription by membership in the Society at $8.00 per
      year for libraries.

18.   International journal of American linguistics. v. 1-   1917-
         Business Manager, Mrs. Elsie Dosch, Indiana University, Bloom-
ington, Ind. Quarterly; $5.00 per year. Subscription includes supple-
mentary Indiana University Publications in Anthropology and Linguistics and Publications of the Indiana University Research Center in
Anthropology, Folklore, and Linguistics.

19.   Journal of American folklore. v. 1-   1888-
         American Folklore Society, Sec.-Treas., Tristam P. Coffin,
Bennett Hall, University of Pennsylvania, Philadelphia 4, Penn.
Quarterly; subscription by membership at $8.50 per year. Subscrip-
tion includes the Society's Memoirs as issued.

20.   Language. v. 1-   1925-
         Linguistic Society of America, Waverly Press, Inc., Mt. Royal
and Guilford Avenues, Baltimore 2, Md. Quarterly; subscription
by membership in the Society at $8.00 per year. Subscription in-
cludes supplementary Language dissertations, Language monographs,
and Bulletin of the Linguistic Society of America.

21.   Man; a record of anthropological science. v. 1-   1901-
         Royal Anthropological Institute of Great Britain and Ireland, 21
Bedford Square, London, W. C. 1. Monthly; 30/- per year.

22.   Man in India. v. 1-   1921-
         18 Church Road, Ranchi, Bihr, India. Quarterly; Rs. 15 per
year.

23.   Oceania; devoted to the study of the native peoples of Australia, New
Guinea and the Islands of the Pacific Ocean. v. 1-   1930-
         University of Sydney, New South Wales, Australia. Quarterly;
40/- per year.

24.   Polynesian Society.
         Journal; a study of the native peoples of the Pacific area.
v. 1-   1892-
         Polynesian Society, Box 5195, Wellington, New Zealand. Quar-
terly; subscription by membership. Estimate: $6.00 per year.
Subscription may include the Society's important Memoir series.

25.   Rhodes-Livingstone journal/Human Problems in British Central
Africa. no. 1-   1944-   Semi-annual.
         Published on behalf of the Rhodes-Livingstone Institute by the
Manchester University Press. Subscription by membership in the
Institute at £1/10/- per year. Membership includes the Journal
and Papers and Communications of the Institute. Address: The
Director, The Rhodes-Livingstone Institute, P. O. Box 900, Lusaka,
Northern Rhodesia.

26.   Royal anthropological institute of Great Britain and Ireland.
         Journal. v. 1-   1871-
         21 Bedford Square, London, W. C. 1. Semi-annual; 40/- per
year.

27.   Société des Américanistes de Paris
          Journal. t. 1-   1895-
          Musée de l'homme, Palais de Chaillot, Place du Trocadéro,
       Paris 16. Annual; 20 NF per year.

28.   Southwestern journal of anthropology. v. 1-   1945-
          University of New Mexico, Albuquerque, N. M. Quarterly, $4.00
       per year.

29.   Word. v. 1-   1945-
          Columbia University, New York 27, for the Linguistic Circle of
       New York. Three times a year; $5.00.

30.   Zeitschrift für Ethnologie. Bd. 1-   1869-
          Organ der Deutschen Gesellschaft für Völkerkunde. Braunschweig,
       Verlag Albert Limbach. Semi-annual; ca. 26 DM per year.

   The more important monographic series which are issued irregularly
and are individually priced are well represented in the subject and area
lists which follow. The more important of these series include:

       American Anthropological Association. Memoirs.
       American Ethnological Society. Monographs and Publications.
       American Museum of Natural History. Anthropological Papers.
       Anthropological Records.
       California. University. Publications in American Archaeology and
          Ethnology.
       Chicago. Natural History Museum. Fieldiana: anthropology.
       Columbia University contributions to anthropology.
       Harvard University. Peabody Museum of Archaeology and Ethnology.
          Memoirs and Papers.
       London School of Economics. Monographs on Social Anthropology.
       Smithsonian institution. Smithsonian Miscellaneous Collections.
       U. S. Bureau of American Ethnology. Annual reports and Bulletins.
       Wenner-Gren Foundation for Anthropological Research. Viking Fund
          Publications in Anthropology.
       Yale University Publications in Anthropology.

                                        II.   BOOKS ON ANTHROPOLOGY
                                                        IN GENERAL

       A. General Bibliographies of Anthropological Works,
             Indices, Outlines

31.   American Universities Field Staff
          A select bibliography: Asia, Africa, Eastern Europe, Latin
       America. New York, 1960, $4.75.

32.   International bibliography of social and cultural anthropology.
        v. 1-   1955-   Paris, UNESCO, 1958-   v. 1, $5.50; v. 2, $6.50;
        v. 3, $7.00.

33.   Murdock, George Peter
            Outline of world cultures. 2d ed., rev. New Haven, HRAF Press,
        1958. (Behavior Science Outlines 3.) $3.00.

34.   Spencer, Robert F., and Elden Johnson
            Atlas for anthropology. Dubuque, Iowa, Brown, 1960, $2.50.

35.   Yale University. Institute of Human Relations.
            Outline of cultural materials, by George P. Murdock and others.
        3d rev. ed. New Haven, Human Relations Area Files, 1950.
        (Behavior Science Outlines, v. 1.) $2.50.

        B. History of Anthropology

36.   Benedict, Ruth (Fulton)
            An anthropologist at work; writings of Ruth Benedict, by Margaret
        Mead. Boston, Houghton-Mifflin, 1959, $6.00.

37.   Bock, Kenneth E.
            The acceptance of histories; toward a perspective of social
        science. Berkeley and Los Angeles, University of California
        Press, 1956. (University of California Publications in Sociology
        and Social Institutions, v. 3, no. 1.) $1.75.

38.   Goldschmidt, Walter Rochs, ed.
            The anthropology of Franz Boas; essays on the centennial of his
        birth. Menasha, Wis., American Anthropological Association, 1959.
        (American Anthropological Association. Memoir no. 89.) Available
        only through Howard Chandler, Publishers, San Francisco, $2.50.

39.   Haddon, Alfred Cort
            History of anthropology. London, Watts, 1949. (Thinkers' Lib-
        rary, no. 42.) 2/6. The first edition (1910) was written with the
        help of Mrs. A. Hingston Quiggin.

40.   Hays, Hoffman Reynolds
            From ape to angel; an informal history of social anthropology.
        1st ed. New York, Knopf, 1958, $7.50; London, Methuen, 1959, 36/-.

41.   Herskovits, Melville Jean
            Franz Boas; the science of man in the making. New York,
        Scribner's, 1953. (Twentieth Century Library.) Out of print; ca.
        $3.00.

42.   Lowie, Robert Harry
            The history of ethnological theory. New York, Farrar & Rine-
        hart, 1937, $5.00.

43.   Lowie, Robert Harry
        Robert H. Lowie, ethnologist; a personal record. Berkeley and
Los Angeles, University of California Press, 1959. $5.00.

44.   Penniman, Thomas Kenneth
        A hundred years of anthropology. With contributions by Beatrice
Blackwood and J. S. Weiner. 2d ed., rev. London, Duckworth, 1952,
30/-.
        U. S. distributor: New York, Macmillan, $5.00.

45.   Resek, Carl
        Lewis Henry Morgan, American scholar. Chicago, University
of Chicago Press, 1960, $4.50.

C. Anthologies, Books of Readings, Collections
   of Articles, Compilations

46.   Adams, Richard N., and Jack J. Preiss, eds.
        Human organization research; field relations and techniques.
Homewood, Ill., published for the Society for Applied Anthropology
by the Dorsey Press, 1960, $8.35.

47.   American Anthropologist.
        Selected papers from the American Anthropologist, 1888-1920.
Edited by Frederica de Laguna for the Publications Committee of
the American Anthropological Association. With an essay on the
beginnings of anthropology in America by A. Irving Hallowell.
Evanston, Ill., Row, Peterson, 1960, $8.00.

48.   Calverton, Victor Francis
        The making of man; an outline of anthropology. New York, The
Modern Library, 1931. Out of print; ca. $2.00.

49.   Casagrande, Joseph Bartholomew, ed.
        In the company of man; twenty portraits by anthropologists. New
York, Harper, 1960, $6.50.

50.   Coon, Carleton Stevens, ed.
        A reader in general anthropology. New York, Holt, 1948, $8.75;
text ed., $6.95.

51.   Diamond, Stanley, ed.
        Culture in history, essays in honor of Paul Radin. New York,
published for Brandeis University by Columbia University Press,
1960, $15.00.

52.   Fried, Morton Herbert, ed.
        Readings in anthropology. New York, Crowell, 1959, 2 v.
    v. 1. Physical anthropology, linguistics, and archeology, $3.00;
    v. 2. Cultural anthropology, $3.25.

53. Goldschmidt, Walter Rochs, ed.
     Exploring the ways of mankind. New York, Holt, Rinehart & Winston, 1960, $6.50; paper: $5.25. First ed. published in 1957 under title: Readings in the ways of mankind.

54. Hoebel, Edward Adamson, Jesse D. Jennings, and Elmer R. Smith, comp.
     Readings in anthropology. New York, McGraw-Hill, 1955, $5.25; paper, $3.75.

55. International Symposium on Anthropology, New York, 1952.
     Anthropology today; an encyclopedic inventory, prepared under the chairmanship of A. L. Kroeber. Chicago, University of Chicago Press, 1953, $9.00.

56. International Symposium on Anthropology, New York, 1952.
     An appraisal of anthropology today, ed. by Sol Tax and others. Chicago, University of Chicago Press, 1953, $7.00.

57. Linton, Ralph, ed.
     Most of the world; the peoples of Africa, Latin America, and the East today. New York, Columbia University Press, 1949, $6.50.

58. Linton, Ralph, ed.
     The science of man in the world crisis. New York, Columbia University Press, 1945, $4.75.

Mead, Margaret, ed.
Coöperation and competition among primitive peoples. See no. 150.

59. Mead, Margaret, and Ruth L. Bunzel, eds.
     The golden age of American anthropology. New York, Braziller, 1960, $10.00.

60. Mead, Margaret, and Rhoda Metraux, eds.
     The study of culture at a distance. Chicago, University of Chicago Press, 1953, $6.00.

61. Murdock, George Peter
     Our primitive contemporaries. New York, Macmillan, 1934, $6.00.

62. Sanders, Irwin Taylor, ed.
     Societies around the world. Prepared at the University of Kentucky by Irwin T. Sanders, editor; Richard B. Woodbury, asst. editor; Frank J. Essene (and others). New York, Dryden Press, 1953, 2 v. Out of print; ca. $10.00.

63. Sanders, Irwin Taylor, ed.
     Societies around the world. Prepared at the University of Kentucky by Irwin T. Sanders, editor; Richard B. Woodbury, asst. editor; Frank J. Essene (and others). A new shorter ed.: Eskimo, Navajo, Baganda, Chinese peasant, Cotton South, English Midlands. Edited in one vol. by Howard Becker. New York, Dryden Press, 1956, $7.75.

64.   Sapir, Edward
        Culture, language, and personality; selected essays edited by
David G. Mandelbaum. 1st paper-bound ed. Berkeley and Los
Angeles, University of California Press, 1956, $1.50.

65.   Shapiro, Harry Lionel, ed.
        Man, culture, and society. New York, Oxford University Press,
1956, $7.75; text ed., $5.75.
        Paper: New York, Oxford University Press, 1960. (Galaxy Books,
32.) $2.25.

66.   Spencer, Robert F., ed.
        Method and perspective in anthropology; papers in honor of Wilson
D. Wallis. Minneapolis, University of Minnesota Press, 1954, $4.50.

67.   Yearbook of Anthropology
        Current anthropology; a supplement to Anthropology today. Edited
by William L. Thomas, Jr. Chicago, University of Chicago Press,
1956, $5.00. (Consists of the first three parts of the Yearbook of
Anthropology, 1955.)

        D. General Textbooks

68.   Beals, Ralph Leon, and Harry Hoijer
        An introduction to anthropology. With the collaboration of Virginia
More Roediger. 2d ed. New York, Macmillan, 1959, $6.90.

69.   Boas, Franz, ed.
        General anthropology, edited by Franz Boas, with contributions
by Ruth Benedict, Franz Boas, Ruth Bunzel, and others. Boston,
New York, Heath, 1938, $6.75.

70.   Boas, Franz
        Race, language and culture. New York, Macmillan, 1940, $6.90.

71.   Chapple, Eliot Dismore, and Carleton Stevens Coon
        Principles of anthropology. New York, Holt, 1942, $6.75.

72.   Coon, Carleton Stevens
        The story of man; from the first human to primitive culture and
beyond. 1st ed. New York, Knopf, 1954, $7.50.

        Firth, Raymond
        Human types. See no. 94.
        Elements of social organization. See no. 164.

73.   Forde, Cyril Daryll
        Habitat, economy, and society; a geographical introduction to
ethnology. London, Methuen, 1934, 25/-; New York, Dutton, 1950,
$5.50.

74.   Gillin, John Philip
       The ways of men, an introduction to anthropology. New York,
       Appleton-Century, 1948, $5.50.

75.   Herskovits, Melville Jean
       Cultural anthropology. New York, Knopf, 1955, $7.50; text ed.,
       $5.50. (Abridged revision of Man and his works.)

76.   Herskovits, Melville Jean
       Man and his works: the science of cultural anthropology. New
       York, Knopf, 1948, $8.00; text ed., $6.00.

77.   Hoebel, Edward Adamson
       Man in the primitive world; an introduction to anthropology. 2d
       ed. New York, McGraw Hill, 1958, $9.00; text ed., $6.95.

78.   Honigmann, John Joseph
       The world of man. New York, Harper, 1959, $7.50.

79.   Keesing, Felix Maxwell
       Cultural anthropology; the science of custom. New York, Rine-
       hart, 1958, $6.00.

80.   Kroeber, Alfred Louis
       Anthropology: race, language, culture, psychology, prehistory,
       New ed., rev. New York, Harcourt, Brace, 1948, $10.00; text ed.
       $7.50.

81.   Linton, Ralph
       The study of man; an introduction. New York, London, Appleton-
       Century, 1936, $5.50.

82.   Titiev, Mischa
       The science of man; an introduction to anthropology. New York,
       Holt, 1954, $7.75; text ed., $6.00.

III.   SOCIAL AND CULTURAL ANALYSIS

A. Books of General Analysis

83.   Anthropological Society of Washington, Washington, D. C.
       Evolution and anthropology: a centennial appraisal. Washington,
       D. C., 1959, $1.50. Betty J. Meggers, ed.

84.   Benedict, Ruth (Fulton)
         Patterns of culture. Boston and New York, Houghton Mifflin,
       1934, $4.00.
         Paper: With an introd. by Franz Boas and a new pref. by
       Margaret Mead. New York, New American Library, 1959.
       (Mentor Books, MD89.) $0.50.

85.   Bidney, David
         Theoretical anthropology. New York, Columbia University
       Press, 1953, $8.50.

86.   Birket-Smith, Kaj
         Primitive man and his ways; pattern of life in some native
       societies. Translated from the Danish by Roy Duffell. London,
       Odhams   Press, 1960, 25/-.
         U. S. distributor: New York, International Publications Service,
       $6.25.

87.   Boas, Franz
         The mind of primitive man. Rev. ed. New York, Macmillan,
       1938, $5.50.

88.   Childe, Vere Gordon
         Social evolution. New York, Schuman, 1951, $3.00.

89.   Dixon, Roland Burrage
         The building of cultures. New York, London, Scribner's, 1928.
       Out of print; ca. $5.00.

90.   Dole, Gertrude Evelyn, and Robert L. Carneiro, eds.
         Essays in the science of culture; in honor of Leslie A. White,
       in celebration of his sixtieth birthday and his thirtieth year of
       teaching at the University of Michigan. New York, Crowell, 1960,
       $6.25.

91.   Durkheim, Emile
         The division of labor in society. Translated from the French
       by George Simpson. Glencoe, Ill., Free Press, 1947, $6.00

92.   Edel, May (Mandelbaum) and Abraham Edel
         Anthropology and ethics. Springfield, Ill., Thomas, 1959, $5.50.

93.   Evans-Pritchard, Edward Evan
         Social anthropology. London, Cohen & West, 1951, 8/6; Glencoe,
       Ill., Free Press, 1952, $3.50.

94.   Firth, Raymond William
         Human types; an introduction to social anthropology. Rev. ed.
       London, Nelson, 1956, 12/6.
         U. S. distributor: New York, Barnes & Noble, $2.50.
         Paper: New York, New American Library, 1958. (Mentor Books,
       MD227.) $0.50.

95.   Firth, Raymond William, ed.
      Man and culture; an evaluation of the work of Bronislaw Malinow-
      ski. London, Routledge & Kegan Paul, 1957, £1/12/-.
      U. S. distributor: New York, Humanities Press, $6.00.

96.   Gennep, Arnold van
      The rites of passage. Translated by Monika B. Vizedom and
      Gabrielle L. Caffee. Introd. by Solon T. Kimball. Chicago, Univer-
      sity of Chicago Press, 1960, $4.50; London, Routledge & Kegan Paul,
      1960, 23/-. Paper: Chicago, University of Chicago Press, 1961
      (Phoenix Books) $1.50.

97.   Goldschmidt, Walter Rochs
      Man's way; a preface to the understanding of human society. New
      York, Holt, 1959, $2.90; trade ed., Cleveland, World Publishing
      Company, $4.00.
      British ed.: Understanding human society. London, Routledge &
      Kegan Paul, 1960. (International Library of Sociology and Social Re-
      construction.) 21/-.

      Hallowell, Alfred Irving
      Culture and experience. See no. 329.

98.   Kluckhohn, Clyde
      Mirror for man; the relation of anthropology to modern life. New
      York, Whittlesey House, 1949, $5.00.
      Paper: Mirror for man, a survey of human behavior and social
      attitudes. Greenwich, Conn., Fawcett, 1957. (A Premier Book.) $0.50.

99.   Kroeber, Alfred Louis
      The nature of culture. Chicago, University of Chicago Press,
      1952, $8.50.

100. La Barre, Weston
      The human animal. Chicago, University of Chicago Press, 1954,
      $6.00.

101. Language, culture, and personality; essays in memory of Edward
      Sapir. Edited by Leslie Spier, A. Irving Hallowell, and Stanley S.
      Newman. Salt Lake City, University of Utah Press, 1960, $3.75
      (a reprint of the Sapir Memorial Publication Fund publication, 1942).

102. Lee, Dorothy D.
      Freedom and culture; essays. Englewood Cliffs, N. J., Prentice-
      Hall, 1959. (A Spectrum Book, S-6.) $1.95.

103. Levy, Marion Joseph
      The structure of society. Princeton, Princeton University
      Press, 1952, $6.00.

104. Linton, Ralph
      The tree of culture. New York, Knopf, 1955, $8.00; text ed.,
      $6.50.
      Paper: Abridged by Adelin Linton. New York, Vintage, 1958.
      (Vintage K76.) $1.25.

105. Lowie, Robert Harry
     An introduction to cultural anthropology. A new and enl. ed. New
     York, Farrar & Rinehart, 1940, $6.50.

106. Lowie, Robert Harry
     Primitive society. New York, Liveright, 1947. (Black and gold
     edition) $3.50.

107. Lowie, Robert Harry
     Selected papers in anthropology. Edited by Cora Du Bois, Berkeley
     and Los Angeles, University of California Press, 1960, $10.00.

     Maine, Sir Henry
     Ancient law. See no. 195.

108. Majumdar, Dhirendra Nath, and T. N. Madan
     An introduction to social anthropology. New York, Asia Pub.
     House, 1960.
     U. S. distributor: Taplinger, $3.95.

109. Malinowski, Bronislaw
     A scientific theory of culture, and other essays; with a preface
     by Huntington Cairns. Chapel Hill, University of North Carolina
     Press, 1944, $3.00.
     Paper: New York, Oxford University Press, 1960. (A Galaxy
     Book, G B 40.) $1.50.

110. Miller, Neal Elgar, and John Dollard
     Social learning and imitation. New Haven, published for the
     Institute of Human Relations by Yale University Press; London,
     H. Milford, Oxford University Press, 1941, $3.50.

111. Morgan, Lewis Henry
     Ancient society; or, researches in the lines of human progress
     from savagery, through barbarism to civilization. London, Rout-
     ledge & Kegan Paul, 1959, 17/6. First published New York, 1877.

112. Nadel, Siegfried Frederick
     The foundations of social anthropology. London, Cohen & West,
     1951, 30/-; Glencoe, Ill., Free Press, 1951, $7.50.

     Nadel, S. F.
     Theory of social structure. See no. 177.

113. Parsons, Talcott, and Neil J. Smelser
     Economy and society; a study in the integration of economic
     and social theory. Glencoe, Ill., Free Press, 1956, $6.00; London,
     Routledge & Kegan Paul, 1956. (International Library of Sociology
     and Social Reconstruction.) £ 1/15/-.

114. Parsons, Talcott
     Essays in sociological theory. 2nd ed., rev. Glencoe, Ill.,
     Free Press, 1954, $6.00.

115. Parsons, Talcott
        The social system. Glencoe, Ill., Free Press, 1951, $7.50;
     London, Tavistock in collaboration with Routledge & Kegan Paul,
     1952, £2/2/-.

116. Parsons, Talcott
        The structure of social action; a study in social theory with
     special reference to a group of recent European writers. 2d ed.
     Glencoe, Ill., Free Press, 1949, $10.00.

117. Piddington, Ralph
        An introduction to social anthropology. Edinburgh, Oliver &
     Boyd, 1950-1957, 2 v., v.1, 25/-; v.2, 30/-; New York, Macmil-
     lan, 1952-1957, $4.75 ea.

118. Radcliffe-Brown, Alfred Reginald
        Method in social anthropology; selected essays. Edited by M.
     N. Srinivas. Chicago, University of Chicago Press, 1958, $3.75.

119. Radcliffe-Brown, Alfred Reginald
        A natural science of society. With a foreword by Fred Eggan.
     Glencoe, Ill., Free Press, 1957, $4.00.

120. Radcliffe-Brown, Alfred Reginald
        Structure and function in primitive society, essays and ad-
     dresses; with a foreword by E. E. Evans-Pritchard and Fred
     Eggan. London, Cohen & West, 1952, 21/-; Glencoe, Ill., Free
     Press, 1952, $6.00.

121. Radin, Paul
        Method and theory of ethnology; an essay in criticism. 1st ed.
     New York and London, McGraw-Hill, 1933. Out of print; ca. $4.00.

122. Radin, Paul
        Primitive man as philosopher: with a foreword by John Dewey.
     2d rev. ed. New York, Dover, 1957, $2.00.

123. Radin, Paul
        The world of primitive man. New York, Schuman, 1953. (The
     Life of Science Library, no. 26.) $5.00.

124. Redfield, Robert
        The little community; viewpoints for the study of a human
     whole. Chicago, University of Chicago Press, 1955, $4.00.

125. Redfield, Robert
        Peasant society and culture; an anthropological approach to
     civilization. Chicago, University of Chicago Press, 1956, $3.25.

126. Redfield, Robert
        The primitive world and its transformations. Ithaca, N. Y.
     Cornell University Press, 1953. (Great Seal Books.) $1.45.

127. Royal Anthropological Institute of Great Britain and Ireland.
Notes and queries on anthropology. 6th ed., rev. and rewritten by a committee of the Royal Anthropological Institute of Great Britain and Ireland. London, Routledge and Kegan Paul, 1951, £1/10/-.

128. Sahlins, Marshall David, and Elman R. Service, eds.
Evolution and culture, by Thomas G. Harding (and others). Foreword by Leslie A. White. Ann Arbor, University of Michigan Press, 1960, $3.75.

129. Sapir, Edward
Selected writings of Edward Sapir in language, culture, and personality; edited by David G. Mandelbaum. Berkeley and Los Angeles, University of California Press, 1949, $8.50.

130. Service, Elman Rogers
A profile of primitive culture. New York, Harper, 1958, $6.00.

131. Shapiro, Harry Lionel
Aspects of culture. New Brunswick, N. J., Rutgers University Press, 1956, $2.75.

132. Slotkin, James Sydney
Social anthropology, the science of human society and culture. New York, Macmillan, 1950, $6.75.

133. Thompson, Edgar Tristram, and Everett C. Hughes, eds.
Race: individual and collective behavior. Glencoe, Ill., Free Press, 1958, $7.50.

134. Thurnwald, Richard
Die menschliche Gesellschaft in ihren ethno-soziologischen grundlagen. Berlin und Leipzig, de Gruyter, 1931-1935. 5 v. Out of print; ca. $60.00.

135. Titiev, Mischa
Introduction to cultural anthropology. New York, Holt, 1959, $8.00; text ed., $6.00.

136. Tylor, Sir Edward Burnett
Anthropology; an introduction to the study of man and civilization. London, Watts, 1946, 2 v. (Thinker's Library.) 2/6.
Abridged paper ed: Abridged and with a foreword by Leslie A. White. Ann Arbor, University of Michigan Press, 1960. (Ann Arbor Paperbacks AA44.) $1.95.

137. Tylor, Sir Edward Burnett
Primitive culture. New York, Harper, 1958, 2 v. (Harper Torchbooks, TB 33-34.)
Contents. v. 1, The origins of culture, $1.75; v. 2, Religion in primitive culture, $1.95.
First published London, 1871.

138. The values of primitive society (radio program)
     The institutions of primitive society, a series of broadcast
talks, by E. E. Evans-Pritchard and others. Oxford, Blackwell,
1954, 8/6; Glencoe, Ill., Free Press, 1954, $3.50.

139. Weber, Max
     From Max Weber: Essays in sociology. Translated, edited,
and with an introduction, by H. H. Gerth and C. Wright Mills.
New York, Oxford University Press, 1946, out of print; London,
Routledge & Kegan Paul, 1948. (International Library of Sociology
and Social Reconstruction.) £1/8/-.
     Paper: New York, Oxford University Press, 1958. (Galaxy
Book, GB 13.) $2.25.

140. Weber, Max
     Theory of social and economic organization. Translated by
A. M. Henderson and Talcott Parsons. Edited with an introd. by
Talcott Parsons. Glencoe, Ill., Free Press, 1957, c. 1947, $6.00.
     A translation of part I of Max Weber's Wirtschaft und Gesell-
schaft.

141. Weyer, Edward Moffatt
     Primitive peoples today. Illus. with 212 photos and 14 maps.
Garden City, N. Y., Doubleday, 1959, $10.00.
     Paper: Garden City, N. Y., Doubleday, 1960. (Dolphin Book,
C200.) $0.95.

142. White, Leslie A.
     The science of culture, a study of man and civilization. New
York, Farrar, Straus, 1949, $6.00.
     Paper: New York, Grove Press, 1958. (Evergreen Books,
E105.) $1.95.

     B. Technology and Economics

     Conklin, Harold C.
     Hanunóo agriculture. See no. 1080.

143. Cottrell, William Frederick
     Energy and society; the relation between energy, social change,
and economic development. New York, McGraw-Hill, 1955, $5.00.

144. Engels, Friedrich
     The origin of the family, private property and the state, in
the light of the researches of Lewis H. Morgan. New York,
International Publishers, 1942, $2.00.

     Firth, Raymond William
     Economics of the New Zealand Maori. See no. 1237.

Firth, Raymond William
Malay fishermen: their peasant economy. See no. 1094.

Firth, Raymond William
Primitive Polynesian economy. See no. 1238.

145. Forbes, Robert James
Man the maker; a history of technology and engineering.
Revised edition. New York, Abelard-Schuman, 1958. (The Life
of Science Library.) $5.00.

Forde, Cyril Daryll
Habitat, economy, and society. See no. 73.

Freeman, J. D.
Iban agriculture. See no. 1097.

Gulliver, P. H.
Family herds. See no. 858.

146. Herskovits, Melville Jean
Economic anthropology; a study in comparative economics.
2d ed., rev., enl., rewritten. New York, Knopf, 1952, $5.75.

147. Herskovits, Melville Jean
Economic life of primitive peoples. New York, London, Knopf,
1940. Out of print; ca. $4.00.
2d ed. has title: Economic anthropology.

148. Hill, Polly
The Gold Coast cocoa farmer: a preliminary survey. London,
Oxford University Press, 1956, $2.60.

Malinowski, Bronislaw
Argonauts of the western Pacific. See no. 1259.
Coral gardens and their magic. See no. 1260.

149. Mauss, Marcel
The gift; forms and functions of exchange in archaic societies.
Trans. by Ian Cunnison. With an intro. by E. E. Evans-Pritchard.
Glencoe, Ill., Free Press, 1954, $3.50.

150. Mead, Margaret, ed.
Cooperation and competition among primitive peoples. Enl.
ed. with a new preface and appraisal. Boston, Beacon Press,
1961, $2.95 (Beacon BP 123). First published New York, 1937.

151. Mumford, Lewis
Technics and civilization. New York, Harcourt, Brace, 1934,
$6.00.

Nash, Manning
Machine age Maya. See no. 1650.

152. Polanyi, Karl, Conrad M. Arensberg, and Harry W. Pearson, eds.
       Trade and market in the early empires; economics in history
       and theory. Glencoe, Ill., Free Press, 1957, $6.00.

153. Quiggin, Alison (Hingston)
       A survey of primitive money; the beginning of currency. With
       an introd. by A. C. Haddon. London, Methuen, 1949. (Methuen's
       Handbooks of Archaeology.) 45/-.
       U. S. distributor: Humanities Press, New York, $8.50.

       Richards, Audrey Isabel
       Economic development and tribal change. See no. 881.
       Land, labour, and diet in Northern Rhodesia. See no. 920.

154. Sayce, Roderick Urwick
       Primitive arts and crafts, an introduction to the study of
       material culture. Cambridge, The University Press, 1933. Out
       of print; ca. $3.00.

155. Singer, Charles Joseph, E. J. Holmyard, and A. R. Hall, eds.
       A history of technology . . . assisted by E. Jaffé, R. H. G.
       Thomson, and J. M. Donaldson. v. 1-2. Oxford, Clarendon Press,
       1954-1956. $26.90 ea.
       Contents: v. 1, From early times to fall of ancient empires;
       v. 2, The Mediterranean civilizations and the Middle Ages.

156. Slotkin, James Sydney
       From field to factory; new industrial employees. Glencoe, Ill.,
       Free Press, 1960, $4.00.

157. Steward, Julian Haynes, ed.
       Irrigation civilizations: a comparative study; a symposium on
       method and result in cross-cultural regularities. Washington,
       Social Science Section, Dept. of Cultural Affairs, Pan American
       Union, 1955. (Pan American Union. Social Science Section.
       Social Science Monographs, 1.) $0.50.

158. Thurnwald, Richard
       Economics in primitive communities. London, published for
       the International Institute of African languages and cultures by
       H. Milford, Oxford University Press, 1932. Out of print; ca.
       $10.00.

159. Usher, Abbott Payson
       A history of mechanical inventions. Rev. ed. Cambridge,
       Mass., Harvard University Press, 1954, $9.00.
       Paper: Boston, Beacon Press, 1959, c1954. (Beacon Paperback
       no. 84.) $2.25.

       Veblen, Thorstein
       Theory of the leisure class. See no. 1622.

Wittfogel, Karl
Oriental despotism. See no. 1211.

C. Social Organization

Aberle, David Friend
The kinship system of the Kalmuk Mongols. See no. 963.

Arensberg, Conrad M., and Solon T. Kimball
Family and community in Ireland. See no. 621.

160. Bachofen, Johann Jakob
Das Mutterrecht. Mit unterstützung von Harald Fuchs, Gustav
Meyer und Karl Schefold hrsg. von Karl Meuli. 3 Aufl. Basel,
Schwabe, 1948, 2 v., 67.35 DM.

Bacon, Elizabeth E.
Obok, a study of social structure in Eurasia. See no. 964.

Barth, Frederik
Principles of social organization in southern Kurdistan. See
no. 673.

Bateson, Gregory
Naven. See no. 1219.

161. Bellah, Robert Neelly
Apache kinship systems. Cambridge, Mass., Harvard University
Press, 1952. (The Harvard Phi Beta Kappa prize essay, 1950.) $2.50.

162. Bott, Elizabeth
Family and social network; roles, norms, and external relationships in ordinary urban families. London, Tavistock, 1957, 30/-.

Clarke, Edith
My mother who fathered me; a study of the family in three
selected communities in Jamaica. See no. 1700.

Colson, Elizabeth
Marriage and the family among the plateau Tonga of Northern
Rhodesia. See no. 904.

Davis, Allison, Burleigh B. Gardner, and Mary R. Gardner
Deep South. See no. 1598.

Dollard, John
Caste and class in a Southern town. See no. 1599.

Dumont, Louis
Hierarchy and marriage alliance in South Indian kinship. See
no. 994.

Edmonson, Munro S.
Status terminology and the social structure of North American
Indians. See no. 1312.

Eggan, Fred, ed.
Social anthropology of North American tribes. See no. 1322.

Eggan, Fred
Social organization of the western Pueblos. See no. 1445.

163. Eisenstadt, Shmuel Noah
From generation to generation; age groups and social structure.
Glencoe, Ill., Free Press, 1956, $6.00; London, Routledge & Kegan
Paul, 1956. (International Library of Sociology and Social Recon-
struction.) £2/2/-.

Elkin, Adolphus Peter
Marriage and the family in Australia. See no. 1235.

Evans-Pritchard, Edward Evan
Kinship and marriage among the Nuer. See no. 852.

164. Firth, Raymond William
Elements of social organization. 2d ed. London, Watts, 1956.
(Josiah Mason Lectures, 1947.) 18/-.

Firth, Raymond William, ed.
Two studies of kinship in London. See no. 623.
We, the Tikopia; a sociological study of kinship in primitive
Polynesia. See no. 1240.

Forde, Cyril Daryll
Marriage and family among the Yakö in southeastern Nigeria.
See no. 811.

Fortes, Meyer
The dynamics of clanship among the Tallensi. See no. 812.

165. Fortes, Meyer, ed.
Social structure: studies presented to A. R. Radcliffe-Brown.
Oxford, Clarendon Press, 1949. Out of print; scarce, but ca. $10.00.

Fortes, Meyer
The web of kinship among the Tallensi. See no. 813.

Freedman, Maurice
Chinese family and marriage in Singapore. See no. 1096.
Lineage organization in southeastern China. See no. 1168.

Ghurye, Govind Sadashiv
Caste and class in India. See no. 1009.

166. Ghurye, Govind Sadashiv
      Family and kin in Indo-European culture. Bombay, New York,
      Oxford University Press, 1955. (University of Bombay Publica-
      tions. Sociology Series, no. 4.) $3.15.

167. Goodenough, Ward H.
      Property, kin, and community on Truk. New Haven, published
      for Dept. of Anthropology, Yale University, by Yale University
      Press, 1951 (reprinted 1961). (Yale University Publications in
      Anthropology, no. 46.) $3.00.

168. Goody, John Rankine, ed.
      The developmental cycle in domestic groups. Cambridge, pub-
      lished for the Dept. of Archaeology and Anthropology at the Uni-
      versity Press, 1958. (Cambridge Papers in Social Anthropology,
      no. 1.) $4.00.

      Hocart, Arthur Maurice
      Caste; a comparative study. See no. 1012.

169. Homans, George C., and David Murray Schneider
      Marriage, authority, and final causes; a study of unilateral
      cross-cousin marriage. Glencoe, Ill., Free Press, 1955. Out of
      print; ca. $3.00.

      Hu, Hsien-chin
      The common descent group in China and its functions. See no.
      1180.

      Hutton, John Henry
      Caste in India. See no. 1015.

170. Josselin de Jong, Jan Petrus Benjamin de
      Lévi-Strauss's theory on kinship and marriage. Leiden, Brill,
      1952. (Mededelingen van het Rijkmuseum voor Volkendunde,
      Leiden, no. 10.) Gld. 3.50.

      Kapadia, Kanailal Motilal
      Marriage and family in India. 2d ed. Bombay, New York,
      Oxford University Press, Indian Branch, 1958, $4.00.

      Karve, Irawati (Karmarkar)
      Kinship organization in India. See no. 1019.

      Leach, Edmund Ronald, ed.
      Aspects of caste in south India, Ceylon and north-west Pakistan.
      See no. 1021.

      Leonard, Olen E., and Charles P. Loomis, eds.
      Readings in Latin American social organization and institutions.
      See no. 1681.

171. Lévi-Strauss, Claude
      Les structures élémentaires de la parenté. 1. éd. Paris,
      Presses universitaires de France, 1949. (Bibliothèque de philos-
      ophie contemporaine. Psychologie et sociologie.) 1,200 fr.

      Lewis, Oscar
      Five families. See no. 1646.

172. Lowie, Robert Harry
      Social organization. New York, Rinehart, 1949, $5.00; London,
      Routledge & Kegan Paul, 1950. (International Library of Sociology
      and Social Reconstruction.) £1/15/-.

      Majumdar, Dhirendra Nath
      Caste and communication in an Indian village. See no. 1026.

173. Malinowski, Bronislaw
      Sex and repression in savage society. London, Kegan Paul,
      Trench, Trubner, 1927. (International Library of Psychology.)
      £1/1/-; New York, Harcourt, Brace, 1927, out of print.
      U. S. distributor: Humanities Press, New York, $4.00.
      Paper: New York, Meridian Books, 1955. (Meridian Books, M15.)
      $1.35.

      Malinowski, Bronislaw
      The sexual life of savages in North-Western Melanesia. See
      no. 1261.

      Marriott, McKim
      Caste ranking and community structure in five regions of India
      and Pakistan. See no. 1030.

      Mayer, Adrian C.
      Caste and kinship in central India. See no. 1033.

      Mead, Margaret
      Male and female. See no. 347.

174. Merton, Robert King
      Social theory and social structure. Rev. and enl. ed. Glencoe,
      Ill., Free Press, 1957, $7.50.

      Mitchell, J. Clyde
      The Yao village; a study in the social structure of a Nyasaland
      tribe. See no. 915.

      Morgan, Lewis Henry
      Ancient society. See no. 111.

175. Morgan, Lewis Henry
      Systems of consanguinity and affinity of the human family.
      Washington, Smithsonian institution, 1870. (Smithsonian contribu-
      tions to knowledge, v. 17, art. 2.) Out of print; rare.

176. Murdock, George Peter
      Social structure. New York, Macmillan, 1949, $4.75.

      Murdock, George Peter, ed.
      Social structure in southeast Asia. See no. 1123.

      Murphy, Robert Francis
      Headhunter's heritage; social and economic change among the
      Mundurucú Indians. See no. 1682.

177. Nadel, Siegfried Frederick
      The theory of social structure; with a memoir by Meyer Fortes.
      Glencoe, Ill., Free Press, 1957, $6.00

178. Parsons, Talcott, and Robert F. Bales
      Family socialization and interaction process . . . in collabora-
      tion with James Olds and others. Glencoe, Ill., Free Press, 1954,
      $6.00; London, Routledge & Kegan Paul, 1956, £1/10/-.

      Pehrson, Robert Niel
      The bilateral network of social relations in Könkämä Lapp
      district. See no. 641.

      Prabhu, Pandhari-nath
      Hindu social organization. See no. 1043.

      Prins, Adriaan Hendrik Johan
      East African age-class systems. See no. 878.

      Radcliffe-Brown, Alfred Reginald, and Cyril Daryll Forde, eds.
      African systems of kinship and marriage. See no. 794.

      Radcliffe-Brown, Alfred Reginald
      Social organization of Australian tribes. See no. 1273.
      Structure and function in primitive society. See no. 120.

179. Rivers, William Halse Rivers
      Social organization . . . ed. by W. J. Perry. New York, Knopf;
      London, Kegan Paul, Trench, Trubner, 1924. Out of print; ca.
      $6.00.

      Sahlins, Marshall David
      Social stratification in Polynesia. See no. 1276.

      Smith, Raymond Thomas
      The Negro family in British Guiana. See no. 1688.

      Smith, W. Robertson
      Kinship and marriage in early Arabia. See no. 753.

      Srinivas, Mysore Narasimhachar
      Marriage and family in Mysore. See no. 1055.

Vreeland, Herbert H.
  Mongol community and kinship. See no. 975.

Young, Michael, and Peter Willmott
  Family and kinship in east London. See no. 637.

D. Laws and Government

180. American Ethnological Society, New York
    Systems of political control and bureaucracy in human
societies. Proceedings of the 1958 Annual Spring Meeting of
the American Ethnological Society, edited by Verne F. Ray.
Seattle, 1958, $2.00.
    Distributor: University of Washington Press, Seattle.

Barnes, James Albert
  Politics in a changing society. See no. 901.

181. Barton, Roy Franklin
    Ifugao law. Berkeley, University of California Press, 1919.
(University of California Publications in American Archaeology
and Ethnology. v. 15, no. 1.) Out of print; ca. $2.50.

Barton, Roy Franklin
  The Kalingas. See no. 1067.

Bohannan, Paul, ed.
  African homicide and suicide. See no. 781.

Bohannan, Paul
  Justice and judgment among the Tiv. See no. 804.

Busia, Kofi Abrefa
  The position of the chief in the modern political system of
the Ashanti. See no. 806.

Cory, Hans
  Sukuma law and custom. See no. 846.

182. Coulborn, Rushton, ed.
    Feudalism in history. With contributions by Joseph R. Strayer
and others. Foreword by A. L. Kroeber. Princeton, Princeton
University Press, 1956, $8.50.

183. Diamond, Arthur Sigismund
    Primitive law. London, Longmans, Green, 1935. Out of print;
ca. $7.00.

184. Elias, Taslim Olawale
    Groundwork of Nigerian law. London, Routledge & Kegan Paul,
1954, £1/10/-.

185. Elias, Taslim Olawale
      The nature of African customary law. Manchester, Manchester
      University Press, 1956, 30/-.
      U. S. distributor: New York, Humanities Press, $6.00.

186. Elias, Taslim Olawale
      Nigerian land law and custom. 3d ed. London, Routledge &
      Kegan Paul, 1962, 42/-.

      Epstein, Arnold Leonard
      Politics in an urban African community. See no. 908.

      Evans-Pritchard, Edward Evan
      The Nuer. See no. 853.

      Fallers, Lloyd A.
      Bantu Bureaucracy. See no. 856.

      Fortes, Meyer, and Edward Evan Evans-Pritchard, eds.
      African political systems. See no. 782.

187. Fustel de Coulanges, Numa Denis
      The ancient city; a study on the religion, laws, and institutions
      of Greece and Rome. Garden City, N. Y., Doubleday, 1956. (A
      Doubleday Anchor Book, A76.) $0.95.

      Gluckman, Max
      Custom and conflict in Africa. See no. 783.
      The judicial process among the Barotse of Northern Rhodesia.
      See no. 911.

      Gullick, J. M.
      Indigenous political systems of western Malaya. See no. 1103.

188. Haar, Barend ter
      Adat law in Indonesia, tr. from the Dutch; ed. with introd. by
      E. Adamson Hoebel and A. Arthur Schiller. New York, International
      Secretariat, Institute of Pacific Relations, 1948. Out of print; ca.
      $5.00.

189. Hanks, Jane (Richardson)
      Law and status among the Kiowa Indians. New York, Augustin,
      1940. (American Ethnological Society. Monographs, 1.) Out of
      print, ca. $3.00.

190. Hoebel, Edward Adamson
      The law of primitive man; a study in comparative legal dyna-
      mics. Cambridge, Harvard University Press, 1954, $5.50.

191. Hoebel, Edward Adamson
      The political organization and law-ways of the Comanche
      Indians. Menasha, Wis., American Anthropological Association,
      1940. (American Anthropological Association. Memoirs, 54.) $2.15.

Hogbin, Herbert Ian
Law and order in Polynesia. See no. 1251.

Holleman, J. F.
Shona customary law. See no. 912.

192. Howell, Paul Philip
A manual of Nuer law, being an account of customary law, its evolution and development in the courts established by the Sudan Government. London, New York, published for the International African Institute by the Oxford University Press, 1954, $6.10.

Leach, Edmund Ronald
Political systems of highland Burma. See no. 1117.

193. Llewellyn, Karl Nickerson, and Edward Adamson Hoebel
The Cheyenne way; conflict and case law in primitive jurisprudence. Norman, University of Oklahoma Press, 1941. (Civilization of the American Indian, no. 21.) $5.00.

194. Lowie, Robert Harry
The origin of the state. New York, Russell and Russell, 1962, $5.00. First published New York, 1927.

195. Maine, Sir Henry James Sumner
Ancient law, its connection with the early history of society and its relation to modern ideas. London & Toronto, Dent; New York, Dutton, 1917. (Everyman's Library 734.) $1.85; London, H. Milford, Oxford University Press. (World's Classics 362.) $1.65.

196. Malinowski, Bronislaw
Crime and custom in savage society. New York, Harcourt Brace, 1926, out of print; London, Kegan Paul, Trench, Trubner, 1926. (International Library of Psychology, Philosophy and Scientific Method.) 16/-.
U. S. distributor: Humanities Press, New York, $3.75.
Paper: Paterson, N. J., Littlefield, Adams, 1959, $1.50.

Meek, Charles Kingsley
Law and authority in a Nigerian tribe. See no. 821.

Middleton, John, And David Tait
Tribes without rulers. See no. 790.

197. Noon, John A.
Law and government of the Grand River Iroquois. New York, Viking Fund, 1949. (Viking Fund Publications in Anthropology, no. 12.) $2.00.

198. Pospisil, Leopold
Kapauku Papuans and their law. New Haven, published for the Dept. of Anthropology, Yale University, 1958. (Yale University Publications in Anthropology, no. 54.) $4.00.

Rattray, Robert Sutherland
Ashanti law and constitution. See no. 830.

Richards, Audrey Isabel
East African chiefs. See no. 880.

Schapera, Isaac
Government and politics in tribal societies. See no. 944.

199. Schapera, Isaac
A handbook of Tswana law and custom. With an introd. by Sir
Charles Rey. 2d ed. London, New York, published for the Interna-
tional African Institute by the Oxford University Press, 1955, $5.60.

Smith, Michael G.
Government in Zazzau. See no. 832.

Southall, Aidan William
Alur Society. See no. 889.

E. Religion

Barnett, Homer G.
Indian shakers. See no. 1356.

Barton, Roy Franklin
The religion of the Ifugaos. See no. 1070.

Bateson, Gregory
Naven. See no. 1219.

Bellah, Robert Neelly
Tokugawa religion. See no. 1144.

Belo, Jane
Trance in Bali. See no. 1074.

200. Benedict, Ruth (Fulton)
The concept of the guardian spirit in North America. Menasha, Wis.,
The American Anthropological Association, 1923. (American Anthro-
pological Association. Memoirs, no. 29.) Out of print; ca. $4.00.

Boas, Franz
The religion of the Kwakiutl Indians. See no. 1358.

201. Campbell, Joseph
The hero with a thousand faces. New York, Pantheon, 1949. (The
Bollingen Series, 17.) $4.00.
Paper: New York, Meridian, 1956, c1949. (Meridian Books,
M22.) $1.55.

Codrington, Robert Henry
The Melanesians. See no. 1232.

202. Durkheim, Emile
The elementary forms of the religious life. Translated by
Joseph Ward Swain. Glencoe, Ill., The Free Press, 1954,
$6.00.

203. Elkin, Adolphus Peter
Studies in Australian Totemism. Sydney, Australian National
Research Council, 1934. (Oceania Monographs, no. 2.) Out of
print; ca. $1.00.

Elwin, Verrier
The religion of an Indian tribe. See no. 1002.

Evans, Ivor Hugh Norman
The religion of the Tempasuk Dusuns of North Borneo. See
no. 1092.

Evans-Pritchard, Edward Evan
Nuer religion. See no. 854.

Evans-Pritchard, Edward Evan
Witchcraft, oracles, and magic among the Azande. See no. 855.

204. Field, Margaret Joyce
Religion and medicine of the Gã people. London, New York,
Oxford University Press, 1937. Out of print; ca. $6.00.

205. Fortes, Meyer
Oedipus and Job in West African religion. Cambridge, University Press, 1959, $2.00.

206. Fortune, Reo Franklin
Manus religion; an ethnological study of the Manus natives of
the Admiralty islands. Philadelphia, American Philosophical
Society, 1935. (Memoirs of the American Philosophical Society,
v. 3.) $1.50.

207. Frazer, Sir James George
The golden bough; a study in magic. Abridged ed. New York,
Macmillan, 1951, $3.95.
The new Golden Bough; a new abridgement of the classic work.
Edited, and with notes and foreword by Theodor H. Gaster. New
York, Criterion, 1959, $8.50.

Geertz, Clifford
Religion of Java. See no. 1100.

Gennep, Arnold van
The rites of passage. See no. 96.

208. Goode, William J.
         Religion among the primitives; with an introd. by Kingsley
      Davis. Glencoe, Ill., Free Press, c1951, $6.00.

209. Handy, Edward Smith Craighill
         Polynesian religion. Honolulu, Hawaii, The Museum, 1927.
      (Bernice P. Bishop Museum Bulletin no. 34.) (Bayard Dominick
      Expedition Publication no. 12.) Out of print; ca. $5.00.

210. Herskovits, Melville Jean, and Frances S. Herskovits
         An outline of Dahomean religious belief. Menasha, Wis., The
      American anthropological association, 1933. (American Anthro-
      pological Association. Memoirs, no. 41.) $0.85.

      Holton, Daniel Clarence
         The national faith of Japan. See no. 1173.
         The political philosophy of modern Shinto. See no. 1174.

211. Howells, William White
         The heathens; primitive man and his religions. 1st ed.
      Garden City, N. Y., Doubleday, 1948, $4.00.

212. Kluckhohn, Clyde
         Navaho witchcraft. Cambridge, Mass., The Museum, 1944.
      (Harvard University. Peabody Museum of American Archaeology
      and Ethnology. Papers, v. 22, no. 2.) Out of print; ca. $4.00.

213. Koppers, Wilhelm
         Primitive man and his world picture. Translated by Edith
      Raybould. London, New York, Sheed & Ward, 1952. Out of print;
      ca. $3.50.

214. La Barre, Weston
         The Peyote cult. Hamden, Conn., Reprinted by Shoe String
      Press, 1959, $4.00.
         (Originally published in 1938 as Yale University Publications
      in Anthropology, no. 19.)

      La Farge, Oliver
         Santa Eulalia; the religion of a Cuchumatan Indian town. See
      no. 1644.

215. Lang, Andrew
         The making of religion. 2d ed. London, New York, Longmans,
      Green, 1900. Out of print; ca. $4.00.

216. Langer, Susanne Katherina (Knauth)
         Philosophy in a new key; a study in the symbolism of reason, rite,
      and art. 3d ed. Cambridge, Harvard University Press, 1957, $4.75.
         Paper: New York, New American Library, 1958. (A Mentor
      Book, MD 101.) $0.50.

217. Leslie, Charles M., ed.
      Anthropology of folk religion. 1st ed. New York, Vintage, 1960.
      (A Vintage Original, V-105.) $1.65.

      Leslie, Charles M.
      Now we are civilized; a study of the world view of the Zapotec
      Indians of Mitla, Oaxaca. See no. 1645.

218. Lessa, William Armand, and Evon Z. Vogt, eds.
      Reader in comparative religion, an anthropological approach.
      Evanston, Ill., Row, Peterson, 1958. $7.25.

219. Lowie, Robert Harry
      Religion of the Crow Indians. New York, 1922. (American Museum
      of Natural History. Anthropological Papers, v. 25, pt. 2.) In print?
      ca. $4.00.

220. Malinowski, Bronislaw
      Magic, science, and religion, and other essays; selected and with
      an introd. by Robert Redfield. Boston, Beacon Press, 1948. Out of
      print.
      Paper: Garden City, N. Y., Doubleday, 1954. (Doubleday Anchor
      A23.) $0.95.

221. Marett, Robert Ranulph
      The threshold of religion. 2d ed., rev. and enl. London, Mac-
      millan, 1914. Out of print; ca. $3.00.

      Mendelsohn, Isaac, ed.
      Religions of the ancient Near East. See no. 737.

      Metraux, Alfred
      Haiti: black peasants and voodoo. See no. 1709.
      Voodoo in Haiti. See no. 1710.

222. Middleton, John
      Lugbara religion; ritual and authority among an east African
      people. London, New York, published for the International African
      Institute by the Oxford University Press, 1960, $6.10.

      Morgan, Kenneth William, ed.
      The religion of the Hindus. See no. 1038.

223. Murphy, Robert Francis
      Mundurucú religion. Berkeley and Los Angeles, University of
      California Press, 1958. (University of California Publications in
      American Archaeology and Ethnology, v. 49, no. 1.) $3.00.

      Nadel, Siegfried Frederick
      Nupe religion. See no. 826.

224. Nilsson, Martin Persson
      Greek popular religion. New York, Columbia University Press,
      1940. (Lectures on the history of religions, sponsored by the Ameri-
      can Council of Learned Societies. n. s., no. 1.) Out of print; ca. $3.00.

225. Norbeck, Edward
      Religion in primitive society, New York, Harper, 1961.

226. Park, Willard Z.
      Shamanism in western North America; a study in cultural rela-
      tionships. Evanston and Chicago, Northwestern University, 1938.
      (Northwestern University. Studies in the Social Sciences, no. 2.)
      Out of print; ca. $8.00.

      Parrinder, Geoffrey
      West African religion. See no. 828.

227. Parsons, Elsie Worthington (Clews)
      Pueblo Indian religion. Chicago, Ill., University of Chicago Press,
      1939, 2 v. Out of print; ca. $9.00.

228. Radin, Paul
      Monotheism among primitive peoples. Basel, Switzerland Ethno-
      graphical Museum, 1954. In print? Fr. 4.-; New York, Bollingen
      Foundation, 1954. (Special publications of Bollingen Foundation, no.
      4.) Out of print. First published London, 1924.

      Radin, Paul
      Primitive man as philosopher. See no. 122.

229. Radin, Paul
      Primitive religion; its nature and origin. New York, Viking, 1937.
      Out of print.
      Paper: New York, Dover, 1957, $1.85.

      Rattray, Robert Sutherland
      Religion and art in Ashanti. See no. 831.

230. Reichard, Gladys Amanda
      Navaho religion, a study in symbolism. New York, Pantheon,
      1950, 2 v. (Bollingen Series, 18.) $10.00.

231. Reichard, Gladys Amanda
      Prayer: the compulsive word. New York, Augustin, 1944. (Ameri-
      can Ethnological Society. Monographs, 7). Out of print; ca. $3.00.

      Richards, Audrey I.
      Chisungu. See no. 918.

232. Schmidt, Wilhelm
      The origin and growth of religion; facts and theories. Translated
      from the original German by H. J. Rose. London, Methuen, 1931.
      Out of print; ca. $5.00.

      Skeat, Walter William
      Malay magic. See no. 1125.

      Slotkin, James S.
      The Peyote religion. See no. 1320.

Smith, William Robertson
　　The religion of the Semites. See no. 754.

Srinivas, Mysore Narasimhachar
　　Religion and society among the Coorgs of South India. See no.
1056.

233. Steiner, Franz
　　Taboo. With a pref. by E. E. Evans-Pritchard. London, Cohen
& West, 1956, 18/-; New York, Philosophical Library, 1956. Out of
print.

234. Tawney, Richard Henry
　　Religion and the rise of capitalism; a historical study. New York,
Harcourt, Brace, 1926 (reprinted 1947). Out of print; ca. $4.00.
　　Paper: New York, New American Library. (Mentor Books, MD
163.) $0.50.

235. Tempels, Placied
　　Bantu philosophy. Translated into English from La philosophie
bantoue, the French version by A. Rubbens of Fr. Tempels' original
work. Colin King, translated. With a foreword to the English ed.
by Margaret Read. Paris, Présence Africaine, 1959. (Collection
Présence Africaine) ca. $2.50.

Tylor, Sir Edward Burnett
　　Religion in primitive culture. (His Primitive culture, v. 2.)
See no. 137.

236. Underhill, Ruth Murray
　　Papago Indian religion. New York, Columbia University Press,
1946. (Columbia University Contributions to Anthropology, no. 33.)
$4.50.

237. Wallis, Wilson Dallam
　　Messiahs, their role in civilization. Washington, D. C., American council on public affairs, 1943, $2.50.

238. Wallis, Wilson Dallam
　　Religion in primitive society. New York, Crofts, 1939. Out of
print; ca. $5.00.

239. Weber, Max
　　Ancient Judaism; translated and edited by Hans H. Gerth & Don
Martindale. Glencoe, Ill., Free Press, 1952, $6.00.

240. Weber, Max
　　The Protestant ethic and the spirit of capitalism. Translated by
Talcott Parsons. With a foreword by R. H. Tawney. New York,
Scribner's, 1948, $4.50.
　　Paper: (Student's edition) New York, Scribner's, 1958, $1.45.

241. Weber, Max
　　The religion of China: Confucianism and Taoism, translated and
edited by Hans H. Gerth. Glencoe, Ill., Free Press, 1951, $6.00.

242. Weber, Max
      The religion of India; the sociology of Hinduism and Buddhism.
      Translated and edited by Hans H. Gerth and Don Martindale.
      Glencoe, Ill., Free Press, 1958, $6.50.

243. Whiting, Beatrice Blyth
      Paiute sorcery. New York, Viking Fund, 1950. (Viking Fund
      Publications in Anthropology, no. 15.) Out of print; ca. $3.00.

      Williams, F. E.
      Orokaiva magic. See no. 1290.

      Williamson, Robert Wood
      Religion and social organization in central Polynesia. See
      no. 1294.
      Religious and cosmic beliefs of central Polynesia. See no.
      1295.

      Wilson, Monica
      Communal rituals of the Nyakyusa. See no. 896.
      Rituals of kinship among the Nyakyusa. See no. 898.

      Worsely, Peter
      The trumpet shall sound. See no. 1297.

244. Yinger, John Milton
      Religion, society, and the individual; an introduction to the
      sociology of religion. New York, Macmillan, 1957, $6.75. Part
      I (322 pages of 655 in complete ed.) available for $5.00.

      F. Art

      a. Art in general

245. Adam, Leonhard
      Primitive art. 3d ed. further rev. and enl. ed. London,
      Baltimore, Penguin, 1954. (Pelican Books A67.) Cloth, 7/6;
      paper, 3/6.

246. The art of Africa, by W. W. Battis and others. Edited and
      arranged by J. W. Grossert, with illus. drawn by the authors
      and L. Jaques-Rosset. Pietermaritzburg, Shuter & Shooter,
      1958, 21/-.

247. Bandi, Hans Georg, and Johannes Maringer
      Art in the ice age, Spanish Levant art, Arctic art . . . in
      execution of a plan by Hugo Obermeier. Translated by Robert
      Allen. New York, Praeger, 1953. Out of print; ca. $10.00.

248. Bennett, Wendell Clark
        Ancient arts of the Andes. With an introd. by René d'Harnon-
court. The Museum of Modern Art, New York, in collaboration
with the California Palace of the Legion of Honor, San Francisco, and the Minneapolis Institute of Arts. New York, Museum
of Modern Art, 1954, $6.50.

        Bliss, Robert Woods
        Pre-Columbian art. See no. 1299.

249. Boas, Franz
        Primitive art. New ed. New York, Dover, 1955, $1.95.

250. Breuil, Henri
        Four hundred centuries of cave art. Trans. by Mary E. Boyle.
Realized by Fernand Windels. Montignac, France, Centre d'études
et de documentation préhistoriques, 1952. In print? 4400 fr.;
paper, 4160 fr.

251. Carter, Dagny (Olsen)
        Four thousand years of China's art. Rev. print. New York,
Ronald Press, 1951, $7.50.

252. Christensen, Erwin Ottomar
        Primitive art. New York, Crowell, 1955. (A Studio publica-
tion.) Reissued in 1959 by Viking, $15.00.

253. Clawson, Hamilton Phelps
        By their works, illustrated from the collections in the Buffalo
Museum of Science. Buffalo, N. Y., Buffalo Society of Natural
Sciences, 1941. In print? ca. $4.00.

        Covarrubias, Miguel
        The eagle, the jaguar, and the serpent. See no. 1309.
        Indian art of Mexico and Central America. See no. 1501.

254. Dockstader, Frederick J.
        Indian art in America; the arts and crafts of the North Ameri-
can Indian. Greenwich, Conn., New York Graphic Society, 1961,
$25.00.

255. Elisofon, Eliot
        The sculpture of Africa; 405 photographs. Text by William
Fagg, pref. by Ralph Linton. New York, Praeger, 1958, $15.00.

256. Elkin, Adolphus Peter, Catherine Berndt, and Ronald Berndt
        Art in Arnhem Land. Melbourne, Cheshire, 1950. Out of
print; ca. $6.00.

257. Frankfort, Henri
        The art and architecture of the ancient Orient. Baltimore,
Penguin, 1955. (The Pelican History of Art, Z 7) $12.50.

258. Gerbrands, Adrianus Alexander
      Art as an element of culture, especially in Negro Africa. Leiden,
      Brill, 1957. (Mededelingen van het Rijksmuseum voor Volkenkunde,
      Leiden, no. 12.) Gld. 10. --.

259. Graziosi, Paolo
      Palaeolithic art. New York, McGraw-Hill, 1960, $35.00.

260. Herskovits, Melville Jean
      Backgrounds of African art. Three lectures given on the Cooke-
      Daniels lecture foundation, in conjunction with an exhibition of Afri-
      can art assembled by the Denver Art Museum, January and February,
      1945. Denver, 1945. Out of print; ca. $4.00.

261. Himmelheber, Hans
      Eskimokünstler. Ergebnisse einer Reise in Alaska. 2 Aufl.
      Eisenach, E. Röth, 1953. (Bücher der Brücke.) Halfcloth, DM
      11.80; cloth, DM 13.40.

262. Hooper, James T., and C. A. Burland
      The art of primitive peoples. With 116 photos of specimens from
      the Hooper collection by R. H. Bomback. London, Fountain Press,
      1953; New York, Philosophical Library, 1954. Out of print; ca. $6.00.

263. Inverarity, Robert Bruce
      Art of the Northwest Coast Indians. Berkeley and Los Angeles,
      University of California Press, 1950, $7.50.

264. Keleman, Pál
      Medieval American art, a survey in two volumes. New York,
      Macmillan, 1943, 2 v., $30.00.
      Medieval American art, masterpieces of the New World before
      Columbus (revised, one vol. ed.) New York, Macmillan, 1956,
      $15.00.

265. Linné, Sigvald
      Treasures of Mexican art; two thousand years of art and art
      handicraft. Translated by Albert Read. Stockholm, Nordisk
      Rotogravyr, 1956, 33 Kr.
      U. S. distributor: Humanities Press, New York, $6.75.

266. Linton, Ralph, and Paul S. Wingert
      Arts of the South Seas . . . in collaboration with René d'Harnon-
      court; color illustrations by Miguel Covarrabias. New York, The
      Museum of Modern Art, 1946. Distributor: Doubleday, New York,
      $3.95.

267. Malraux, André
      The voices of silence. Translated by Stuart Gilbert. Garden City,
      N. Y., Doubleday, 1953, $25.00.

268. Redfield, Robert, Melville J. Herskovits, and Gordon F. Eckholm
      Aspects of primitive art. New York, Museum of Primitive Art;
      distributed by University Publishers, 1959. (New York Museum of
      Primitive Art; Lecture Series, no. 1.) $2.75.

269. Reichard, Gladys Amanda
    Melanesian design, a study of style in wood and tortoiseshell carv-
    ing. New York, Columbia University Press, 1933. (Columbia Univer-
    sity contributions to anthropology, v. 18.) Out of print; ca. $10.00.

270. Roy, Claude
    The art of the savages. Translated by Eh. S. Seldon. New York,
    Golden Griffin, 1958. (Essential Encyclopedia.) $6.50.

    Spinden, Herbert Joseph
    Maya art and civilization. See no. 1528.

271. Symposium on the Artist in Tribal Society, London, 1957.
    The artist in tribal society; proceedings of a symposium held at
    the Royal Anthropological Institute. Edited by Marian W. Smith. Lon-
    don, Routledge & Kegan Paul, 1961 (Royal Anthropological Institute of
    Great Britain and Ireland. Occasional publication, no. 15) 25/-; New
    York, Free Press of Glencoe, 1961, $4.75.

272. Tischner, Herbert
    Oceanic art. 96 photos. by Friedrich Hewicker; text by Herbert
    Tischner. New York, Pantheon, 1954, $8.50; London, Thames and
    Hudson, 1954, 42/-.

273. Trowell, Kathleen Margaret
    African design. New York, Praeger, 1960, $7.50.

    b. Music

274. Dahlbach, Karl
    New methods in vocal folk music research. Oslo, Oslo Uni-
    versity Press, 1958. (Publication from Norwegian Folk Music
    Institute, no. 2.) 12 Kr.

275. Herskovits, Melville Jean, and Frances S. Herskovits
    Suriname folk-lore . . . with transcriptions of Suriname songs
    and musicological analysis by Dr. M. Kolinski. New York, Colum-
    bia University Press, 1936. (Columbia University Contributions to
    Anthropology, v. 27.) Pt. III, pp. 491-760: Suriname music, by M.
    Kolinski. Out of print; ca. $7.00.

276. Jones, A. M.
    Studies in African music. London, New York, Oxford University
    Press, 1959, 2 v., $23.55.

277. Karpeles, Maud, ed.
    The collecting of folk music and other ethnomusicological
    material; a manual for field workers. 1st ed. London, Inter-
    national Folk Music Council and the Royal Anthropological Insti-
    tute of Great Britain and Ireland, 1958, 6/-.

278. Kunst, Jaap
      Ethnomusicology; a study of its nature, its problems, methods
      and representative personalities to which is added a bibliography.
      3d much enl. ed. of Musicologica. The Hague, Nijhoff, 1959, $6.30.

279. McAllester, David Park
      Enemy way music; a study of social and esthetic values as seen
      in Navaho music. Cambridge, The Museum, 1954. (Reports of the
      Rimrock Project; Values Series, no. 3.) (Papers of the Peabody
      Museum of American Archaeology and Ethnology, v. 41, no. 3.)
      $2.65.

280. Nettl, Bruno
      Music in primitive culture. Cambridge, Harvard University
      Press, 1956, $5.00.

281. Nettl, Bruno
      North American Indian musical styles. Philadelphia, American
      Folklore Society, 1954. (Memoirs of the American Folklore
      Society, v. 45.) $2.50.

282. Sachs, Curt
      The history of musical instruments. New York, Norton, 1940,
      $8.95.

283. Tracey, Hugh
      Chopi musicians, their music, poetry, and instruments. London,
      New York, Oxford University Press, 1948. Out of print; ca. $6.00.

      c. Folklore and literature

284. African folktales and sculpture. Folktales selected and edited by
      Paul Radin, with the collaboration of Elinore Marvel. Introd. to
      tales by Paul Radin. Sculpture selected with an introd. by James
      Johnson Sweeney. New York, Pantheon, 1952. (Bollengen Series,
      32.) $10.00.

      Barton, Roy Franklin
      The mythology of the Ifugaos. See no. 1068.

285. Beckwith, Martha Warren
      Folklore in America, its scope and method. Poughkeepsie, N.Y.
      Vassar College, The Folklore Foundation, 1931. (Publications of the
      Folklore Foundation. no. 11.) Out of print? Estimate: $4.00.

286. Benedict, Ruth (Fulton)
      Zuni mythology. New York, Columbia University Press, 1935.
      2 v. (Columbia University Contributions to Anthropology, v. 21.)
      Out of print; ca. $8.00.

287. Clark, Ella E.
      Indian legends of the Pacific Northwest; illustrated by Robert
Bruce Inverarity. Berkeley and Los Angeles, University of California Press, 1953. Paper, $1.95.

Codrington, Robert Henry
      The Melanesians. See no. 1232.

288. Eberhard, Wolfram, ed. and tr.
      Chinese fairy tales and folk tales. London, Kegan Paul, Trench,
Trubner, 1937; out of print; New York, Dutton, 1938, out of print;
ca. $5.00.

Elwin, Verrier
      Myths of middle India. See no. 1001.

Frazer, Sir James George
      The Golden bough. See no. 207.

289. Funk & Wagnalls standard dictionary of folklore, mythology, and
legend. Maria Leach, editor, Jerome Fried, associate editor.
New York, Funk & Wagnalls, 1949-1950, 2 v., $20.00.

Grey, Sir George
      Polynesian mythology and ancient traditional history of the
Maori. See no. 1246.

290. Herskovits, Melville Jean, and Frances S. Herskovits
      Dahomean narrative; a cross-cultural analysis. Evanston, Ill.,
Northwestern University Press, 1958. (Northwestern University
African Studies, no. 1.) $6.50.

Herskovits, Melville J. and Frances S. Herskovits
      Suriname folklore. See no. 275.

291. Jacobs, Melville
      The content and style of an oral literature; Clackamas Chinook
myths and tales. Chicago, University of Chicago Press, 1959,
$5.00. Also published as Viking Fund Publications in Anthropology,
no. 26.

292. Krappe, Alexander Haggerty
      The science of folklore. London, Methuen, 1930; New York,
L. MacVeagh, Dial Press, 1930. Out of print; ca. $4.00.

293. Kroeber, Theodora
      The inland whale. Foreword by Oliver LaFarge. Drawings by
Joseph Crivy. Bloomington, Indiana University Press, 1959, $4.50.
(Calif. Indian Legends.)

294. Panchatantra, English.
      The Panchatantra, translated from the Sanskrit, by Arthur W.
Ryder. Chicago, Ill., The University of Chicago Press, 1925, $6.00.

295. Propp, Vladimir IAkovlevich
     Morphology of the folktale. Edited with an introduction
by Svatava Pirkova-Jakobson. Translated by Laurence Scott.
Bloomington, Ind., 1958. (Publication of the Indiana University Research Center in Anthropology, Folklore, and Linguistics, 10.) (International Journal of American Linguistics,
v. 24, no. 4, pt. 3.) (Bibliographical and special series of
the American Folklore Society, v. 9.) $5.00.

296. Radin, Paul
     The trickster; a study in American Indian mythology. With
commentaries by Karl Kerényi and C. G. Jung. London, Routledge and Kegan Paul, 1955, £1/1/-.

297. Raglan, Fitz Roy Richard Somerset, baron
     The hero; a study in tradition, myth, and drama. London,
Watts, 1949. (The Thinkers Library, no. 133.) 3/6.
     Paper: New York, Vintage, 1956. (Vintage Books, K 32.)
$1.25.

298. Sydow, Carl Wilhelm von
     Selected papers on folklore. Published on the occasion
of his 70th birthday. Copenhagen, Rosenkilde & Bagger, 1948.
In print? 28 Kr.

299. Taylor, Archer
     The Proverb. Cambridge, Mass., Harvard University Press,
1931. Out of print; ca. $5.00.

300. Thompson, Stith
     The folktale. New York, Dryden Press, 1946, $7.00.

301. Thompson, Stith
     Four symposia on folklore; held at the Midcentury Inter-
national Folklore Conference, Indiana University, July 21-
August 4, 1950. Bloomington, Indiana University Press, 1953.
(Indiana University Publications Folklore Series, no. 8.)
$3.50.

302. Thompson, Stith, ed.
     Tales of the North American Indians, selected and anno-
tated by Stith Thompson. Cambridge, Mass., Harvard University Press, 1929. Out of print; ca. $6.00.

303. Toor, Frances
     A treasury of Mexican folkways. The customs, myths,
folklore, traditions, beliefs, fiestas, dances, and songs of
the Mexican people. Illustrated with 10 color plates, 100
drawings by Carlos Merida, and 170 photographs. New York,
Crown, 1947, $7.50.

d. Plastic and graphic arts

304. Adair, John
     The Navaho and Pueblo silversmiths. Norman, University of
Oklahoma Press, 1944. (The Civilization of the American Indian,
25.) $5.00.

     African folktales and sculpture, by Paul Radin and James Johnson
Sweeney. See no. 284.

305. Amsden, Charles Avery
     Navajo weaving; its technic and history; foreword by Fred-
erick Webb Hodge. Albuquerque, University of New Mexico Press,
1949. Out of print; ca. $7.00.

     Archer, William George
     The vertical man; a study in primitive Indian sculpture. See
no. 976.

306. Bunzel, Ruth Leah
     The Pueblo potter; a study of creative imagination in primi-
tive art. New York, Columbia University Press, 1929. (Columbia university contributions to anthropology, v. 8.) Out of print;
ca. $10.00.

307. Bushnell, Geoffrey Hext Sutherland, and Adrian Digby
     Ancient American pottery. London, Faber and Faber, 1955,
35/-; New York, Pitman, 1955. (The Faber Monographs on
Pottery and Porcelain) $8.50.

308. Laming, Annette
     Lascaux: paintings and engravings. Translated by Eleanore
Frances Armstrong. Harmondsworth, Middlesex, Baltimore, Md.,
Penguin, 1959. (Pelican Books, A419.) $1.25.

309. O'Neale, Lila Morris
     Textiles of highland Guatemala. Drawings by Lucretia Nelson.
Washington, D. C., 1945. (Carnegie institution of Washington.
Publication 567.) Out of print; ca. $6.00.

310. Poulík, Josef
     Prehistoric art, including some recent cave-culture discoveries
and subsequent developments up to Roman times. Photographs
and graphic arrangements by W. and B. Forman. Translated by
R. Finlayson Samsour. London, Spring Books, 1956. Out of print?
ca. $7.00.

311. Robinson, Alambert E.
     The basket weavers of Arizona. Photos. by Robert H. Peebles.
Albuquerque, University of New Mexico Press, 1954. Out of print;
ca. $7.50.

312. Tschopik, Harry
      Navaho pottery making; an inquiry into the affinities of Navaho painted pottery. Cambridge, Mass., The Museum, 1941. (Papers of the Peabody Museum of American Archaeology and Ethnology, Harvard University. v. 17, no. 1.) $1.75.

313. Underwood, Leon
      Bronzes of West Africa. London, Tiranti, 1949, 9/-.
      U. S. distributor: Transatlantic Arts, Hollywood-by-the-Sea, Florida, $2.50.

314. Underwood, Leon
      Figures in wood of West Africa. London, Tiranti, 1947, 9/-.
      U. S. distributor: Transatlantic Arts, Hollywood-by-the-Sea, Florida, $2.50.

315. Underwood, Leon
      Masks of West Africa. London, Tiranti, 1948, 9/-.
      U. S. distributor: Transatlantic Arts, Hollywood-by-the-Sea, Florida, $2.50.

316. Wildschut, William, and John C. Ewers
      Crow Indian beadwork; a descriptive and historical study. New York, Museum of the American Indian, Heye Foundation, 1959. (New York [City] Museum of the American Indian, Heye Foundation. Contributions, v. 16.) $3.50.

G. Culture and Personality

317. Aberle, David Friend
      The psychosocial analysis of a Hopi life-history. Berkeley and Los Angeles, University of California Press, 1951. (Comparative Psychology Monographs, v. 21, no. 107.) $3.50.

318. Akiga
      Akiga's story; the Tiv tribe as seen by one of its members; translated and annotated by Rupert East. London, New York, published for the International Institute of African Languages and Cultures by the Oxford University Press, 1939. Out of print; ca. $8.00.

319. Baba of Karo
      Baba of Karo, a woman of the Muslim Hausa. Autobiography recorded by Mary Felice Smith. With an introd. and notes by M. G. Smith; pref. by Daryll Forde. London, Faber & Faber, 1954, 25/-; New York, Philosophical Library, 1955. Out of print.

Barton, Roy Franklin
      Philippine pagans; the autobiographies of three Ifugaos. See no. 1069.

Bateson, Gregory, and Margaret Mead
Balinese character, a photographic analysis. See no. 1071.

Bateson, Gregory
Naven. See no. 1219.

Benedict, Ruth (Fulton)
The chrysanthemum and the sword. See no. 1145.

Brown, Roger
Words and things. See no. 440.

Carstairs, G. Morris
The twice-born. See no. 983.

Casagrande, Joseph B., ed.
In the company of man. See no. 49.

320. Dennis, Wayne
The Hopi child. New York, London, D. Appleton-Century Co.,
Inc., for the Institute for Research in the Social Sciences, Uni-
versity of Virginia, 1940. (Virginia. University. Institute for
Research in the Social Sciences. Institute monograph, no. 26.)
Out of print; ca. $4.00.

321. Devereux, George
Reality and dream; psychotherapy of a Plains Indian. Prefaces
by Karl A. Menninger and Robert H. Lowie. Psychological tests
edited and interpreted by Robert R. Holt. New York, International
Universities Press, 1951, $7.50.

322. Dollard, John
Criteria for the life history, with analyses of six notable documents. New Haven, Pub. for the Institute of Human Relations by
Yale University Press; London, Oxford University Press, H. Milford, 1935; out of print. New York, Smith, 1949, $3.25.

323. Dollard, John, and Neal E. Miller
Personality and psychotherapy; an analysis in terms of learning, thinking, and culture. 1st ed. New York, McGraw-Hill, 1950,
$6.75.

Du Bois, Cora
People of Alor. See no. 1085.

324. Erikson, Erik Homburger
Childhood and society. 1st ed. N. Y., Norton, 1950, $5.50.

325. Ford, Clellan Stearns, and Frank A. Beach
Patterns of sexual behavior. With a foreword by Robert Latou
Dickinson. 1st ed. New York, Harper, 1951, $5.75.
Paper: New York, Ace Books, 1961, $0.75.

Ford, Clellan Stearns
   Smoke from their fires; the life of a Kwakiutl chief. See no.
1364.

326. Freud, Sigmund
   Civilization and its discontents . . . authorized translation by
Joan Riviere. London, L. and Virginia Woolf at The Hogarth
Press, 1930. (International Psycho-analytical Library, ed. by
Ernest Jones, no. 17.) 10/6.
   U. S. distributor: New York, Hillary House, $2.75.
   Paper: Translated from the German by Joan Riviere. Garden
City, N. Y., Doubleday, 1958. (Doubleday Anchor Books, A 130.)
$0.95.

327. Freud, Sigmund
   Totem and taboo; some points of agreement between the mental
lives of savages and neurotics. Authorized translation by James
Strachey. London, Routledge & Kegan Paul, 1950, 15/-; New York,
Norton, 1952, c1950, $4.50.
   Paper: Totem and taboo; resemblances between the psychic
lives of savages and neurotics; authorized translation with an
introduction by A. A. Brill. New York, Modern Library, 1960.
(Modern Library of the World's Best Books, P 67.) $0.95.

Gladwin, Thomas, and Seymour B. Sarason
   Truk: man in paradise. See no. 1245.

Gorer, Geoffrey
   The American people, a study in national character. See no.
1602.
   Exploring English character. See no. 626.
   People of Great Russia. See no. 660.

328. Gottschalk, Louis Reichenthal, Clyde Kluckhohn, and Robert Angell
   The use of personal documents in history, anthropology, and
sociology, prepared for the Committee on Appraisal of Research.
New York, Social Science Research Council, 1945. (Social Science
Research Council, Bulletin 53.) $1.50.

329. Hallowell, Alfred Irving
   Culture and experience. Philadelphia, University of Pennsylvania Press, 1955. (Publications of the Philadelphia Anthropological Society, v. 4.) $8.50.

330. Haring, Douglas Gilbert, comp.
   Personal character and cultural milieu; a collection of readings.
3d rev. ed. Syracuse, N. Y., Syracuse University Press, 1956,
$7.50.

331. Hilger, Inez
   Field guide to the ethnological study of child life. New Haven,
Human Relations Area Files Press, 1960. (Behavior Science
Field Guides, v. 1.) $1.25.

Honigmann, John Joseph
Culture and ethos of Kaska society. See no. 1345.

332. Honigmann, John Joseph
Culture and personality. New York, Harper, 1954, $5.00.

333. Hsu, Francis L. K., ed.
Aspects of culture and personality; a symposium. New York,
Abelard-Schuman, 1954, $4.00.

334. Hsu, Francis L. K., ed.
Psychological anthropology; approaches to culture and personality. Homewood, Ill., Dorsey Press, 1961. (The Dorsey
series in anthropology and sociology) $10.60.

335. Interdisciplinary Conference, New York, 1947.
Culture and personality, ed. by S. Stansfeld Sargent and Marian
W. Smith. New York, Viking Fund, 1949. Out of print; ca. $3.00.

336. Kaplan, Bert
A study of Rorschach responses in four cultures. Cambridge,
The Museum, 1954. (Harvard University. Peabody Museum of
American Archaeology and Ethnology. Papers, v. 42, no. 2; Re-
ports on the Ramah Project, no. 6.) Out of print; ca. $3.00.

337. Kaplan, Bert, ed.
Studying personality cross-culturally. Evanston, Ill., Row,
Peterson, 1961, $8.50.

338. Kardiner, Abram
The individual and his society; the psychodynamics of primitive social organization . . . with a foreword and two ethnological reports by Ralph Linton. New York, Columbia University
Press, 1939, $6.50.

339. Kardiner, Abram, and Lionel Ovesey
The mark of oppression; a psychosocial study of the American
Negro. New York, Norton, 1951. Out of print; ca. $5.00.

340. Kardiner, Abram
The psychological frontiers of society . . . with the collabora-
tion of Ralph Linton, Cora Du Bois, and James West. New York,
Columbia University Press, 1945, $6.50.

341. Kluckhohn, Clyde, Henry A. Murray, and David M. Schneider, eds.
Personality in nature, society, and culture. 2d ed., rev. and
enl. New York, Knopf, 1953, $8.75; text ed. $6.50.

Landy, David
Tropical childhood. See no. 1707.

Language, culture, and personality; essays in memory of Edward
Sapir. See no. 101.

Lantis, Margaret
  Eskimo childhood and interpersonal relationship. See no. 1336.

342. Laubscher, Barend Jacob Frederick
  Sex, custom, and psychopathology; a study of South African
  pagan natives. London, Routledge, 1937, £1/12/-; New York,
  McBride, 1938. Out of print.
  U. S. distributor: New York, Humanities Press, $7.50.

343. Left Handed, Navaho Indian
  Son of Old Man Hat, a Navaho autobiography recorded by
  Walter Dyk, with an introduction by Edward Sapir. New York,
  Harcourt, Brace, 1938. Out of print; ca. $5.00.

Leighton, Dorothea (Cross), and Clyde Kluckhohn
  Children of the people, the Navajo individual and his development. See no. 1460.

Lewis, Oscar
  Life in a Mexican village: Tepoztlan restudied. See no. 1647.

344. Linton, Ralph
  The cultural background of personality. New York, London,
  Appleton-Century, 1945, $2.00; London, Kegan Paul, Trench,
  Trubner, 1947. (International Library of Sociology and Social
  Reconstruction.) 14/-.

345. Macgregor, Gordon
  Warriors without weapons; a study of the society and personality development of the Pine Ridge Sioux. With the collaboration
  of Royal B. Hassrick and William E. Henry. Chicago, University
  of Chicago Press, 1946. Out of print; ca. $4.00.

Malinowski, Bronislaw
  Sex and repression in savage society. See no. 173.

346. Mead, Margaret and Martha Wolfenstein, eds.
  Childhood in contemporary cultures. Chicago, University of
  Chicago Press, 1955, $7.50.

Mead, Margaret
  Coming of age in Samoa. See no. 1262.

Mead, Margaret, and Frances C. Macgregor
  Growth and culture. See no. 1119.

347. Mead, Margaret
  Male and female, a study of the sexes in a changing world.
  New York, Morrow, 1949, $5.00; London, Gollancz, 1950, 18/-.
  Paper; New York, New American Library, 1955. (A Mentor
  Book, MD 150.) $0.50.

Mead, Margaret
  Sex and temperament in three primitive societies. See no. 1267.

Mead, Margaret, and Rhoda Metraux, eds.
The study of culture at a distance. See no. 60.

Miner, Horace M., and George De Vos
Oasis and Casbah. See no. 738.

348. Opler, Marvin Kaufmann, ed.
Culture and mental health; cross-cultural studies. New York,
Macmillan, 1959, $8.75.

349. Piers, Gerhart, and Milton B. Singer
Shame and guilt, a psychoanalytic and a cultural study.
Springfield, Ill., Thomas, 1953. (American Lecture Series,
Publication no. 171; American Lectures in Psychiatry.) $3.25.

350. Pike, Kenneth Lee
Language in relation to a unified theory of the structure
of human behavior. Preliminary ed. Glendale, Calif., Summer
Institute of Linguistics, 1954-1955, 2 v.: Pt. 1, $5.00; Pt. 2,
$2.00.

351. Potter, David Morris
People of plenty; economic abundance and the American char-
acter. Chicago, University of Chicago Press, 1954. (Charles R.
Walgreen Foundation Lectures.) $4.25.
Paper: Chicago, University of Chicago Press, 1958. (Phoenix
Books P28.) $1.35.

Raum, O. F.
Chaga childhood. See no. 879.

Read, Margaret
Children of their fathers; growing up among the Ngoni of
Nyasaland. See no. 916.

352. Róheim, Géza
Psychoanalysis and anthropology; culture, personality and the
unconscious. New York, International Universities Press, 1950.
Out of print; ca. $10.00.

353. Rohrer, John Harrison, and Munro S. Edmonson, eds.
The eighth generation: cultures and personalities of New
Orleans Negroes. Co-authors: Harold Lief, Daniel Thompson,
and William Thompson. New York, Harper, 1960, $6.00.

Sapir, Edward
Culture, language, and personality; selected essays edited by
D. G. Mandelbaum. See no. 64.
Selected writings. See no. 129.

Simmons, Leo W., ed.
Sun chief. See no. 354.

Spindler, George D.
Sociocultural and psychological processes in Menomini acculturation. See no. 373.

Spiro, Melford
Children of the Kibbutz. See no. 755.

354. Talayesva, Don C.
Sun chief; the autobiography of a Hopi Indian, edited by Leo
W. Simmons. New Haven, Published for the Institute of Human
Relations by Yale University Press; London, H. Milford, Oxford
University Press, 1942, $4.00.

355. Wallace, Anthony
Culture and society. New York, Random House, 1961. (Studies
in anthropology, 1.) $0.95.

356. Whiting, John Wesley Mayhew
Becoming a Kwoma; teaching and learning in a New Guinea
tribe . . . with a foreword by John Dollard. New Haven, Pub.
for the Institute of Human Relations by Yale University Press;
London, H. Milford, Oxford University Press, 1941, $3.75.

357. Whiting, John Wesley Mayhew, and Irvin L. Child
Child training and personality development: a cross-cultural
study. New Haven, Yale University Press, 1953, $5.50.

358. Wilbur, George B., and Warner Muensterberger, eds.
Psychoanalysis, and culture, essays in honor of Géza Róheim.
New York, International Universities Press, 1951, $10.00.

Winter, Edward H.
Beyond the mountains of the moon. See no. 899.

H. Culture Change and Acculturation

359. American Ethnological Society, New York
Cultural stability and cultural change. Proceedings of the
1957 Annual Spring Meeting of the American Ethnological Society,
edited by Verne F. Ray. Seattle, 1957, $2.50.
Distributor: University of Washington Press.

Bailey, F. G.
Caste and the economic frontier. See no. 978.

360. Barnett, Homer Garner
Innovation: the basis of cultural change. 1st ed. New York,
McGraw-Hill, 1953, $7.50.

361. Barnouw, Victor
       Acculturation and personality among the Wisconsin Chippewa.
       Menasha, American Anthro. Assn., 1950. (Memoirs of the Ameri-
       can Anthropological Association, no. 72.) $2.00.

       Caudill, William A.
       Japanese-American personality and acculturation. See no. 1596.

       Firth, Raymond William
       Social change in Tikopia. See no. 1239.

362. Foster, George McClelland
       Culture and conquest: America's Spanish heritage. New York,
       Wenner-Gren Foundation for Anthropological Research, 1960.
       (Viking Fund publications in anthropology, no. 27.) $5.00.

       Fujii, Yukio, and T. Lynn Smith
       The acculturation of the Japanese immigrants in Brazil. See
       no. 1673.

363. Gearing, Frederick O., Robert McC. Netting, and Lisa R. Peattie,
       eds.
       Documentary history of the Fox project, 1948-1959; a program
       in action anthropology, directed by Sol Tax. Chicago, Dept. of
       Anthropology, University of Chicago, 1960, $8.50.

       Hallowell, Alfred Irving
       Culture and experience. See no. 329.

364. Herskovits, Melville Jean
       Acculturation: the study of culture contact. Gloucester, Mass.,
       Smith, 1958, $3.00. First published New York, Augustin, 1938.

       Hogbin, Herbert Ian
       Experiments in civilization; the effects of European culture
       on a native community in the Solomon islands. See no. 1250.

365. Hogbin, Herbert Ian
       Social change. London, Watts, 1958. (Josiah Mason Lectures,
       1957.) 21/-.

       Hogbin, Herbert Ian
       Transformation scene; the changing culture of a New Guinea
       Village. See no. 1252.

366. International African Institute
       Methods of study of culture contact in Africa; with an
       introductory essay by B. Malinowski. London, New York, Ox-
       ford University Press, 1938 (reprinted 1959). (International
       African Institute. Memorandum 15.) 8/-.

367. Keesing, Felix Maxwell
    Culture change; an analysis and bibliography of anthropological
    sources to 1952. Stanford, Calif., Stanford University Press, 1953.
    Stanford Anthropological Series, no. 1.) $3.50.

368. Linton, Ralph, ed.
    Acculturation in seven American Indian tribes. New York, London,
    Appleton-Century, 1940. Out of print; ca. $10.00.

    Little, Kenneth Lindsay
    The Mende of Sierra Leone. See no. 819.

369. Locke, Alain LeRoy, and Bernhard J. Stern, eds.
    When peoples meet, a study in race and culture contacts. Rev.
    ed. New York, Hinds, Hayden & Eldridge, 1946. Out of print; ca.
    $4.00.

370. Malinowski, Bronislaw
    The dynamics of culture change; an inquiry into race relations in
    Africa. Edited by Phyllis M. Kaberry. New Haven, Yale University
    Press; London, H. Milford, Oxford University Press, 1945, $4.00.
        Paper: New Haven, Yale University Press, 1961. (Yale Paper-
    bounds) $1.45.

    Mead, Margaret
    The changing culture of an Indian tribe. See no. 1406.
    New lives for old. See no. 1266.

    Paul, Benjamin D., ed.
    Health, culture, and community. See no. 576.

    Redfield, Robert
    A village that chose progress; Chan Kom revisited. See no.
    1655.

371. Siegel, Bernard Joseph, ed.
    Acculturation; critical abstracts, North America. Bernard J.
    Siegel, editor, assisted by Rose Wax. Stanford, Calif., Stanford
    University Press, 1955. (Stanford Anthropological Series, no. 2.)
    $4.00.

372. Spicer, Edward Holland, ed.
    Human problems in technological change, a casebook. New
    York, Russell Sage Foundation, 1952, $4.00.

373. Spindler, George D.
    Sociocultural and psychological processes in Menomini accul-
    turation. Berkeley and Los Angeles, University of California
    Press, 1955. (University of California Publications in Culture
    and Society, v. 5.) Out of print; ca. $3.50.

374. Steward, Julian Haynes
    Theory of culture change; the methodology of multilinear evolu-
    tion. Urbana, University of Illinois Press, 1955, $4.00.

375. Tax, Sol, ed.
        Acculturation in the Americas. Chicago, University of Chicago
      Press, 1952. (International Congress of Americanists. 29th, New
      York, 1949. Selected papers, v. 2.) Out of print; ca. $7.50.

      Tax, Sol, ed.
        Heritage of conquest. See no. 1657.

      Thompson, Laura
        Culture in crisis; a study of the Hopi Indians. See no. 1480.

      Tumin, Melvin Marvin
        Caste in a peasant society. See no. 1659.

376. Vogt, Evon Zartman
        Navaho veterans; a study of changing values. Cambridge, The
      Museum, 1951. (Reports of the Rimrock Project. Values Series, no. 1.)
      (Papers of the Peabody Museum of American Archaeology and
      Ethnology, Harvard University, v. 41, no. 1.) $3.00.

377. Wilson, Godfrey, and Monica (Hunter) Wilson
        The analysis of social change, based on observations in central
      Africa. Cambridge, England, The University Press, 1945 (reprinted
      1954), $2.50.

      Wilson, Monica (Hunter)
        Reaction to conquest. See no. 952.

378. World Federation for Mental Health
        Cultural patterns and technical change; a manual edited by
      Margaret Mead. Paris, UNESCO, 1953. (Tensions and Technology
      Series.) $2.50.
        Paper: New York, New American Library, 1955. (A Mentor
      Book, MD 134.) $0.50.

IV. ARCHAEOLOGY AND CULTURE HISTORY

A. General

379. American Association for the Advancement of Science. Section on
      Anthropology.
        Asia and North America; Transpacific contacts. Assembled by
      Marian W. Smith for the Society for American Archaeology and The
      Amer. Assn. for the Adv. of Sci., Salt Lake City, Soc. for Am.
      Archaeo., 1953. (Society for American Archaeology, Memoirs, no.
      9.) $1.50.

380. Bibbey, Geoffrey
Testimony of the spade. 1st ed. New York, Knopf, 1956, $6.75.

Braidwood, Robert John
The Near East and the foundations for civilization. See no. 677.

381. Braidwood, Robert John
Prehistoric Men. Drawings by Susan T. Richert. 3d ed., issued in coöperation with The Oriental Institute, The University of Chicago. Chicago, 1957. (Chicago. Natural History Museum. Popular Series; Anthropology no. 37.) $1.25.

382. Breuil, Henri
Beyond the bounds of history; scenes from the Old Stone Age. English translation by Mary E. Boyle. Foreword by J. C. Smuts. London, Gawthorn, 1949, 12/6.

383. Breuil, Henri, and Raymond Lantier
Les hommes de la pierre ancienne (paléolithique et mésolithique) Nouv. éd. revue et augm. avec 32 photos. hors texte. Paris, Payot, 1959. (Bibliothèque Scientifique.) 2,200 fr.

Childe, Vere Gordon
The dawn of European civilization. See no. 581.
Man makes himself. See no. 681.
New light on the most ancient East. See no. 682.
Piecing together the past. See no. 408.

384. Childe, Vere Gordon
A short introduction to archaeology. London, Muller, 1956 (Man and Society Series), 10/6; New York, Macmillan, 1958, $2.50.

Childe, Vere Gordon
Social evolution. See no. 88.

385. Childe, Vere Gordon
What happened in history. New ed. London, Parrish, 1960, 30/-.
Paper: New York, Penguin, 1946. (Pelican Books, A108) $0.85.

386. Clark, John Grahame Douglas
Archaeology and society; reconstructing the prehistoric past. 3d ed. rev. London, Methuen, 1957, 25/-; New rev. ed. Cambridge, Mass., Harvard University Press, 1957, $5.00.
Paper: London, Methuen, 1960. (University Paperbacks, UP1.) 12/6.
U. S. distributor: New York, Barnes & Noble, Inc., $1.95.

Clark, J. G. D.
Prehistoric Europe; the economic basis. See no. 584.

387. The concise encyclopedia of archaeology.
      Edited by Leonard Cottrell. The contributors: P. J. Adams
      and others. 1st ed. New York, Hawthorn, 1960, $12.95.

      Coon, Carleton S.
         The seven caves. See no. 688.
         The story of man. See no. 72.

388. Daniel, Glyn Edmund
      A hundred years of archaeology. London, Duckworth, 1950.
      (The Hundred Years Series.) 30/-.
      U. S. distributor: Macmillan, New York, $3.50.

389. De Terra, Helmut, and Thomas Thomson Patterson
      Studies on the ice age in India and associated human cultures.
      Washington, D. C., Carnegie Institution of Washington, 1939.
      (Carnegie Institution of Washington. Publication no. 493.) Out of
      print; ca. $7.50.

      Fox, Sir Cyril Fred
         The personality of Britain. See no. 592.

390. Kroeber, Alfred Louis
      Configurations of culture growth. Berkeley and Los Angeles,
      University of California Press, 1944, $7.50.

      Kroeber, Alfred Louis
      Cultural and natural areas of native North America. See
      no. 1315.

391. Kroeber, Alfred Louis
      Style and civilizations. Ithaca, N. Y., Cornell University Press,
      1957, $3.00.

      Leakey, Louis S. B.
         Adam's ancestors. See no. 524.

      Linton, Ralph
         The tree of culture. See no. 104.

392. Oakley, Kenneth P.
      Man the tool-maker. 4th ed. London, British Museum (Natural
      History) 1958, 4/-; Chicago, University of Chicago Press, 1957.
      (Phoenix Books, P20.) $1.25.

393. Peake, Harold John Edward, and Herbert John Fleure
      The horse and the sword. New Haven, Yale University Press;
      London, H. Milford, Oxford University Press, 1933. (*Their* The
      corridors of time, 8.) $2.40.

394. Peake, Harold John Edward, and Herbert John Fleure
      Hunters and artists. New Haven, Yale University Press; Lon-
      don, H. Milford, Oxford University Press, 1927. (*Their* The
      corridors of time, 2.) $2.40.

395. Peake, Harold John Edward, and Herbert John Fleure
    The law and the prophets. New Haven, Yale University Press;
    London, H. Milford, Oxford University Press, 1936. *(Their* The
    corridors of time, 9.) $2.40.

396. Peake, Harold John Edward, and Herbert John Fleure
    Merchant venturers in bronze. New Haven, Yale University
    Press; London, H. Milford, Oxford University Press, 1931.
    (Their The corridors of time, 7.) $2.40.

397. Peake, Harold John Edward, and Herbert John Fleure
    Peasants and potters. New Haven, Yale University Press;
    London, H. Milford, Oxford University Press, 1927. *(Their* The
    corridors of time, 3.) $2.40.

398. Peake, Harold John Edward, and Herbert John Fleure
    Priests and Kings. New Haven, Yale University Press; London,
    H. Milford, Oxford University Press, 1927. *(Their* The corridors
    of time, 4.) $2.40.

399. Peake, Harold John Edward, and Herbert John Fleure
    The steppe and the sown. New Haven, Yale University Press;
    London, H. Milford, Oxford University Press, 1928. *(Their* The
    corridors of time, 5.) $2.40.

400. Peake, Harold John Edward, and Herbert John Fleure
    Times and places. Oxford, The Clarendon Press, 1956. *(Their*
    The corridors of time, 10.) $6.75.

401. Peake, Harold John Edward, and Herbert John Fleure
    The way of the sea. New Haven, Yale University Press; London,
    H. Milford, Oxford University Press, 1929. *(Their* The corridors
    of time, 6.) $2.40.

402. Piggott, Stuart
    Approach to archaeology. London, Black, 1959, 15/-; Cam-
    bridge, Harvard University Press, 1959, $3.00.

403. Thompson, Raymond Harris, ed.
    Migrations in new world culture history. Tucson, University
    of Arizona Press, 1958. (Arizona. University. Social Science
    Bulletin no. 27.) $1.00.

404. White, Leslie A.
    The evolution of culture; the development of civilization to the
    fall of Rome. New York, McGraw-Hill, 1959, $10.00; text ed.,
    $7.50.

405. Wooley, Sir Charles Leonard
    History unearthed; a survey of eighteen archaeological sites
    throughout the world. London, Benn, 1958, 12/6.

B. Methods, Theory, and Techniques

406. Atkinson, Richard John Copland
        Field archeology. 2d ed., rev. London, Methuen, 1953, 17/6.

407. Bradford, John
        Ancient landscapes; studies in field archaeology. London, Bell,
        1957, 84/-.

408. Childe, Vere Gordon
        Piecing together the past; the interpretation of archaeological
        data. London, Routledge & Kegan Paul, 1956, 18/-; New York,
        Praeger, 1956, $3.95.

409. Conference on Archaeological Field and Laboratory Techniques,
        New York, 1950
        Essays on archaeological methods; proceedings of a conference
        held under the auspices of the Viking fund. Edited by James B.
        Griffin. Ann Arbor, University of Michigan Press, 1951. (Michi-
        gan. University. Museum of Anthropology. Anthropological
        Papers, no. 8.) $1.50.

410. Cookson, Maurice Bruce
        Photography for archaeologists. Foreword by Sir Mortimer
        Wheeler. London, Parrish, 1954, 15/-.

411. Cornwall, Ian Wolfram
        Bones for the archaeologist. London, Phoenix House, 1956,
        50/-; New York, Macmillan, 1956, $7.50.

412. Cornwall, Ian Wolfram
        Soils for the archaeologist. London, Phoenix House, 1958,
        50/-; New York, Macmillan, 1958, $7.50.

413. Crawford, Osbert Guy Stanhope
        Archaeology in the field. London, Phoenix House, 1953 (re-
        printed 1960), 45/-; New York, Praeger, 1953 (Books That Matter),
        out of print.

414. Daniel, Glyn Edmund
        The three ages; an essay on archaeological method. Cambridge,
        University Press, 1943; out of print; ca. $2.00.

415. Douglass, Andrew Ellicott
        Dating Pueblo Bonito and other ruins of the Southwest. Wash-
        ington, 1935. (National Geographic Society. Contributed Technical
        Papers. Pueblo Bonito Series. no. 1.) Out of print? ca. $2.00.

416. Douglass, Andrew Ellicott
        Tree rings and chronology. Tucson, Ariz., University of
        Arizona, 1937. (University of Arizona Bulletin, v. 8, no. 4.
        Physical Science Bulletin no. 1.) Out of print; ca. $1.00.

417. Ehrich, Robert W., ed.
Relative chronologies in Old World archaeology. Chicago,
University of Chicago Press, 1954, $2.50.

418. Flint, Richard Foster
Glacial and Pleistocene geology. New York, Wiley, 1957, $12.50.
(Based on the author's Glacial geology and the Pleistocene epoch,
1947.)

419. Goodwin, Astley John Hilary
Method in prehistory. An introduction to the discipline of prehistoric archaeology, with special reference to South African conditions. 2nd ed. Cape Town, South African Archaeological Society,
1953. (South African Archaeological Society. Handbook Series,
no. 1.) 22/6; paper, 17/6.

420. Heizer, Robert Fleming, and Sherburne F. Cook, eds.
The application of quantitative methods in archaeology. Chicago,
Quadrangle Books, 1960. (Wenner-Gren Foundation for Anthropologi-
cal Research. Viking Fund Publications in Anthropology, no. 28.)
$7.50.

421. Heizer, Robert Fleming, ed.
The archaeologist at work; a source book in archaeological
method and interpretation. New York, Harper, 1959, $8.00.

422. Heizer, Robert Fleming, ed.
A guide to archaeological field methods. 3rd rev. ed. Palo Alto,
Calif., National Press, 1958, $5.00; paper, $4.00. (First published
in 1949 under title: A manual of archaeological field methods.)

423. Johnson, Frederick, ed.
Radiocarbon dating; a report on the program to aid in the
development of the method of dating. Salt Lake City, Utah, Society
for American Archaeology, 1951. (Society for American Archaeology. Memoirs, no. 8.) $1.50.

424. Kenyon, Kathleen Mary
Beginning in archaeology. 2nd rev. ed. with sections on Ameri-
can archaeology, by Saul S. Weinberg and Gladys D. Weinberg.
London, Phoenix House, 1961, 16/-; New York, Praeger, 1961,
$4.75.
Paper: New York, Praeger, 1961 (Praeger paperbacks, PPS-
41) $2.45.

425. Libby, Willard F.
Radiocarbon dating. 2d ed. Chicago, University of Chicago
Press, 1955, $4.50.

426. Martin, Paul Sidney
Digging into history; a brief account of fifteen years of archaeological work in New Mexico. Drawings by Gustaf Dalstrom. Chicago,
1959. (Chicago. Natural History Museum. Popular Series: Anthropology, no. 38.) $1.50.

Piggott, Stuart
Approach to archaeology. See no. 402.

427. Plenderleith, Harold James
The preservation of antiquities and works of art; treatment, repair, and restoration. London, New York, Oxford University Press, 1956, $13.50.

428. Shepard, Anna Osler
Ceramics for the archaeologist. Washington, Carnegie Institution of Washington, 1956. (Carnegie Institution of Washington. Publication 609.) $2.00.

429. Society for American Archaeology.
Seminars in archaeology: 1955. Organized and edited by Robert Wauchope, chairman, Richard K. Beardsley and others. Salt Lake City, 1956. (Society for American Archaeology Memoirs, no. 11.) (American Antiquity, v. 22, no. 2, pt. 2.) $2.00.

430. Stallings, William Sidney
Dating prehistoric ruins by tree-rings. Santa Fe, N. M., Printed by Clarks Studio, 1939. (General Series, Bulletin no. 8, Laboratory of Anthropology, Santa Fe, New Mexico.) Out of print; ca. $1.00.

431. Taylor, Walter Willard
A study of archaeology. Menasha, Wis., American Anthropological Association, 1958. (American Anthropological Association. Memoirs, no. 69.) Out of print; ca. $4.00.

432. Thompson, Raymond Harris
Modern Yucatecan Maya pottery making. Salt Lake City, Utah, 1958. (Society for American Archaeology. Memoirs, no. 15.) (American Antiquity, v. 23, no. 4, pt. 2, April, 1958.) $2.50.

433. Wheeler, Sir Robert Eric Mortimer
Archaeology from the earth. Oxford, Clarendon Press, 1954, $4.50.
Paper: Harmondsworth, Middlesex, Penguin, 1956, 3/6.

434. Willey, Gordon Randolph, and Philip Phillips
Method and theory in American archaeology. Chicago, University of Chicago Press, 1958, $4.75.

435. Woolley, Sir Charles Leonard
Digging up the past. Harmondsworth, Middlesex, Penguin, 1956. (Pelican Books, A4.) $0.95.

436. Zeuner, Friedrich Eberhard
Dating the past, an introduction to geochronology; 4th ed., rev. and enl. London, Methuen, 1958, 50/-.
U. S. distributor: New York, Longmans, Green & Co., $10.00.

437. Zeuner, Friedrich Eberhard
      The Pleistocene period; its climate, chronology, and faunal suc-
      cessions. London, Hutchinson's Scientific & Technical, 1959, 42/-.

V. LANGUAGE AND WRITING

438. Bloch, Bernard, and George L. Trager
      Outline of linguistic analysis. Baltimore, Md., published by
      Linguistic Society of America at the Waverley Press, 1942; Ann
      Arbor, Edwards, 1948. (Special publications of the Linguistic
      Society of America.) $1.00.

439. Bloomfield, Leonard
      Language. New York, Holt, 1933, $6.75.

440. Brown, Roger William
      Words and things. Glencoe, Ill., Free Press, 1958, $6.75

441. Carroll, John Bissell
      The study of language; a survey of linguistics and related
      disciplines in America. Cambridge, Harvard University Press,
      1953, $4.75.

442. Chadwick, John
      The decipherment of linear B. Cambridge, University Press,
      1958, $3.75.
      Paper: New York, Modern Library, 1960. (Modern Library
      P65.) $0.95.

443. Diringer, David
      The alphabet; a key to the history of mankind. Foreword by
      Sir Ellis Minns. New York, Philosophical Library, 1948, out of
      print; London, New York, Hutchinson's Scientific & Technical, 1948,
      out of print; ca. $7.00. New, 2 v. ed. in preparation; to be pub-
      lished by Hutchinson at £7/7/-.

444. Driver, Godfrey Rolles
      Semitic writing from pictograph to alphabet. Rev. ed. London,
      published for the British Academy by Oxford University Press, 1954.
      (The Schweich Lectures of the British Academy, 1944.) $6.90.

445. Estrich, Robert M., and Hans Sperber
      Three keys to language. New York, Rinehart, 1952. $5.00.

446. Friedrich, Johannes
      Extinct languages. Translated from the original German by
      Frank Gaynor. New York, Philosophical Library, 1957. Out of
      print; ca. $5.00.

447. Gelb, Ignace J.
      A study of writing; the foundations of grammatology. Chicago,
      University of Chicago Press, 1952. Out of print; ca. $5.00.

448. Gleason, Henry Allan
      An introduction to descriptive linguistics. New York, Holt,
      1955, $6.00.

449. Greenberg, Joseph Harold
      Essays in linguistics. Chicago, University of Chicago Press,
      1957, $3.00.
      Also issued as Viking Fund Publication in Anthropology, no. 24.

450. Greenberg, Joseph Harold
      Studies in African linguistic classification. Reprinted from the
      Southwestern Journal of Anthropology for the Language and Communi-
      cation Research Center, Columbia University and the Program of
      African Studies, Northwestern University. New Haven, Compass,
      1955, $2.50.

451. Hall, Robert Anderson
      Leave your language alone! Ithaca, N. Y., Linguistica, 1950,
      $3.00.

452. Harris, Zellig Sabbettai
      Methods in structural linguistics. Chicago, University of
      Chicago Press, 1951, $10.00.

453. Haugen, Einar Ingvald
      Bilingualism in the Americas: a bibliography and research guide.
      Gainesville, Fla., American Dialect Society; obtainable from the
      University of Alabama Press, University, Ala., 1956. (American
      Dialect Society. Publication 26.) No price.

454. Heffner, Roe-Merrill Secrist
      General phonetics. With a foreword by W. W. Twaddell.
      Madison, University of Wisconsin Press, 1949, $3.75.

455. Henle, Paul, ed.
      Language, thought and culture, by Roger W. Brown and others.
      Ann Arbor, University of Michigan Press, 1958, $4.95.

456. Hill, Archibald A.
      Introduction to linguistic structures; from sound to sentence
      in English. New York, Harcourt, Brace, 1958, $10.50; text ed.,
      $7.50.

457. Hockett, Charles Francis
      A course in modern linguistics. New York, Macmillan, 1958, $7.50.

458. Hockett, Charles Francis
      A manual of phonology. Baltimore, Waverley Press, 1955.
      (Indiana. University. Publications in Anthropology and Linguistics.
      Memoir 11.) $3.50.

459. Hoenigswald, Henry M.
     Language change and linguistic reconstruction. Chicago,
     University of Chicago Press, 1960, $5.00.

460. Hoijer, Harry, ed.
     Language in culture; proceedings of a conference on the inter-
     relations of language and other aspects of culture. With papers
     by Franklin Fearing and others. Chicago, University of Chicago
     Press, 1954. (Comparative Studies of Cultures and Civilizations,
     no. 3.) $4.50.
     Also published as American Anthropological Association Memoir
     no. 79.

461. Jespersen, Otto
     Language; its nature, development, and origin. London, Allen
     & Unwin, 1922, 25/-; New York, Macmillan, 1949, $4.75.

462. Jones, Daniel
     The phoneme: its nature and use. Cambridge, Heffer, 1950,
     25/-.

463. Karlgren, Bernhard
     Sound and symbol in Chinese. London, Oxford University Press,
     H. Milford, 1923 (reprinted 1946). (The World's Manuals. Language
     and Literature Series.) Out of print; ca. $3.00.

     Language, culture, and personality; essays in memory of Edward
          Sapir. See no. 101.

464. Martinet, André, and Uriel Weinreich, eds.
     Linguistics today. New York, 1954. (Linguistic Circle of New
     York. Publication no. 2.) Out of print; ca. $5.00.

465. Meillet, Antoine, and Marcel Cohen, eds.
     Les langues du monde, par un groupe de linguistes sous la
     direction de A. Meillet et Marcel Cohen. Nouv. éd. Paris, Centre
     National de la Recherche Scientifique; H. Champion, dépositaire,
     1952, 2 v., $13.06.

466. Miller, George A.
     Language and communication. New York, McGraw-Hill, 1951,
     $6.50.

467. Nida, Eugene Albert
     Morphology, the descriptive analysis of words. 2d and completely
     new ed., based on actual-language materials. Ann Arbor, Univer-
     sity of Michigan Press, 1949. (Michigan. University. Publications.
     Linguistics, v. 2.) $3.75.

468. Ogden, Charles Kay, and Ivor A. Richards
     The meaning of meaning; a study of the influence of language
     upon thought and of the science of symbolism. With suppl. essays

by B. Malinowski and F. G. Crookshank. 8th ed. New York. Har-
court, Brace, 1956, $5.50; London, Routledge & Kegan Paul, 1956.
(International Library of Psychology, Philosophy, and Scientific
Method.) £1/8/-.
   Paper: New York, Harcourt, Brace, 1959. (Harvest Books,
HB-29.) $2.25.

469. Osgood, Cornelius, ed.
   Linguistic structures of native America by Harry Hoijer, L.
Bloomfield, M. R. Haas and others. New York, 1946. (Wenner-
Gren Foundation for Anthropological Research. Viking Fund
Publications in Anthropology, no. 6.) Out of print; ca. $4.50.

470. Pike, Kenneth Lee
   Phonemics, a technique for reducing languages to writing. Ann
Arbor, University of Michigan Press. (University of Michigan.
Publications. Linguistics, v. 3.) $3.00.

Sapir, Edward
   Culture, language, and personality; selected essays edited by
David G. Mandelbaum. See no. 64.

471. Sapir, Edward
   Language, an introduction to the study of speech. New York,
Harcourt, Brace, 1921. Out of print.
   Paper: New York, Harcourt, Brace, 1957. (Harvest Books,
HB-7.) $1.15.

Sapir, Edward
   Selected writings in language, culture, and personality. See
no. 129.

472. Saussure, Ferdinand de
   Course in general linguistics, edited by Charles Bally and
Albert Sechehaye in collaboration with Albert Reidlinger. Trans.
from the French by Wade Baskin. New York, Philosophical
Library, 1959, $6.00.

473. Sturtevant, Edgar Howard
   An introduction to linguistic science. New Haven, Yale University Press; London, G. Cumberlege, Oxford University Press,
1947, $5.00.
   Paper: New Haven, Yale University Press, 1960. (A Yale Paper-
bound, Y-17.) $1.45.

474. Voegelin, Charles Frederick, and Erminie (Wheeler) Voegelin
   Map of North America Indian languages, comp. and drawn by
C. F. and E. W. Voegelin. New York, J. J. Augustin, agent, 1944.
(American Ethnological Society. Publication, 20.) In print? ca.
$3.00. (The Society's publications are now handled by University
of Washington Press, Seattle.)

475. Weinreich, Uriel
     Languages in contact, findings and problems. With a pref. by
André Martinet. New York, Linguistic Circle of New York, 1953.
(Linguistic Circle of New York. Publication no. 1.) Out of print;
ca. $3.50.

476. Whorf, Benjamin Lee
     Language, thought, and reality; selected writings. Edited and
with an introd. by John B. Carroll. Foreword by Stuart Chase.
Cambridge, Technology Press of Massachusetts Institute of Technology, 1956, $7.00.

                                        VI. PHYSICAL ANTHROPOLOGY

     A. General (Texts, Readings, Essays)

477. Benedict, Ruth (Fulton)
     Race: science and politics. Rev. ed. New York, Viking, 1943,
$3.50.
     Paper: Including The races of mankind, by Ruth Benedict and
Gene Weltfish. New York, Viking, 1959. (Compass Books, C42.)
$1.25.

478. Boyd, William Clouser
     Genetics and the races of man; an introduction to modern
physical anthropology. 1st ed. Boston, Little, Brown, 1950, $6.75;
text ed.: Boston, Heath, 1950, $5.25.

479. Boyd, William Clouser, and Isaac Asimov
     Races and people. Illustrated by John Bradford. New York,
Abelard-Schuman, 1955, $2.75.

480. Comas, Juan
     Manual of physical anthropology. Rev. and enl. English ed.
Springfield, Ill., Thomas, 1960, $17.50.

481. Coon, Carleton Stevens, Stanley M. Garn, and Joseph B. Birdsell
     Races; a study of the problem of race formation in Man.
Springfield, Ill., Thomas, 1950. (American Lecture Series, Publication no. 77. American Lectures in Physical Anthropology.) Out
of print; ca. $5.00.

482. Count, Earl Wendel, ed.
     This is race; an anthology selected from the international
literature on the races of man. New York, Schuman, 1950. Out
of print; ca. $6.00.

483. Dobzhansky, Theodosius Grigorievich
      Evolution, genetics, and man. New York, Wiley, 1955, $5.50.

484. Dunn, Leslie Clarence, and Theodosius Dobzhansky
      Heredity, race, and society. Rev. and enl. ed. New York, New
      American Library, 1952. (A Mentor Book, M74.) $0.50.

      Fried, Morton Herbert, ed.
      Physical anthropology (v. 1 of *his* Readings in anthropology).
      See no. 52.

485. Garn, Stanley M.
      Human races. Springfield, Ill., Thomas, 1961, $5.50.

486. Garn, Stanley M.
      Readings on race. Springfield, Ill., Thomas, 1960, $6.75.

487. Hrdlička, Aleš
      Practical anthropometry. 4th ed. Edited by T. D. Stewart. Phila-
      delphia, The Wistar Institute of Anatomy and Biology, 1952, $5.00.

      Korn, Noel, and Harry Reece Smith, ed.
      Human evolution: readings in physical anthropology. See no. 522.

488. Martin, Rudolf
      Lehrbuch der Anthropologie in systematischer Darstellung, mit
      besonderer Berücksichtigung der anthropologischen Methoden. 3
      völlig. umgearb. und erweiterte Aufl. von Karl Saller. Stuttgart,
      Fischer, 1957-
      To be complete in 4 vols. Price if ordered by subscription be-
      fore publication is completed, $96.00; after publication, $108.00.

489. Montagu, Ashley
      A handbook of anthropometry. With a section on The measure-
      ment of body composition, by Josef Brozek. Springfield, Ill.,
      Thomas, 1960, $5.00.
      186 pages extracted and reprinted as a whole from the author's
      An introduction to physical anthropology (third edition).

490. Montagu, Ashley
      An introduction to physical anthropology. 3d ed. Springfield,
      Ill., Thomas, 1960, $14.50; Oxford, Blackwell Scientific Publica-
      tions, 1960, 116/-.

491. Montagu, Ashley
      Man's most dangerous myth: the fallacy of race. Foreword by
      Aldous Huxley. 3d ed., rev. and enl. New York, Harper, 1952, $5.00.

492. Mourant, Arthur Ernest, Ada C. Kopec, and Kazimiera Domanie-
      Sobczak
      The ABO blood groups; comprehensive tables and maps of world
      distribution. Oxford, Blackwell Scientific Publications, 1958, 42/-;
      Springfield, Ill., Thomas, 1958. (Royal Anthropological Institute.
      Occasional paper, no. 13.) $8.50.

493. Mourant, Arthur Ernest
     The distribution of human blood groups. With a foreword by
     H. J. Fleure. Oxford, Blackwell Scientific Publications, 1954,
     42/-; Springfield, Ill., Thomas, 1954, $8.75.

494. Spuhler, James N., ed.
     Natural selection in man; papers of the Wenner-Gren supper
     conference, held at the University of Michigan, April 12, 1957,
     during a meeting of the American Society of Human Genetics and
     the American Association of Physical Anthropologists. Detroit,
     Wayne State University Press, 1958, $1.50.
     (Originally published as Memoir no. 86 of the American Anthro-
     pological Association and as part of the February, 1958, issue of
     Human Biology [v. 30, no. 1].)

495. Symposium on the Evolution of Man's Capacity for Culture,
     Chicago, 1957.
     The evolution of man's capacity for culture; six essays by J.
     N. Spuhler and others, with a summary by Leslie A. White arranged
     by J. N. Spuhler. Detroit, Wayne State University Press, 1959,
     $3.50.
     First published in the February, 1959, issue of Human Biology.

     B. Human Evolution

496. American Anthropological Association
     The processes of ongoing human evolution, ed. by Gabriel W.
     Lasker. Detroit, Wayne State University Press, 1960, $3.75.
     Six lectures presented at the 58th annual meeting of the Ameri-
     can Anthropological Association, Mexico City, Dec. 28, 1959.

497. Barnett, Samuel Anthony, ed.
     A century of Darwin. Cambridge, Mass., Harvard University
     Press, 1958, $5.75.

498. Boule, Marcellin, and Henri V. Vallois
     Fossil men: a textbook of human palaeontology . . . with a new
     introduction by Kenneth P. Oakley. London, Thames and Hudson,
     1957, 84/-; New York, Dryden Press, 1957, $9.50.
     Translated by Michael Bullock.
     U. S. edition lacks subtitle.

499. Broom, Robert, Gerritt Willem Hendrik Schepers
     The South African fossil ape-man, the Australopithecinae . . .
     with a pref. by J. C. Smuts. Pretoria, 1946. (Transvaal Museum,
     Pretoria. Memoir no. 2). £1/7/6.

500. Broom, Robert, J. T. Robinson, and Gerritt Willem Hendrik Schepers
     Sterkfontein ape-man Plesianthropus. Pretoria, Transvaal
     Museum, 1949. (Transvaal Museum, Pretoria. Memoir no. 4). 17/6.

Contents: Further evidence of the structure of the Sterkfontein ape-man Plesianthropus, by R. Broom and J. T. Robinson. The brain casts of the recently discovered Plesianthropus skulls, by G. W. H. Schepers.

501. Broom, Robert, and J. T. Robinson
      Swartkrans ape-man, *Paranthropus crassidens.* Pretoria, Transvaal Museum, 1952. (Transvaal Museum, Pretoria. Memoir no. 6.) £1/12/6.

502. Carpenter, Clarence Ray
      A field study in Siam of the behavior and social relations of the gibbon (Hylobates lar). With an introduction by Professor A. H. Schultz. Baltimore, Md., The Johns Hopkins Press, 1941. (Comparative Psychology Monographs; v. 16, serial no. 84, December, 1940.) Out of print; ca. $2.00.
      Present publisher: University of California Press.

503. Carpenter, Clarence Ray
      A field study of the behavior and social relations of howling monkeys. Baltimore, Md., The Johns Hopkins Press, 1934. (Comparative Psychology Monographs, v. 10, serial no. 48, May, 1934.) $2.25.
      Present publisher: University of California Press.

504. Clark, Sir Wilfrid Edward Le Gros
      The antecedents of man; an introduction to the evolution of the primates. Edinburgh, University Press, 1959. (Edinburgh University Publications. Science and Mathematics Texts, 2.) 21/-; Chicago, Quadrangle Books, 1960, $6.00.

505. Clark, Sir Wilfrid Edward Le Gros
      The fossil evidence for human evolution; an introduction to the study of paleoanthropology. Chicago, University of Chicago Press, 1955, $6.00.

506. Clark, Sir Wilfrid Edward Le Gros
      The foundations of human evolution. Line drawings by Christine Court. Eugene, Oregon State System of Higher Education, 1959. (Condon Lectures, 1959.) $1.00.

507. Clark, Sir Wilfrid Edward Le Gros
      History of the primates, an introduction to the study of fossil man. 7th ed. London, Printed by order of the Trustees of the British Museum, 1960, 15/-; 2d Phoenix Books ed. Chicago, University of Chicago Press, 1959. (Phoenix Books, P21.) $1.25.

508. Cold Spring Harbor, N. Y. Biological Laboratory.
      Origin and evolution of man. Cold Spring Harbor, 1950. (*Its* Symposia on quantitative biology, v. 15.) $12 to libraries; $8 to individuals.

509. Dart, Raymond Arthur
      The osteodontokeratic culture of Australopithecus prometheus.
      Parow, Cape Times, 1957. (Transvaal Museum, Pretoria. Memoir
      no. 10.) £1/1/-.

510. Darwin, Charles Robert
      The origin of species by means of natural selection; or, The
      preservation of favored races in the struggle for life. New York,
      Modern Library, 1936. (Includes *his* The descent of man and
      selection in relation to sex.) (A Modern Library Giant, G27.)
      $2.95.
      ____ A variorum text, edited by Morse Peckham. Philadelphia,
      University of Pennsylvania Press, 1959, $15.00.
      ____ Introduction by Sir Arthur Keith. London, Dent; New York,
      Dutton, 1934. (Everyman's Library, no. 811.) $1.95.
      ____ A reprint of the 6th ed. with a pref. by G. R. de Beer.
      London, New York, Oxford University Press, 1951. (The World's
      Classics, 11.) $1.85.
      Paper: Introd. by Sir Julian Huxley. New York, New American
      Library, 1958. (A Mentor Book, MD 222.) $0.75. Garden City,
      N. Y., Doubleday, 1960. (Dolphin Book, C172.) $0.95.

      Dobzhansky, Theodosius Grigorievich
      Evolution, genetics, and man. See no. 483.

511. Dunn, Leslie Clarence
      Heredity and evolution in human population. Cambridge, Mass.,
      Harvard University Press, 1959 (Harvard Books in Biology, no. 1),
      $3.50.

512. Early man in the Far East. A Symposium of the American
      Association of Physical Anthropologists and the American
      Anthropological Association, December 28, 1946. Edited by
      W. W. Howells. Detroit, American Association of Physical
      Anthropologists, 1949. (Studies in Physical Anthropology, no. 1.)
      Out of print? ca. $2.00.

513. Eiseley, Loren C.
      Darwin's century; evolution and the men who discovered it.
      1st ed. Garden City, N. Y., Doubleday, 1958. (Doubleday Anchor
      Books.) $5.00; London, Gollancz, 1959, 21/-.
      Paper: New York, Doubleday, 1961. (A Doubleday Anchor
      Book.) $1.45.

514. Eiseley, Loren C.
      The firmament of time. 1st ed. New York, Atheneum, 1960,
      $3.50.

515. Eiseley, Loren C.
      The immense journey. New York, Random House, 1957, $3.50.
      Paper: New York, Modern Library, 1959. (Modern Library of
      the World's Best Books, P47.) $0.95.

516. Hooton, Earnest Albert
    Man's poor relations. Garden City, N. Y., Doubleday, Doran,
    1942. Out of print; ca. $4.00.

517. Hooton, Earnest Albert
    Up from the ape. Rev. ed. New York, Macmillan, 1946,
    $8.00.

518. Howells, William White
    Mankind in the making; the story of human evolution. Draw-
    ings by Janis Cirulis. Garden City, N. Y., Doubleday, 1959, $4.95.

519. Huxley, Thomas Henry
    Man's place in nature. Introd. by Ashley Montagu. Ann Arbor,
    University of Michigan Press, 1959, $4.40.
        Paper: Ann Arbor, University of Michigan Press, 1959. (Ann
    Arbor Paperbacks, AA24.) $1.75.
        (First published in 1863 under title: Evidence as to man's
    place in nature.)

520. Joint Expedition of the British school of archaeology in Jerusalem
        and the American school of prehistoric research, 1929-1937.
        The stone age of Mount Carmel. Oxford, Clarendon Press,
    1937-1939. 2 v.
        v. 1, Excavations at the Wady el-Mughara, by D. A. E. Garrod
    and D. M. A. Bate; v. 2, The fossil human remains from the
    Levalloiso-Mousterian by T. D. McCown and Sir Arthur Keith.
    Out of print; ca. $40.00.

521. Koenigswald, Gustav Heinrich Ralph von
    Meeting prehistoric man. Translated from the German by
    Michael Bullock. London, New York, Thames & Hudson, 1956,
    21/-; New York, Harper, 1956, $3.50.

522. Korn, Noel, and Harry Reece Smith, eds.
    Human evolution; readings in physical anthropology. New York,
    Holt, 1959, $7.50; text ed., $5.50.

523. Lasker, Gabriel W.
    The evolution of man; a brief introduction to physical anthro-
    pology. New York, Holt, Rinehart and Winston, 1961, $3.50.

524. Leakey, Louis Seymour Bazett
    Adam's ancestors; an up-to-date outline of the old stone age
    (Palaeolithic) and what is known about man's origin and evolution.
    4th ed., completely rewritten. London, Methuen, 1953, 21/-.
        Paper: New York, Harper, 1960. (Harper Torchbooks, Tb1019.)
    $1.60.

525. Mellersh, H. E.
    The story of man; human evolution to the end of the stone age.
    London, Hutchinson, 1959, 21/-; New York, Viking, 1960, $4.50.
        U. S. edition has title: Story of early man.

526. Moody, Paul Amos
    Introduction to evolution. 1st ed. New York, Harper, 1953,
    $6.00.

527. The Non-human primates and human evolution. Arr. by James
    A. Gavan. In memory of Earnest Albert Hooton, 1887-1954.
    Detroit, Wayne University Press, 1955, $3.50.
    First published in the Sept., 1954, issue of Human Biology.

528. Oparin, Aleksandr Ivanovich
    The origin of life. Translated from the Russian by Ann
    Synge. 3d. rev. and enl. ed. New York, Academic Press, 1957,
    $7.50; Edinburgh, Oliver & Boyd, 1957, 35/-.
    Edinburgh edition has title: The origin of life on the earth.

529. Piveteau, Jean
    Vers la forme humaine; le problème biologique de l'homme;
    les époques de l'intelligence. Primates; paléontologie humaine.
    Paris, Masson, 1957. (*His* Traité de Paléontologie, v. 7.) 13,500
    fr., paper; 14,500 fr., boards.

530. Robinson, John Talbot
    The dentition of the Australopithecinae. Pretoria, Transvaal
    Museum, 1956. (Transvaal museum memoir no. 9) £2.

531. Roe, Anne, And George Gaylord Simpson, eds.
    Behavior and evolution. New Haven, Yale University Press,
    1958, $10.00.

532. Romer, Alfred Sherwood
    Vertebrate paleontology. 2d ed. Chicago, University of Chicago
    Press, 1945, $8.50.

533. Romer, Alfred Sherwood
    The vertebrate story. 4th ed. Chicago, University of Chicago
    Press, 1959, $7.00.
    A revised and enlarged edition of Man and the vertebrates.

534. Simpson, George Gaylord
    The major features of evolution. New York, Columbia Univer-
    sity Press, 1953. (Columbia Biological Series, no. 17.) $7.50.

535. Simpson, George Gaylord
    The meaning of evolution, a study of the history of life and of
    its significance for man. New Haven, Yale University Press, 1949.
    (The Terry Lectures.) $5.00.
    Paper: New Haven, Yale University Press, 1960, $1.45.

536. Stirton, Ruben Arthur
    Time, life, and man; the fossil record. New York, Wiley, 1959.
    $9.00; text ed., $7.50.

537. Tax, Sol, ed.
         Evolution after Darwin. Chicago, University of Chicago Press,
      1960, 3 v.
         Contents. v. 1, Evolution of life: its origin, history and future,
      $10.00; v. 2, Evolution of man: mind, culture, and society, $10.00.
      v. 3, Issues in evolution: the University of Chicago Centennial
      discussions, ed. by Sol Tax and Charles Callender, $7.50. Set,
      $25.00.

538. Weidenreich, Franz
         Apes, giants, and man. Chicago, University of Chicago Press,
      1946, $3.50.

539. Weidenreich, Franz
         Giant early man from Java and south China. New York, 1945.
      (Anthropological Papers of the American Museum of Natural
      History. v. 40, pt. 1.) In print? ca. $2.00.

540. Weidenreich, Franz
         Morphology of Solo Man. Introd. by G. H. R. von Koenigswald.
      New York, 1951. (Anthropological Papers of the American Museum
      of Natural History. v. 43, pt. 3.) In print? ca. $2.50.

541. Weidenreich, Franz
         The shorter anthropological papers . . . published in the period
      1939-1948; a memorial volume. Compiled by S. L. Washburn and
      David Wolffson. New York, The Viking Fund, 1949. Out of print?
      ca. $3.00.

542. Weidenreich, Franz
         Skull of Sinanthropus pekinensis; a comparative study on a
      primitive hominid skull. Pehpei, Chungking, Geological Survey
      of China, 1943.
         U. S. distributor: Hafner, New York, $5.00.

543. Weiner, Joseph Sidney
         The Piltdown forgery. London, New York, Oxford University
      Press, 1955, $2.00.

      C. Human Genetics

      Boyd, William Clouser
         Genetics and the races of man; an introduction to modern
      physical anthropology. See no. 478.

544. Cold Spring Harbor, N. Y. Biological Laboratory.
         Population genetics: the nature and causes of genetic varia-
      bility in populations. Cold Spring Harbor, N. Y., The Biological
      Laboratory, 1955. (Cold Spring Harbor Symposia on Quantitative
      Biology, v. 20.) $12 to libraries; $8 to individuals.

545. Corner, George Washington
   Ourselves unborn; an embryologist's essay on man. New Haven, Yale University Press, 1944. (The Terry Lectures.) Out of print; ca. $5.00.

546. Dobzhansky, Theodosius Grigorievich
   Genetics and the origin of species. 3d ed., rev. New York, Columbia University Press, 1951. (Columbia Biological Series, 11.) $6.00.

547. Gates, Reginald Ruggles
   Human genetics. New York, Macmillan, 1946, 2 v., $28.00.

548. Haldane, John Burdon Sanderson
   New paths in genetics. New York and London, Harper, 1942. Out of print; ca. $4.00.

549. Herskovits, Melville Jean
   The anthropometry of the American Negro. New York, Columbia University Press, 1930. (Columbia University Contributions to Anthropology, v. 11.) Out of print; ca. $5.00.

550. Neel, James Van Gundia, and William J. Schull
   Human heredity. Chicago, University of Chicago Press, 1954 (The College Library of Biological Sciences). $8.50.

551. Race, Robert Russell, and Ruth Sanger
   Blood groups in man. With a foreword by Sir Ronald Fisher. 3rd ed. Springfield, Ill., Thomas, 1958, $8.50; Oxford, Blackwell Scientific Publications, 1958, 42/-.

552. Stern Curt
   Principles of human genetics. 2d ed. San Francisco, Freeman, 1960, $9.00.

553. Wallace, Bruce, and Theodosius Dobzhansky
   Radiation, genes, and man. New York, Holt, 1959, $4.75; text ed., $3.50.

D. Somatology

554. Essays on growth and form presented to D'Arcy Wentworth Thompson. Edited by W. E. LeGros Clark and P. B. Medawar. Oxford, Clarendon Press, 1945. Out of print; ca. $6.00.

555. Garn, Stanley M., and Zvi Shamir
   Methods for research in human growth. Springfield, Ill., Thomas, 1958, $4.75.

556. Krogman, Wilton Marion
    A bibliography of human morphology, 1914-1939. Chicago, Ill., University of Chicago Press, 1941. (The University of Chicago Publications in Anthropology. Physical Anthropology Series.) Out of print; ca. $5.00.

557. McKern, Thomas W., and T. D. Stewart
    Skeletal age changes in young American males; analysed from the standpoint of age identification. Natick, Mass., 1957. (U. S. Army. Quartermaster Corps. Environmental Protection Research Division. Technical report, EP-45.) No price.

558. Parpart, Arthur Kemble, ed.
    The chemistry and physiology of growth, by J. H. Northrop and others. Princeton, Princeton University Press, 1949. Out of print; ca. $5.00.

559. Reynolds, Earle L.
    Distribution of subcutaneous fat in childhood and adolescence. Evanston, Ill., Child Development Publications, 1951. (Fels Monograph Series, no. 1.) (Monographs of the Society for Research in Child Development, v. 15, serial no. 50, no. 2, 1950.) No price; estimate: $4.00.

560. Sanders, Barkev Sahak
    Environment and growth. Baltimore, Warwick & York, 1934. Out of print; ca. $4.00.

561. Sobotta, Johannes
    Atlas of descriptive human anatomy. Edited and translated by Eduard Uhlenhuth. 7th English ed. New York, Hafner, 1957, 3 v., $40.00.

VII. APPLIED ANTHROPOLOGY

Adams, Richard N., and Jack J. Preiss, eds.
Human organization research. See no. 46.

562. Anthropological Society of Washington, Washington, D. C.
    Some uses of anthropology: theoretical and applied. Joseph B. Casagrande, Thomas Gladwin, editors. Washington, 1956, $1.50.

563. Balandier, Georges
    L'anthropologie appliqué aux problèmes des pays sous-développés. Paris, Cours de droit, 1955. Estimate: $3.00.

564. Barnett, Homer Garner
        Anthropology in administration. Evanston, Ill., Row Peterson,
        1956. Out of print; ca.$5.00.

565. Brown, G. Gordon, and Alexander McDonald Bruce
        Anthropology in action; an experiment in the Iringa district of
        the Iringa province, Tanganyika territory . . . with an intro. by
        P. E. Mitchell. London, published for the International Institute
        of African Languages and Cultures by the Oxford University Press,
        H. Milford, 1935. Out of print; ca. $6.00.

566. Clark, Margaret
        Health in the Mexican-American culture; a community study. Ber-
        keley and Los Angeles, University of California Press, 1959, $6.50.

567. Foster, George McClelland
        Problems in intercultural health programs; memorandum to the
        Committee on Preventive Medicine and Social Science Research.
        New York, 1958. (Social Science Research Council. Pamphlet no.
        12.) $0.50.

568. Galdston, Iago, ed.
        Medicine and anthropology. New York, International Universities
        Press, 1959. (New York Academy of Medicine. Lectures to the
        laity, no. 21.) $3.00.

      Gearing, F. O., R. M. Netting, and L. R. Peattie, eds.
      Documentary history of the Fox project, 1948-1959. See no. 363.

569. Hailey, William Malcolm Hailey, baron
        Native administration in British African territories. London,
        H. M. Stationery Off., 1950-1953. 5 v. Contents: Pt. 1. East
        Africa: Uganda, Kenya, Tanganyika. Pt. 2. Central Africa: Zanzi-
        bar, Nyasaland, Northern Rhodesia. Pt. 3. West Africa: Nigeria,
        Gold Coast, Sierra Leone, Gambia. Pt. 4. A general survey of
        the system of native administration. Pt. 5. The High Commission
        territories: Basutoland, the Bechuanaland Protectorate and Swazi-
        land. I, 18/5; II, 10/10; III, 18/5; IV, 5/3; V, 23/2.

570. Leighton, Alexander Hamilton
        The governing of men; general principles and recommendations
        based on experience at a Japanese relocation camp. Princeton,
        N. J., Princeton University Press, 1945. Out of print; ca. $5.00.

571. Leighton, Alexander Hamilton
        Human relations in a changing world; observations on the use
        of the social sciences. 1st ed. New York, Dutton, 1949. Out of
        print; ca. $5.00.

572. Loomis, Charles Price
        Studies in applied and theoretical social science at Michigan
        State College. East Lansing, Michigan State College Press, 1950,
        $5.00.

Macgregor, Gordon
Warriors without weapons. See no. 345.

573. Mair, Lucy Philips
Studies in applied anthropology. London, University of London,
Athlone Press, 1957. (London School of Economics. Monographs
on Social Anthropology, no. 16.) 13/6.

574. Mandelbaum, David Goodman
Soldier groups and Negro soldiers. Berkeley, University of
California Press, 1952, $2.75.

575. Mayer, Philip
Two studies in applied anthropology in Kenya. With an introd.
by Arthur Phillips. London, Published by H. M. Stationery Off.
for the Colonial Office, 1951. (Gt. Brit. Colonial Office. Colonial
Research Studies, no. 3.) 2/8.

576. Paul, Benjamin David, ed.
Health, culture, and community; case studies of public reactions to health programs. New York, Russell Sage Foundation,
1955, $5.00.

577. Salz, Beate R.
The human element in industrialization; a hypothetical case
study of Ecuadorean Indians. Menasha, Wis., American Anthropological Association, 1955. (American Anthropological Association. Memoir no. 85.) $3.75.

578. Saunders, Lyle
Cultural difference and medical care; the case of the Spanish-
speaking people of the Southwest. New York, Russell Sage Foundation, 1954, $4.50.

579. Smithsonian Institution. Institute of Social Anthropology.
A cross-cultural anthropological analysis of a technical aid
program, based on field analyses by Charles Erasmus (and
others) of the Smithsonian Institution's Institute of Social Anthropology, with the coöperation of the Health and Sanitation Division of the Institute of Inter-American Affairs, and the Ministry of Health Servicios of Brazil, Colombia, Mexico, and Peru.
Edited by George Foster, director of the Institute of Social Anthropology. Washington, Smithsonian Institution, 1951. Out of print?
Estimate: $3.00.

Spicer, Edward Holland, ed.
Human problems in technological change. See no. 372.

580. Spindler, George D., ed.
Education and anthropology. Pref. by Lawrence K. Frank. Stanford, Calif., Stanford University Press, 1955, $5.50.

VIII. PUBLICATIONS DEALING WITH PEOPLES OF SPECIFIC AREAS, INCLUDING ARCHAEOLOGY, CULTURE HISTORY, AND CONTEMPORARY ETHNOLOGY

A. Europe

1. Archaeology

a. General

581. Childe, Vere Gordon
Dawn of European civilization. 6th ed., rev. London, Routledge & Kegan Paul, 1958, £2/2/-; New York, Knopf, 1958, $7.50.

582. Childe, Vere Gordon
Prehistoric migrations in Europe. Oslo, Aschehoug; Cambridge, Mass., Harvard University Press, 1950. (Instituttet for Sammenlignende Kulturforskning. Series A: Forelesninger, 20.) Harvard edition out of print.
Scandinavian distributor: Copenhagen, Munksgaard, Kr. 31.50.

583. Childe, Vere Gordon
The prehistory of European society. How and why the prehistoric barbarian societies of Europe behaved in a distinctively European way. Harmondsworth, Middlesex, Penguin, 1958. (Pelican books, A415.) $0.95.

584. Clark, John Grahame Douglas
Prehistoric Europe; the economic basis. London, Methuen, 1952, 60/-.

585. Fleure, Herbert John
The peoples of Europe. London, Oxford University Press, H. Milford, 1922. Out of print; ca. $3.00.

586. Hawkes, Charles Francis Christopher
The prehistoric foundations of Europe to the Mycenean age. London, Methuen, 1940. Out of print; ca. $5.00.

b. West and British Isles

587. Atkinson, Richard John Copland
Stonehenge. London, Hamilton, 1956, 16/-.

588. Childe, Vere Gordon
    Prehistoric communities of the British Isles. 2d ed. London,
    Chambers, 1947. Out of print?; ca. $6.00.

589. Clark, John Grahame Douglas
    Excavations at Star Carr; an early Mesolithic site at Seamer
    near Scarborough, Yorkshire. With chapters by D. Walker and
    others and with an appendix by John W. Moore. Cambridge, Uni-
    versity Press, 1954, $11.50.

590. Clark, John Grahame Douglas
    The Mesolithic age in Britain. Cambridge, University Press,
    1932. Out of print; ca. $6.00.

591. Daniel, Glyn Edmund
    The Megalith builders of western Europe. London, Hutchinson,
    1958, 18/-; New York, Praeger, 1959, $3.50.

592. Fox, Sir Cyril Fred
    The personality of Britain, its influence on inhabitant and
    invader in prehistoric and early historic times. With numerous
    distribution maps including a series specially prepared by Lily
    F. Chitty. 4th ed. Cardiff, National Museum of Wales, 1947,
    7/6.

593. Hawkes, Jacquetta (Hopkins), and Christopher Hawkes
    Prehistoric Britain. Rev. ed. Harmondsworth, Middlesex,
    Penguin, 1958 (Pelican Books, A115.) $0.95.

594. Lacaille, Armand Donald
    The stone age in Scotland. London, New York, Oxford Univer-
    sity Press, 1954. (Publications of the Wellcome Historical Medi-
    cal Museum, new ser., no. 6.) $8.80.

    Laming, Annette
    Lascaux: paintings and engravings. See no. 308.

595. Movius, Hallam Leonard
    The Irish stone age, its chronology, development and relation-
    ships. Cambridge, University Press, 1942. Out of print; ca.
    $9.00.

596. Piggott, Stuart
    British prehistory. London, New York, Oxford University
    Press, 1949. (The Home University Library of Modern Knowl-
    edge, 205.) $1.40.

597. Piggott, Stuart
    The neolithic cultures of the British Isles; a study of the
    stone-using agricultural communities of Britain in the second
    millennium B. C. Cambridge, University Press, 1954, $15.00.

598. Piggott, Stuart
         Scotland before history, an essay. With illustrations by Keith
      Henderson. London, New York, Nelson, 1958, 15/-.

      c. North

599. Bronsted, Johannes
         The Vikings. Translated by Estrid Bannister-Good. Baltimore,
      Penguin, 1960. (Pelican Books, A459.) $1.25.

600. Burnham, Robert Edward
         Who are the Finns? A study in prehistory. London, Faber &
      Faber, 1946. Out of print; ca. $3.00.

601. Clark, John Grahame Douglas
         The Mesolithic settlement of northern Europe; a study of the
      food-gathering peoples of northern Europe during the early post-
      glacial period. Cambridge, University Press, 1936. Out of print;
      ca. $7.50.

602. Gjessing, Gutorm
         Circumpolar Stone Age. Kobenhavn, E. Munksgaard, 1944 (Acta
      arctica, fasc. 2). 12 Danish Kr.

603. Klindt-Jensen, Ole
         Denmark before the Vikings. London, Thames and Hudson,
      1957, 25/-; New York, Praeger, 1957, $6.50. (Ancient Peoples
      and Places, v. 4.)

604. Lauring, Palle
         Land of the Tollund man; the prehistory and archaeology of
      Denmark. Translated by Reginald Spink; photos. by Lennart
      Larsen. 1st English ed. London, Lutterworth Press, 1957, 30/-;
      New York, Macmillan, 1958, $6.00.

605. Shetelig, Haakon, and Hjalmar Falk
         Scandinavian archaeology. Translated by E. V. Gordon.
      Oxford, Clarendon Press, 1937, $6.75.

606. Sjøvold, Thorleif
         The Oseberg find and the other Viking ship finds. Translated
      by Mary Fjeld. Oslo, Universitetes Oldsaksamling, 1957. Esti-
      mate: $2.00.

      d. Central

607. Childe, Vere Gordon
         The Danube in prehistory. Oxford, Clarendon Press, 1929.
      Out of print; ca. $12.00.

608. Grahmann, Rudolph
      The lower palaeolithic site of Markkleeberg and other com-
      parable localities near Leipzig. Edited by Hallam L. Movius,
      Jr., Philadelphia, American Philosophical Society, 1955. (Ameri-
      can Philosophical Society. Transactions, new ser., v. 45, pt. 6.)
      $2.00.

      e. South

      Bandi, Hans Georg, and Johannes Maringer
      Art in the ice age, Spanish Levant art. See no. 247.

609. Bloch, Raymond
      The Etruscans. Translated by Stuart Hood. London, Thames
      and Hudson, 1958, 25/-; New York, Praeger, 1958. (Ancient
      Peoples and Places. v. 7.) $6.50.

610. Hall, Harry Reginald Holland
      The civilization of Greece in the bronze age. London,
      Methuen, 1928. Out of print; ca. $5.00.

611. MacKendrick, Paul Lachlan
      The mute stones speak; the story of archaeology in Italy.
      New York, St. Martin's Press, 1960, $7.50.

612. Obermaier, Hugo
      Fossil man in Spain . . . with an introduction by Henry Fair-
      field Osborn. New Haven, published for the Hispanic society of
      America by the Yale University Press, 1924. Out of print; ca.
      $10.00.

613. Randall-MacIver, David
      Italy before the Romans. Oxford, Clarendon Press, 1928,
      $1.60.

614. Whatmough, Joshua
      The foundations of Roman Italy. London, Methuen, 1937, 30/-.
      U. S. distributor: New York, Humanities Press, $6.00.

      f. East

615. Gimbutas, Marija (Alseikaite)
      The prehistory of Eastern Europe. Edited by Hugh Hencken.
      Cambridge, Mass., Peabody Museum, 1956- . (American School
      of Prehistoric Research. Bulletin no. 20- .) No. 20, $7.50.
      Contents: Pt. 1, Mesolithic, neolithic and copper age cultures in
      Russia and the Baltic area.

616. Golomshtok, Eugene Alexandrovich
        The old stone age in European Russia. Philadelphia, American
      Philosophical Society, 1938. (American Philosophical Society.
      Transactions, new ser., v. 29, pt. 2.) Out of print; ca. $4.00.

617. Mongait, Aleksandr L'vovich
        Archaeology in the U.S.S.R. Translated from the Russian by
      David Skvirsky. Moscow, Foreign Languages Pub. House, 1959.
      U. S. distributor: New York, Heinman, $10.00.

618. Vernadsky, George
        The origins of Russia. Oxford, Clarendon Press, 1959, $5.60.

      2. Contemporary

      a. General

619. Coon, Carleton Stevens
        The races of Europe. New York, Macmillan, 1939, $15.00.

      b. West and British Isles

620. Arensberg, Conrad Maynadier
        The Irish countryman; an anthropological study. Gloucester,
      Mass., Smith, 1959 (c1937), $3.00.

621. Arensberg, Conrad Maynadier, and Solon T. Kimball
        Family and community in Ireland. Gloucester, Mass., P. Smith,
      1959, $5.00. First published Cambridge, Mass., Harvard Univer-
      sity Press, 1940.

622. Dennis, Norman, Fernando Henriques, and Clifford Slaughter
        Coal is our life; an analysis of a Yorkshire mining community.
      London, Eyre & Spottiswoode, 1956, 25/-.

623. Firth, Raymond William, ed.
        Two studies of kinship in London. London, University of Lon-
      don, Athlone Press, 1956. (London School of Economics. Mono-
      graphs on Social Anthropology, no. 15.) 13/6.
      U. S. distributor: New York, Humanities Press, 1957, $2.75.

624. Frankenberg, Ronald
        Village on the border; a social study of religion, politics and
      football in a North Wales community. With an introd. by Max
      Gluckman. London, Cohen & West, 1957, 18/-.
      U. S. distributor: New York, Humanities Press, $3.75.

625. Gadourek, Ivan
      A Dutch community; social and cultural structure and process
      in a bulb-growing region in the Netherlands. Leiden, H. E. Sten-
      fert Kroese, 1956. (Publications of the Netherlands' Institute of
      Preventive Medicine, 30.) 28.50 fl.

626. Gorer, Geoffrey
      Exploring English character. New York, Criterion, 1955,
      standard ed. $5.00; complete ed. $8.50; London, Cresset Press,
      1955, standard ed. 30/-; complete ed. 63/-.

627. Hammond, John Lawrence Le Breton, and Barbara Hammond
      The village labourer, 1760-1832; a study in the government of
      England before the Reform bill. New ed. London, New York,
      Longmans, Green, 1920. Out of print; ca. $5.00.

628. Keur, John Yak and Dorothy L. Keur
      The deeply rooted; a study of a Drents community in the
      Netherlands. Assen, Printed at the Royal Van Gorcum, 1955.
      (Monographs of the American Ethnological Society, 25.)
      U. S. distributor: Seattle, University of Washington Press,
      $3.00.

629. Little, Kenneth Lindsay
      Negroes in Britain; a study of racial relations in English
      society. London, Kegan Paul, Trench, Trubner, 1948 (Interna-
      tional Library of Sociology and Social Reconstruction). £1/5/-.
      U. S. distributor: Humanities Press, New York, $5.00.

630. Metraux, Rhoda Bubendey, and Margaret Mead
      Themes in French culture; a preface to a study of French
      community. Stanford, Stanford University Press, 1954. (Hoover
      Institute Studies. Series D: Communities, no. 1.) $1.50.

631. Mogey, John M.
      Family and neighborhood: two studies in Oxford. London,
      Oxford University Press, 1956, $4.80.

632. Rees, Alwyn D.
      Life in a Welsh countryside, a social study of Llanfihangel
      yng Ngwynfa. Cardiff, University of Wales Press, 1950, 12/6.

633. Turney-High, Harry Holbert
      Château-Gérard; the life and times of a Walloon Village.
      Columbia, University of South Carolina Press, 1953. Out of
      print; ca. $5.00.

634. Venables, Ursula
      Life in Shetland, a world apart. Edinburgh, Oliver & Boyd,
      1956, 15/-.

635.   Williams, William Morgan
       Gosforth: the sociology of an English village. Glencoe, Ill.,
       Free Press, 1956, $5.00. London ed. (Routledge & Kegan Paul)
       has title: The sociology of an English village: Gosforth. £1/5/-.

636.   Wylie, Laurence William
       Village in the Vaucluse. Cambridge, Mass., Harvard Univer-
       sity Press, 1957, $5.50.

637.   Young, Michael Dunlop, and Peter Willmott
       Family and kinship in east London. Foreword by Richard M.
       Titmuss. London, Routledge & Kegan Paul, 1957. (Institute of
       Community Studies. Reports, no. 1.)   £1/5/-; Glencoe, Ill.,
       Free Press, 1957, $5.00.

       c. North

638.   Bosi, Roberto
       The Lapps. Translated by James Cadell. London, Thames &
       Hudson, 1960, 30/-; New York, Praeger, 1960, $6.50. (Ancient
       Peoples and Places, v. 17.)

639.   Collinder, Björn
       The Lapps. Princeton, Princeton University Press for the
       American Scandinavian Foundation. New York, 1949, $3.75.

640.   Gjessing, Gutorm
       Changing Lapps; a study in culture relations in northernmost
       Norway. London, published for Dept. of Anthropology, London
       School of Economics and Political Science, 1954. (Monographs
       on Social Anthropology, no. 13.) 12/-.
       U. S. distributor: New York, Humanities Press, $2.50.

641.   Pehrson, Robert Niel
       The bilateral network of social relations in Könkämä Lapp
       district. Bloomington, Ind., 1957. (Indiana. University. Publi-
       cations: Slavic and East European series, v. 5.) Indiana. Uni-
       versity. Research center in Anthropology, Folklore, and Lin-
       guistics. Publication, 3/ International Journal of American
       Linguistics, v. 23, no. 1, pt. 2.) $2.50.

642.   Rodnick, David
       The Norwegians, a study in national culture. Washington,
       Public Affairs Press, 1955, $3.25.

643.   Turi, Johan Olafsson
       Turi's book of Lappland; edited and translated into Danish by
       Emilie Demant Hatt, translated from the Danish by E. Gee Nash.
       New York and London, Harper, 1931. Out of print; ca. $4.00.

644. Whitaker, Ian
   Social relations in a nomadic Lappish community. Oslo, Norsk folkemuseum, 1955. (Samiske samlinger, bd. 2.) In print? Estimate: $3.00.

   d. Central

645. Lowie, Robert Harry
   The German people, a social portrait to 1914. New York, Toronto, Farrar & Rinehart, 1945, $2.00.

646. Lowie, Robert Harry
   Toward understanding Germany. Chicago, University of Chicago Press, 1954, $6.00.

647. Rodnick, David
   Postwar Germans, an anthropologist's account. New Haven, Yale University Press, 1948. Out of print; ca. $4.00.

   e. South

648. Banfield, Edward C.
   The moral basis of a backward society . . . with the assistance of Laura Fasano Banfield. Photos. by the author. Glencoe, Ill., Free Press; Chicago, Research Center in Economic Development and Cultural Change, University of Chicago, 1958, $4.00.

   Foster, George McClelland
   Culture and conquest: America's Spanish heritage. See no. 362.

649. Gallop, Rodney
   A Book of the Basques. London, Macmillan, 1930. Out of print; ca. $6.00.

650. Halpern, Joel Martin
   A Serbian village. Illustrated by Barbara Kerewsky Halpern. New York, Columbia University Press, 1958, $6.00. (A condensed version of the author's doctoral dissertation published in 1956 under title: Social and cultural change in a Serbian village.)

651. Megas, Georgios A.
   Greek calendar customs. Athens, Press and Information Dept., Prime Minister's Office, 1958. Distributed by Ministry of Information, Greek Govt. Estimate: $2.00.

652. Pitt-Rivers, Julian Alfred
      The people of the Sierra. Introd. by E. E. Evans-Pritchard.
      London, Weidenfeld and Nicolson, 1954, 18/-; New York, Criterion,
      1954, out of print.

653. Rayner, Louisa
      Women in a village; an Englishwoman's experiences and im-
      pressions of life in Yugoslavia under German occupation. Lon-
      don, Heineman, 1957, 21/-.

654. West, Rebecca, pseud.
      Black lamb and grey falcon; a journey through Yugoslavia.
      New York, Viking, 1943, $6.95. First published in 1941.

      f. East

655. Barnett, Clifford R.
      Poland, its people, its society, its culture . . . in collabora-
      tion with Robert J. Feldman and others. New Haven, HRAF
      Press, 1958. (Survey of World Cultures.) $7.50.
      Paper: New York, Grove, 1958. (Evergreen E129.) $2.45.

656. Benet, Sula
      Song, dance, and customs of peasant Poland. With a preface
      by Margaret Mead. New York, Roy, 1951, $3.50.

657. Durham, Mary Edith
      Some tribal origins, laws and customs of the Balkans. London,
      Allen & Unwin, 1928. Out of print, ca. $3.00.

658. Field, Henry, comp.
      Contributions to the anthropology of the Soviet Union. Wash-
      ington, Smithsonian Institution, 1948. (Smithsonian miscellaneous
      collections, v. 110, no. 13.) $2.00.

659. Fitzsimmons, Thomas, ed.
      RSFSR, Russian Soviet Federated Socialist Republic. Contribu-
      tors: Clifford R. Barnett and others. New Haven, Human Rela-
      tions Area Files, 1957, 2 v. (Country Survey Series.) $8.50.

660. Gorer, Geoffrey, and John Rickman
      The people of Great Russia; a psychological study. London,
      Cresset Press, 1949, 10/6; New York, Chanticleer Press, 1950,
      out of print.

661. Hasluck, Margaret Masson (Hardie)
      The unwritten law in Albania. Edited by J. H. Hutton. Cam-
      bridge, University Press, 1954, $6.50.

662. Mead, Margaret
Soviet attitudes toward authority; an interdisciplinary approach
to problems of Soviet character. The RAND Corporation. 1st ed.
New York, McGraw-Hill, 1951. (The RAND Series.) Distributed
by Morrow, $5.00.

663. Sanders, Irwin Taylor
Balkan village. Lexington, University of Kentucky Press, 1949,
$4.00.

664. Thomas, William Isaac, and Florian Znaniecki
The Polish peasant in Europe and America. New York, Dover,
1958, 2 v., $12.50.

665. Tomašić, Dinko Antun
Personality and culture in Eastern European politics. New
York, Stewart, 1948. (Library of Policy Sciences.) Out of print;
ca. $4.00.

666. Zborowski, Mark, and Elizabeth Herzog
Life is with people; the Jewish little-town of eastern Europe.
Foreword by Margaret Mead. New York, International Universi-
ties Press, 1952, $5.00.

B. Middle East (including North Africa)

667. Albright, William Foxwell
The archaeology of Palestine. Rev. ed. Harmondsworth,
Middlesex, Baltimore, Penguin, 1960. (Pelican Books, A199.)
$0.95. First published 1954.

668. Albright, William Foxwell
From the stone age to Christianity; monotheism and the his-
torical process. 2d ed., with a new introd. Baltimore, Johns
Hopkins Press, 1957, $5.00.
Paper: Garden City, N. Y., Doubleday, 1957. (Doubleday
Anchor Books, A100.) $1.45.

669. Aldred, Cyril
The Egyptians. New York, Praeger, 1961, $6.50; London,
Thames & Hudson, 1961, 30/-. (Ancient Peoples and Places, v. 18.)

670. Ammar, Hamed
Growing up in an Egyptian village; Silwa, province of Aswan.
London, Routledge & Kegan Paul, Ltd., 1954. (International Library
of Sociology and Social Reconstruction.) 28/-.

671. Ayrout, Henry Habib
The fellaheen. Tr. by Hilary Wyament, with a foreword by
M. Taher Pasha. Cairo, R. Schindler, 1945, ca. $7.50. Out of print?

672. Barbour, Nevill, ed.
      A survey of North West Africa (the Maghrib). London, New
      York, Oxford University Press, 1959, $5.60.

673. Barth, Fredrik
      Principles of social organization in southern Kurdistan. Oslo,
      Brødrene Jørgensen boktr., 1953. (Universitetets Etnografiske
      Museum Bulletin 7.) 20 Kr.

674. Baumgärtel, Elise
      The cultures of prehistoric Egypt. Rev. ed. London, published
      on behalf of the Griffith Institute, Ashmolean Museum, Oxford, by
      Oxford University Press, 1955-1960. 2 v. Pt. 1, out of print,
      ca. $8.00; Pt. 2, $10.10.

675. Berque, Jacques
      Structures sociales du Haut-Atlas. 1. ed. Paris, Presses
      Universitaires de France, 1955. (Bibliothèque de Sociologie Con-
      temporaine. Serie B: Travaux du centre d'études sociologiques.)
      1,800 fr.

676. Bovill, E. W.
      The golden trade of the Moors. London, New York, Oxford
      University Press, 1958, $7.00. (A rewriting of the author's
      Caravans of the old Sahara.)

677. Braidwood, Robert John
      The Near East and the foundations for civilization; an essay
      in appraisal of the general evidence. Eugene, Oregon State Sys-
      tem of Higher Education, 1952 (Condon Lectures.) $1.00.

678. Briggs, Lloyd Cabot
      Tribes of the Sahara. Cambridge, Mass., Harvard University
      Press, 1960, $6.00.

679. Caton-Thompson, Gertrude, and Elinor W. Gardner
      The Desert Fayum. London, The Royal Anthropological Insti-
      tute of Great Britain and Ireland, 1934. 2 v. In print? Estimate:
      $6.00.

680. Chiera, Edward
      They wrote on clay; the Babylonian tablets speak today . . . edited
      by George G. Cameron. Chicago, University of Chicago Press, 1938,
      $5.00.
      Paper: Chicago, University of Chicago Press, 1956, c1938.
      (Phoenix Books, P2.) $1.25.

681. Childe, Vere Gordon
      Man makes himself. 3d ed. London, Watts, 1956. Cloth ed.
      8/6, paper, 5/-.
      Paper: New York, New American Library, 1951. (A Mentor
      Book, MD 154.) $0.50.

682. Childe, Vere Gordon
        New light on the most ancient east. 4th ed. London, Routledge
      & Kegan Paul, 1952; £1/15/-; New York, Praeger, 1953. Out of
      print. 4th ed. reprinted with corrections, Routledge & Kegan Paul,
      1954. First published 1928 under title: The most ancient East.
        Paper: New York, Grove Press, 1957. (Evergreen Books,
      E-72.) $1.95.

683. Clarke, Bryan Campbell
        Berber village; the story of the Oxford University Expedition
      to the High Atlas Mountains of Morocco. London, Longmans,
      1959, 18/-

684. Cline, Walter Buchanan
        Notes on the people of Siwah and El Garah in the Libyan
      desert. Menasha, Wis., George Banta, 1936. (General Series on
      Anthropology, no. 4.) Out of print; ca. $3.00.

685. Contenau, Georges
        Everyday life in Babylon and Assyria. New York, St. Martin's
      Press, 1954, $6.00.

686. Coon, Carleton Stevens
        Caravan: the story of the Middle East. Rev. ed. New York,
      Holt, 1958, $4.50.

687. Coon, Carleton Stevens
        Cave explorations in Iran, 1949. Philadelphia, University Mu-
      seum, University of Pennsylvania, 1951. (Museum Monographs.)
      $1.50.

688. Coon, Carleton Stevens
        The seven caves; archaeological explorations in the Middle
      East. 1st ed. New York, Knopf, 1956, $5.75.

689. Coon, Carleton Stevens
        Tribes of the Rif. Cambridge, Mass., Peabody Museum of
      Harvard University, 1931. (Harvard African Studies, v. 9.) $10.00.

690. Coult, Lyman H.
        An annotated research bibliography of studies in Arabic, Eng-
      lish, and French, of the fellah of the Egyptian Nile, 1798-1955.
      With the assistance of Karim Durzi. Coral Gables, Fla., Uni-
      versity of Miami Press, 1958, $3.00.

691. Cressey, George Babcock
        Crossroads; land and life in southwest Asia. Chicago, Lippin-
      cott, 1960, $15.00; text ed., $8.95.

692. Dickson, Harold Richard Patrick
        Kuwait and her neighbors. Edited for publication by Clifford
      Witting. London, Allen & Unwin, 1956, 75/-.
        U. S. distributor: Macmillan, New York, $12.75.

693. Doughty, Charles Montagu
      Travels in Arabia Deserta . . . with an introduction by T. E.
      Lawrence. New and definitive ed. London, Cape, 1936, 2 v.,
      £4/14/6; New York, Random House, 1936, 2 v. in 1, $7.50.
      Abridgment: Passages from Arabia Deserta, selected by Ed-
      ward Garnett, New York, Liveright, 1931, $2.50; London, Cape,
      1931, 12/6.
      Abridgment in paper: Garden City, N. Y., Doubleday, 1955.
      (A Doubleday Anchor Book, A50.) $1.45.

694. Edwards, Iorwerth Eiddon Stephen
      The pyramids of Egypt. Drawings by John Cruikshank Rose. Har-
      mondsworth, Middlesex, Penguin, 1949. (Pelican Books, A168.) 2/6.

      Ehrich, Robert W., ed.
      Relative chronologies in Old World Archaeology. See no. 417.

695. Eisenstadt, Shmuel Noah
      The absorption of immigrants; a comparative study based
      mainly on the Jewish community in Palestine and the State of
      Israel. London, Routledge & Kegan Paul, 1954. (International
      Library of Sociology and Social Reconstruction.) £1/5/-; Glen-
      coe, Ill., Free Press, 1955, out of print.

696. Ettinghausen, Richard
      A selected and annotated bibliography of books and periodicals
      in Western languages dealing with the Near and Middle East, with
      special emphasis on medieval and modern times. Completed sum-
      mer, 1951. With supplement, December, 1953. Washington, Middle
      East Institute, 1954, $2.50.

697. Evans-Pritchard, Edward Evan
      The Sanusi of Cyrenaica. Oxford, Clarendon Press, 1949, $5.60.

698. Field, Henry
      Ancient and modern man in southwestern Asia. Coral Gables,
      Fla., University of Miami Press, 1956, $7.50.

699. Field, Henry
      The anthropology of Iraq.
      Pt. 1, no. 1, The upper Euphrates. no. 2, The lower Euphrates-
      Tigris region. Chicago, Field Museum of Natural History, 1940.
      (Fieldiana: Anthropology, v. 30.) No. 1, out of print; no. 2, $6.50.
      Pt. 2, no. 1, The Northern Jazira; no. 2-3; Kurdistan and con-
      clusions. Cambridge, Peabody Museum, 1951-1952. (Papers of
      the Peabody Museum of Archaeology and Ethnology, Harvard Uni-
      versity, v. 46.) Pt. 2, no. 1-2, $13.35; bound in cloth, $16.35.

700. Field, Henry
      Bibliography on Southwestern Asia. Coral Gables, Fla., Uni-
      versity of Miami Press, 1953-   v. 1-2, $3.00 ea.; v. 3, $6.00;
      v. 4, $12.00; v. 5-6, $6.00 ea.; $32.00 for set.

701. Field, Henry
Contributions to the anthropology of Iran. Chicago, 1939. 2 v.
(Chicago. Natural History Museum. Fieldiana: Anthropology.
v. 29, no. 1-2.) $12.00.

702. Field, Henry
Contributions to the anthropology of the Faiyum, Sinai, Sudan,
Kenya. Berkeley and Los Angeles, University of California Press,
1952, $4.00.

703. Fisher, William Bayne
The Middle East; a physical, social, and regional geography. 3d
ed. London, Methuen; New York, Dutton, 1956, $6.95. (Methuen's
advanced geographies.)

704. Frankfort, Henri
Ancient Egyptian religion; an interpretation. New York, Columbia University Press, 1948. (Lectures on the history of religions,
sponsored by the American Council of Learned Societies, new ser.,
no. 2.) Out of print; ca. $3.00.

705. Frankfort, Henri
Before philosophy; the intellectual adventure of ancient man. An
essay on speculative thought in the ancient Near East. Harmondsworth, Middlesex, Penguin, 1959. (Pelican Books, A198.) $0.95.
Originally published 1946 under title The intellectual adventure of
ancient man.

706. Frankfort, Henri
The birth of civilization in the Near East. Bloomington, Indiana
University Press, 1951, $4.50.
Paper: Garden City, N. Y., Doubleday, 1956. (Doubleday
Anchor Books, A89.) $0.95.

707. Frankfort, Henri
Kingship and the gods, a study of ancient Near Eastern religion
as the integration of society and nature. Chicago, University of
Chicago Press, 1948. (Oriental Institute Essay.) $9.00.

708. Geiger, Bernhard
Peoples and languages of the Caucasus; a synopsis, by Bernhard
Geiger and others. 's-Gravenhage, Mouton, 1959. (Janua linguarum,
nr. 6.) f 8.-.
U. S. distributor: New York, Humanities Press, $2.50.

709. Ghurschman, Roman
Iran, from the earliest times to the Islamic conquest. Harmondsworth, Penguin, 1954. (Pelican Books, A239.) $0.95.

710. Gibb, Sir Hamilton Alexander Rosskeen, and Harold Bowen
Islamic society and the west; a study of the impact of Western
civilization on Moslem culture in the Near East. London, New
York, Oxford University Press, 1950-   v. 1, Islamic society in
the eighteenth century. Pt. 1, 1950, $4.00; pt. 2, 1957, $5.60.

711. Granqvist, Hilma Natalia
Birth and childhood among the Arabs; studies in a Muhammadan
village in Palestine. Helsingfors, Söderström, 1947.
Scandinavian distributor: Munksgaard, Copenhagen, Kr. 25.-.
U. S. distributor: Humanities Press, New York, $6.00.

712. Granqvist, Hilma Natalia
Child problems among the Arabs; studies in a Muhammadan
village in Palestine. Helsingfors, Södorström, 1950.
Scandinavian distributor: Munksgaard, Copenhagen, Kr. 30.-.
U. S. distributor: Humanities Press, New York, $6.00.

713. Granqvist, Hilma Natalia
Marriage conditions in a Palestinian village. Helsingfors, Akade-
mische buchhandlung, 1931-1935, 2 v. (Finska vetenskaps-societeten
Helsingfors. Commentationes humanarum litterarum. III, 8; IV, 8.)
Out of print; ca. $15.00.

714. Gulick, John
Social structure and culture change in a Lebanese village. New
York, Wenner-Gren Foundation for Anthropological Research, 1955.
(Viking Fund Publications in Anthropology, no. 21.) Out of print;
ca. $3.50.

715. Gurney, Oliver Robert
The Hittites. 2d ed. London, Baltimore, Penguin, 1952. (Pelican Books, A259.) 3/6.

716. Harris, George Lawrence
Iraq: its people, its society, its culture. In collaboration with
Moukhtar Ani and others. New Haven, HRAF Press, 1958. (Survey
of World Cultures.) $7.00.

717. Harris, George Lawrence
Jordan: its people, its society, its culture . . . in collaboration
with Moukhtar Ani and others. New Haven, HRAF Press, 1958.
(Survey of World Cultures.) $5.50.
Paper: New York, Grove Press, 1958. (Evergreen Books E-132.)
$1.95.

Joint Expedition of the British school of archaeology in Jerusalem
and the American school of prehistoric research, 1929-1937. The
stone age of Mount Carmel. See no. 520.

718. Jurji, Edward Jabra
The Middle East, its religion and culture. Philadelphia, West-
minster Press, 1956, $3.00.

719. Kenyon, Kathleen Mary
Archaeology in the Holy Land. New York, Praeger, 1960. $6.95.

720. Kenyon, Kathleen Mary
Digging up Jericho. London, Benn, 1957, 30/-; New York,
Praeger, 1957. $6.00. New York ed. has subtitle: The results
of the Jericho excavations, 1952-1956.

721. Klunzinger, Karl Benjamin
Upper Egypt: its people and its products. A descriptive account of the manners, customs, superstitions, and occupations of the people of the Nile valley, the desert, and the Red Sea coast, with sketches of the natural history and geology. With a prefatory notice by Dr. Georg Schweinfurth. London, Blackie, 1878; New York, Scribner, Armstrong, 1878. Out of print; ca. $3.50.

722. Kramer, Samuel Noah
History begins at Sumer. Garden City, N. Y., Doubleday, 1959. (Doubleday Anchor Books, A175.) $1.45. Published in 1956 under title: From the tablets of Sumer.

723. Kramer, Samuel Noah, ed.
Mythologies of the ancient world. Contributions by Rudolf Anthes and others. Chicago, Quadrangle Books, 1961, $7.50.
Paper: Garden City, N. Y., Doubleday, 1961. (Anchor Books, A229.) $1.45.
Contributions to a symposium at the 1959 annual meeting of the American Anthropological Association and the American Folklore Society.

724. Lambton, Ann Katherine Swynford
Landlord and peasant in Persia; a study of land tenure and land revenue administration. London, New York, Oxford University Press, 1953, $8.00.

725. Lammens, Henri
Islam: beliefs and institutions . . . translated from the French by Sir E. Denison Ross. London, Methuen, 1929. Out of print; ca. $5.00.

726. Lane, Edward William
Manners and customs of the modern Egyptians. 3d ed. London, Dent; New York, Dutton, 1908. (Everyman's Library, 315.) $1.95.
Title shortened in later printings to The modern Egyptians.

727. Levy, Reuben
Social structure of Islam, being the second edition of the sociology of Islam. Cambridge, University Press, 1957, $9.50.

728. Lewis, Bernard
The Arabs in history. London, New York, Hutchinson's, 1950, $2.25.
Paper: New York, Harper, 1960. (Harper Torch Books. TB 1029.) $1.35.

729. Lipsky, George Arthur
Saudi Arabia: its people, its society, its culture. In collaboration with Moukhtar Ani and others. New Haven, HRAF Press, 1959. (Survey of World Cultures, 4.) $7.00.

730. Lloyd, Seton
Early Anatolia; the archaeology of Asia Minor before the Greeks. With a note on the anthropology of the ancient inhabitants of Anatolia by Muzaffer Senyurek. Baltimore, Penguin, 1956. (Pelican Books, A354.) $0.95.

731. Lloyd, Seton
    Foundations in the dust; a story of Mesopotamian exploration.
    Harmondsworth, Eng., Penguin, 1955. (Pelican Books A336.) $0.85.
    Previously published, London, Oxford University Press, 1947.

732. London. University. School of Oriental and African Studies. Library.
    Index Islamicus, 1906-1955. A catalogue of articles on Islamic
    subjects in periodicals and other collective publications, com-
    piled by J. D. Pearson, librarian, with the assistance of Julia F.
    Ashton. Cambridge, Heffer, 1958, £5/5/-.

733. Lucas, Alfred
    Ancient Egyptian materials and industries. 3d ed., rev. Lon-
    don, Arnold, 1948, 25/-.

734. McBurney, Charles Brian Montagu
    The stone age of Northern Africa. Harmondsworth, Middlesex;
    Baltimore, Penguin, 1960. (Pelican Books, A342.) $1.45.

735. Massé, Henri
    Persian beliefs and customs. Translated from the French by
    Charles A. Messner. New Haven, Human Relations Area Files,
    1954. (Behavior Science Translations.) $4.75.

736. Maxwell, Gavin
    People of the reeds. New York, Harper, 1957, $4.50; London,
    New York, Longmans, Green, 1957, 21/-. English edition has
    title: A reed shaken by the wind.

737. Mendelsohn, Isaac, ed.
    Religions of the ancient Near East; Sumero-Akkadian religious
    texts and Ugaritic epics. New York, Liberal Arts Press, 1955.
    (The Library of Religion, v. 4.) $4.50; paper, $1.75.

738. Miner, Horace Mitchell, and George De Vos
    Oasis and casbah: Algerian culture and personality in change.
    Ann Arbor, University of Michigan, 1960. (Michigan. University.
    Museum of Anthropology. Anthropological papers, no. 15.) $2.50.

739. Miner, Horace Mitchell
    The primitive city of Timbuctoo. Princeton, published for the
    American Philosophical Society by Princeton University Press, 1953.
    (Memoirs of the American Philosophical Society, v. 32.) $5.00.

740. Murray, George William
    Sons of Ishmael; a study of the Egyptian Bedouin. London,
    Routledge, 1935. Out of print; ca. $4.00.

741. Musil, Alois
    The manners and customs of the Rwala Bedouins . . . published
    under the patronage of the Czech academy of sciences and arts
    and of Charles R. Crane. New York, 1928. (American Geographi-
    cal Society. Oriental Explorations and Studies no. 6.) $8.00.

742. Pallis, Svend Aage Frederik Dichmann
The antiquity of Iraq; a handbook of Assyriology. Copenhagen, Munksgaard, 1956, Kr. 120.-.

743. Patai, Raphael
Cultures in conflict; three lectures on the socio-cultural problems of Israel and her neighbors. 2d ed. rev. and enl. New York, 1961. (Heizl Institute Pamphlets, 21.) Price unknown; estimate: $1.00.

744. Patai, Raphael
Golden river to golden road: society, culture, and change in the Middle East. Philadelphia, University of Pennsylvania Press, 1962. $7.50.

745. Patai, Raphael
Israel between East and West, a study in human relations. Philadelphia, Jewish Publication Society of America, 1953. Out of print; ca. $4.50.

746. Patai, Raphael
Jordan, Lebanon, and Syria; an annotated bibliography. New Haven, HRAF Press, 1957. (Behavior Science Bibliographies.) $6.50.

747. Patai, Raphael
The kingdom of Jordan. Princeton, Princeton University Press, 1958, $5.00.

748. Patai, Raphael
Sex and family in the Bible and the Middle East. 1st ed. Garden City, N. Y., Doubleday, 1959, $3.95.
Paper: New York, Doubleday, 1960. (Dolphin C 40.) $0.95.

749. Peake, Frederick Gerard
A history of Jordan and its tribes. Coral Gables, Fla., University of Miami Press, 1958, $6.00.

750. Perkins, Ann Louise
The comparative archaeology of early Mesopotamia. Chicago, University of Chicago Press, 1949. (Chicago. University. Oriental Institute. Studies in Ancient Oriental Civilization, no. 25.) $5.00.

751. Planhol, Xavier de
The world of Islam; Le monde islamique; essay de géographie religieuse. Ithaca, N. Y., Cornell University Press, 1959, $2.00.

752. Rodd, Frances James Rennell
The people of the veil; being an account of the habits, organisation and history of the wandering Tuareg tribes which inhabit the mountains of Air or Asben in the Central Sahara. London, Macmillan, 1926. Out of print; ca. $10.00.

753. Smith, William Robertson
        Kinship and marriage in early Arabia. Cambridge, University
        Press, 1885; new ed., with additional notes by the author and by
        Professor Ignaz Goldziher, Budapest; ed. by Stanley A. Cook.
        London, Black, 1903. Out of print; ca. $6.00.

754. Smith, William Robertson
        The religion of the Semites; the fundamental institutions. New
        York, Meridian, 1956. (The Meridian Library, ML4.) $2.25.
        First published in 1889 as the first series of the author's
        Lectures on the religion of the Semites (Burnett Lectures, Aber-
        deen University, 1888-1889.)

755. Spiro, Melford E.
        Children of the Kibbutz . . ., with the assistance of Audrey G.
        Spiro. Cambridge, Mass., Harvard University Press, 1958, $10.00.

756. Spiro, Melford E.
        Kibbutz: venture in Utopia. Cambridge, Mass., Harvard Uni-
        versity Press, 1956, $4.50.

757. Symposium on Urbanization and Cultural Development in the
        Ancient Near East, University of Chicago, 1958.
        City invincible; a Symposium on Urbanization and Cultural
        Development in the Ancient Near East held at the Oriental Insti-
        tute of the University of Chicago, December 4-7, 1958. Edited for
        the Planning Committee by Carl H. Kraeling and Robert M. Adams.
        Chicago, University of Chicago Press, 1960 (Chicago. University.
        Oriental Institute. Special publication.) $6.00.

758. Thesiger, Wilfred
        Arabian sands. 1st ed. New York, Dutton, 1959, $5.95.

759. Ullens de Schooten, Marie Thérèse
        Lords of the mountains; southern Persia and the Kashkai tribe.
        London, Chatto & Windus, 1956. Out of print; ca. $3.00.

760. Von Grunebaum, Gustave Edmund
        Islam; essays in the nature and growth of a cultural tradition.
        New ed. with addenda. London, Routledge & Kegan Paul, 1961, 25/-.
        First published as American Anthropological Association Memoir,
        no. 81. Comparative Studies of Cultures and Civilizations, no. 4.

761. Von Grunebaum, Gustave Edmund, ed.
        Studies in Islamic cultural history; with contributions by Werner
        Caskel and others. English translation by I. Lichtenstadter. Men-
        asha, Wis., American Anthropological Association, 1954. (Com-
        parative studies in Cultures and Civilizations, no. 2.) (American
        Anthropological Association. Memoir no. 76.) $1.40.

762. Von Grunebaum, Gustave Edmund, ed.
        Unity and variety in Muslim civilization. Chicago, University
        of Chicago Press, 1955. (Comparative Studies of Cultures and
        Civilization.) $6.50.

763. Vreeland, Herbert Harold, ed.
    Iran. Contributors: Clifford R. Barnett and others. New
Haven, Human Relations Area Files, 1957. (Country Survey
Series, 3.) $8.00.

764. Warriner, Doreen
    Land and poverty in the Middle East. London & New York,
Royal Institute of International Affairs, 1948. (Middle East Economic and Social Studies.) Out of print? ca. $3.00.

765. Warriner, Doreen
    Land reform and development in the Middle East; a study of
Egypt, Syria, and Iraq. London, New York, Royal Institute of
International Affairs, 1957, $2.90.

Weber, Max
    Ancient Judaism. See no. 239.

766. Westermarck, Edvard Alexander
    Marriage ceremonies in Morocco. London, Macmillan, 1914.
Out of print; ca. $6.00.

767. Westermarck, Edvard Alexander
    Ritual and belief in Morocco. London, Macmillan, 1926. 2 v.
Out of print; ca. $9.00.

768. Westermarck, Edvard Alexander
    Wit and wisdom in Morocco; a study of native proverbs . . .
with the assistance of Shereef 'Abdes-Salem el-Baqqali. New
York, Liveright, 1931; London, Routledge, 1930. Out of print;
ca. $7.50.

769. Wilbur, Donald Newton, ed.
    Afghanistan. Contributors: Elizabeth E. Bacon and others.
New Haven, Human Relations Area Files, 1956. (Country Survey
Series.) Out of print; ca. $8.00.

770. Wilber, Donald Newton
    Annotated bibliography of Afghanistan. New Haven, Human Rela-
tions Area Files, 1956. (Behavior Science Bibliographies.) $5.50.

771. Wilson, John Albert
    The burden of Egypt; an interpretation of ancient Egyptian cul-
ture. Chicago, University of Chicago Press, 1951, $6.00.
    Paper ed., with changed title: The culture of ancient Egypt.
Chicago, University of Chicago Press, 1956. (Phoenix Books, P
11.) $1.50.

772. Woolley, Sir Charles Leonard
    Excavations at Ur; a record of twelve years' work. London,
Benn, 1954, 15/-.
    U. S. distributor: Barnes & Noble, New York, $3.50.
    Also published by Crowell, New York, 1954. Out of print.

773. Woolley, Sir Charles Leonard
     A forgotten Kingdom, being a record of the results obtained
     from the excavations of two mounds, Atchana and Al Mina, in
     the Turkish Hatay. Rev. ed. London, Parrish, 1959, 30/-.

774. Woolley, Sir Charles Leonard
     Ur of the Chaldees; a record of seven years of excavation.
     2d ed. London, Benn, 1950. Out of print; ca. $2.50.

775. Woolley, Sir Charles Leonard
     Ur: the first phases. London and New York, Penguin, 1946.
     (The King Penguin Books) out of print; ca. $1.00.

776. Wulsin, Frederick Roelker
     The prehistoric archaeology of northwest Africa. Cambridge,
     Mass., The Museum, 1941. (Harvard University. Peabody Museum
     of American Archaeology and Ethnology. Papers, v. 19, no. 1.)
     $3.25.

C. Africa sub-Sahara

a. General

Ethnographic survey of Africa
     In addition to the monographs listed below, special reference
should be called to the Ethnographic survey of Africa, a monographic series which aims to publish socio-cultural outlines for
all the peoples of the continent south of the Sahara. The volumes
thus far published cover perhaps one-half the area and cost an
average of $2.25 each. The Survey has several publishers and is
divided as follows:

   (a) Ethnographic survey of Africa. Western Africa. no. 1-
       1950-   London, International African Institute, 1950-
       Fourteen titles published.

   (b) Ethnographic survey of Africa. Western Africa. French
       series. no. 1-   1954-   Paris, Presses Universitaires
       de France, 1954-   . Eight titles published.
          Also published in the series: Monographies Ethnologiques
       Africaines.

   (c) Ethnographic survey of Africa. North-Eastern Africa.
       no. 1-   1955-   London, International African Institute,
       1955-   . Three titles published.

   (d) Ethnographic survey of Africa. East Central Africa.
       no. 1-   1950-   . London, International African Institute,
       1950-   . Eleven titles published.

(e) Ethnographic survey of Africa. Madagascar. no. 1-
     1959-   . Paris, Presses Universitaires de France,
     1959-   . One title published. Also published in the series:
     Monographies Ethnologiques. Les peuple malgache.

(f) Ethnographic survey of Africa. West Central Africa. no. 1-
     1951-   . London, International African Institute, 1951-   .
     Four titles published.

(g) Ethnographic survey of Africa. Central Africa, Belgian
     Congo. no. 1-   1954-   . London, International African
     Institute, 1954-   . Five titles published. Also published
     in the series: Annales du Musée du Congo Belge. Sciences
     de l'homme. Monographies Ethnographiques.

(h) Ethnographic survey of Africa. Southern Africa, no. 1-
     1952-   . London, International African Institute, 1952-   .
     Four titles published.

777. Afrika-Institiut (Netherlands)
      The future of customary law in Africa. L'avenir du droit
coutumier en Afrique. Symposium-colloque, Amsterdam, 1955.
Organized by the Afrika Institiut, Studiecentrum, Leiden, in
collaboration with the Royal Tropical Institute, Amsterdam.
Leiden, Universitaire Pers Leiden, 1956, Gld. 19.75.

778. Alimen, Henriette
      Prehistory of Africa, tr. by Alan Houghton Broderick. London,
Hutchinson, 1957, 63/-.

The art of Africa, by W. W. Battis.   See no. 246.

779. Bascom, William Russell, and Melville J. Herskovits, eds.
      Continuity and change in African cultures. Chicago, University
of Chicago Press, 1959, $7.00.

780. Baumann, Hermann, and Diedrich Westermann
      Les peuples et les civilizations de l'Afrique, par H. Baumann.
Suivi de Les langues et l'éducation, par D. Westermann. Traduc-
tion française par L. Homburger. Pref. de Théodore Monod.
Paris, Payot, 1948 (reprinted 1957). (Bibliothèque Scientifique.)
17.00 NF.

781. Bohannan, Paul, ed.
      African homicide and suicide. Princeton, N. J., Princeton
University Press, 1960, $6.00.

Elias, Taslim Olawale
The nature of African customary law. See no. 185.

Elisofon, Eliot
The sculpture of Africa. See no. 255.

178   REXFORD S. BECKHAM

782. Fortes, Meyer, and Edward Evan Evans-Pritchard, eds.
        African political systems. London, published for the International
     African Institute by the Oxford University Press, 1940, $3.40.
        Paper ed. announced by International African Institute for
     Spring 1961.

783. Gluckman, Max
        Custom and conflict in Africa. Oxford, Blackwell, 1955, 12/6;
     Glencoe, Ill., Free Press, 1956, $3.50.

     Greenberg, Joseph Harold
     Studies in African linguistic classification. See no. 450.

784. Hailey, William Malcolm Hailey, baron
        An African survey; a study of problems arising in Africa south
     of the Sahara, by Lord Hailey. Rev. ed. London, New York, Ox-
     ford University Press, 1957, $16.80.

785. International African Institute
        African worlds; studies in the cosmological ideas and social
     values of African peoples. London, New York, Oxford University
     Press, 1954, $5.20.

786. International African Institute
        Select annotated bibliography of tropical Africa, compiled under
     the direction of Daryll Forde. New York, 1956. In print? No
     price.

787. International African Institute
        Social implications of industrialization and urbanization in
     Africa, south of the Sahara. Paris, UNESCO, 1956. (Tensions
     and Technology Series.) $11.00; paper, $9.00.
        U. S. distributor: International Document Service, Columbia
     University Press.

788. Kimble, George Herbert Tinley
        Tropical Africa. New York, Twentieth Century Fund, 1960,
     2 v., $15.00.

789. Leakey, Louis Seymour Bazett
        Stone age Africa; an outline of prehistory in Africa. London,
     Oxford University Press, H. Milford, 1936. Out of print; ca.
     $5.00.

790. Middleton, John, and David Tait, eds.
        Tribes without rulers; studies in African segmentary sys-
     tems. Pref. by E. E. Evans-Pritchard. London, Routledge &
     Kegan Paul, 1958, £1/8/-.
        U. S. distributor: New York, Humanities Press, $5.50.

791. Murdock, George Peter
        Africa: its people and their culture history. New York,
     McGraw-Hill, 1959, $11.75; text ed., $8.75.

792. Ottenberg, Simon, and Phoebe Ottenberg, eds.
     Cultures and societies of Africa. New York, Random House,
     1960, $7.50.

793. Pan African Congress on Prehistory, 3rd, Livingstone, 1955
     Proceedings. Ed. by J. Desmond Clark, assisted by Sonia Cole.
     London, Chatto & Windus, 1957, 75/-.
     U. S. distributor: New York, Humanities Press, $15.00.

794. Radcliffe-Brown, Alfred Reginald, and Cyril Daryll Forde, eds.
     African systems of kinship and marriage. London, New York,
     published for the International African Institute by the Oxford Uni-
     versity Press, 1950, $6.40.
     Paper ed. announced by International African Institute for 1961 at
     18/-.

795. Seligman, Charles Gabriel
     Races of Africa. 3d ed. London, New York, Oxford University
     Press, 1957. (The Home University Library of Modern Knowledge,
     144.) $1.40.

796. Stillman, Calvin W., ed.
     Africa in the modern world. Chicago, University of Chicago
     Press, 1955. (Harris Foundation Lectures, 1953.) $6.00.

797. Westermann, Diedrich
     The African today and tomorrow. With a foreword by the Rt.
     Hon. Lord Lugard. 3d ed. London, New York, published for the
     International African Institute by Oxford University Press, 1949,
     $2.25.

798. Westermann, Diedrich
     Geschichte Afrikas; Staatenbildungen südlich der Sahara. Köln,
     Greven-Verlag, 1952, DM 41.

799. Wieschhoff, Heinrich Albert
     Anthropological bibliography of Negro Africa. New Haven,
     American Oriental Society, 1948. (American Oriental Series,
     v. 23.) $7.00.

800. Wolfe, Alvin William
     Field guide to West and Central Africa. Washington, National
     Academy of Sciences, National Research Council, 1959. (National
     Research Council. Committee on International Anthropology.
     Field Guide Series no. 2.) (National Research Council. Publication
     702.) $1.25.

     b. West

801. Apter, David Ernest
     The Gold Coast in transition. Princeton, Princeton University
     Press, 1955, $6.00.

Baba of Karo
Baba of Karo, a woman of the Muslim Hausa. Autobiography
recorded by M. F. Smith. See no. 319.

802. Banton, Michael P.
West African city; a study of tribal life in Freetown. London,
published for the International African Institute by the Oxford
University Press, 1957, $5.60.

803. Beckett, W. H.
Akokoaso, a survey of a Gold Coast village. London, published
for the London School of Economics and Political Science by P.
Lund, Humphries, 1944. (Monographs on Social Anthropology,
10.) 8/6.

804. Bohannan, Paul
Justice and judgment among the Tiv. London, New York,
published for the International African Institute by Oxford
University Press, 1957, $6.40.

805. Bowen, Elenore Smith, pseud.
Return to laughter. 1st American ed. New York, Harper,
1954, $3.50.

806. Busia, Kofi Abrefa
The position of the chief in the modern political system of
Ashanti; a study of the influence of contemporary social changes
on Ashanti political institutions. London, New York, published
for the International African Institute, by the Oxford University
Press, 1951, $3.40.

807. Christensen, James Boyd
Double descent among the Fanti. New Haven, Human Relations
Area Files, 1954. (Behavior Science Monographs.) $2.50.

808. Coker, G. B. A.
Family property among the Yorubas. With a foreword by
Maxime de Comarmond. London, Sweet & Maxwell, 1958, 45/-.

809. Delavignette, Robert Louis
Freedom and authority in French West Africa. London, New
York, published for the International African Institute by the Ox-
ford University Press, 1950, $2.40.

Elias, Taslim Olawale
Groundwork of Nigerian law. See no. 184.
Nigerian land law and custom. See no. 186.

810. Fage, J. D.
An introduction to the history of West Africa. 2d ed. Cambridge, Cambridge University Press, 1960, $3.00.

811. Forde, Cyril Daryll
       Marriage and family among the Yakö of southeastern Nigeria.
       2d ed. London, published for the International African Institute
       by P. Lund, Humphries, 1951. (London School of Economics.
       Monographs on Social Anthropology, no. 5.) 10/6.

812. Fortes, Meyer
       The dynamics of clanship among the Tallensi, being the first
       part of an analysis of the social structure of a trans-Volta tribe.
       London, New York, published for the International African Institute
       by the Oxford University Press, 1945, $5.80.

       Fortes, Meyer
       Oedipus and Job in West African religion. See no. 205.

813. Fortes, Meyer
       The web of kinship among the Tallensi; the second part of an
       analysis of the social structure of a Trans-Volta tribe. London, New
       York, published for the International African Institute by the Oxford
       University Press, 1949, $7.20.

814. Green, Margaret Mackesen
       Ibo village affairs, chiefly with reference to the village of
       Umueke Agbaja. London, Sidgwick & Jackson, 1947. Out of print;
       ca. $3.00.

815. Greenberg, Joseph Harold
       The influence of Islam on a Sudanese religion. New York,
       Augustin, 1946. (Monographs of the American Ethnological
       Society, 10.) Out of print; ca. $3.50.

       Herskovits, Melville Jean, and Frances S. Herskovits
       Dahomean narrative. See no. 290.

816. Herskovits, Melville Jean
       Dahomey, an ancient West African Kingdom. New York City,
       Augustin, 1938, 2 v., $20.00.

       Herskovits, Melville Jean, and Frances S. Herskovits
       An outline of Dahomean religious belief. See no. 210.

       Hill, Polly
       The Gold Coast cocoa farmer. See no. 148.

817. Hopen, C. Edward
       The pastoral Fulbe family in Gwandu. London, published for
       the International African Institute by the Oxford University Press,
       1958, $4.80.

818. Kaberry, Phyllis Mary
       Women of the grassfields; a study of the economic position of
       women in Bamenda, British Cameroons. London, H. Majesty's
       Stationery Office, 1952. (Gt. Brit. Colonial Office. Colonial
       Research Publication no. 14.) 32/10.

819. Little, Kenneth Lindsay
      The Mende of Sierra Leone; a West African people in
      transition. London, Routledge & Kegan Paul, 1951. (Interna-
      tional Library of Sociology and Social Reconstruction.) Out of
      print; ca. $6.00.

820. Lystad, Robert A.
      The Ashanti; a proud people. New Brunswick, N. J., Rutgers
      University Press, 1958, $5.00.

821. Meek, Charles Kingsley
      Law and authority in a Nigerian tribe; a study in indirect
      rule. With a foreword by the Right Hon. Lord Lugard. Lon-
      don, New York, Oxford University Press, 1937. Out of print;
      ca. $5.00.

822. Meek, Charles Kingsley
      The northern tribes of Nigeria; an ethnographical account of
      the northern provinces of Nigeria together with a report on the
      1921 decennial census. London, Oxford University Press, H. Mil-
      ford, 1925. 2 v. Out of print; ca. $15.00.

823. Meek, Charles Kingsley
      A Sudanese kingdom; an ethnographical study of the Jukun-
      speaking peoples of Nigeria. With introduction by H. R. Palmer.
      London, Kegan Paul, Trench, Trubner, 1931, £1/15/-.
      U. S. distributor: New York, Humanities Press, $7.50.

824. Meek, Charles Kingsley
      Tribal studies in northern Nigeria. London, Kegan Paul, Trench
      Trubner, 1931, 2 v., £1/10/- ea.
      U. S. distributor: New York, Humanities Press, $15.00.

825. Nadel, Siegfried Frederick
      A black Byzantium; the kingdom of the Nupe in Nigeria . . .
      with a foreword by the Right Hon. Lord Lugard. London, New
      York, published for the International African Institute by the
      Oxford University Press, 1942, $5.20.

826. Nadel, Siegfried Frederick
      Nupe religion. Glencoe, Ill., Free Press, 1954, out of print.
      London, Routledge & Kegan Paul, 1954. £1/5/-.
      U. S. distributor: New York, Humanities Press, $5.00.

827. Niven, Cecil Rex
      A short history of the Yoruba peoples. London, New York,
      Longmans, Green, 1958, 5/-.

828. Parrinder, Geoffrey
      West African religion, illustrated from the beliefs and prac-
      tices of the Yoruba, Ewe, Akan and kindred peoples. With a
      foreword by Edwin Smith. London, Epworth Press, 1949. Out
      of print; ca. $3.50.

829. Rattray, Robert Sutherland
        Ashanti. Oxford, Clarendon Press, 1923 (reprinted 1956). 35/-.

830. Rattray, Robert Sutherland
        Ashanti law and constitution. Oxford, Clarendon Press, 1929
        (reprinted 1956). 30/-.

831. Rattray, Robert Sutherland
        Religion and art in Ashanti. With chapters by G. T. Bennett,
        Vernon Blake, H. Dudley Buxton, R. R. Marett, C. G. Seligman.
        Oxford, Clarendon Press, 1927 (reprinted 1954). 45/-.

832. Smith, Michael Garfield
        Government in Zazzau, 1800-1950. London, New York, pub-
        lished for the International African Institute by the Oxford Uni-
        versity Press, 1960, $8.00.

833. Stenning, Derrick J.
        Savannah nomads; a study of the Wodaabe pastoral Fulani of
        Western Bornu Province, Northern Region, Nigeria. With a fore-
        word by Daryll Forde. London, published for the International
        African Institute by Oxford University Press, 1959, $6.40.

834. Thompson, Virginia McLean, and Richard Adloff
        The emerging states of French Equatorial Africa. Stanford,
        Calif., Stanford University Press, 1960, $8.75.

835. Thompson, Virginia McLean, and Richard Adloff
        French West Africa. Stanford, Calif., Stanford University
        Press, 1957, $8.50.

836. Trimmingham, John Spencer
        Islam in West Africa. Oxford, Clarendon Press, 1959, $4.80.

        c. East

837. Arkell, Anthony John
        A history of the Sudan: from the earliest times to 1821. With
        a foreword by Sir John Harold MacMichael. London, University
        of London, Athlone Press, 1955, 21/-.

838. Beattie, John
        Bunyoro, an African kingdom. New York, Holt, 1960. (Case
        Studies in Cultural Anthropology.) $1.75; text ed., $1.25.

839. Budge, Sir Ernest Alfred Thompson Wallis
        A history of Ethiopia, Nubia and Abyssinia (according to the
        hieroglyphic inscriptions of Egypt and Nubia, and the Ethiopian
        chronicles). London, Methuen, 1928. 2 v. Out of print; ca.
        $50.00.

840. Butt, Audrey
       The Nilotes of the Anglo-Egyptian Sudan and Uganda. London,
       International African Institute, 1952. (Ethnographic Survey of
       Africa: east central Africa, pt. 4.) 15/-.

841. Clark, John Desmond
       The prehistoric cultures of the Horn of Africa; an analysis
       of the stone age cultural and climatic succession in the Somali-
       lands and eastern parts of Abyssinia. With a foreword by M.
       C. Burkitt. Cambridge, University Press, 1954, (Occasional
       Publications of the Cambridge Museum of Archaeology and
       Ethnology, 2.) $22.50.

842. Cole, Sonia Mary
       Early man in East Africa. London, Macmillan, 1958. (Treasury
       of East African History Series.) 4/-.
       U. S. distributor: St. Martins Press, New York, $1.25.

843. Cole, Sonia Mary
       The prehistory of East Africa. Harmondsworth, Middlesex,
       Penguin, 1954. (Pelican Books, A316.) $0.65.

844. Cory, Hans, and M. M. Hartnoll
       Customary law of the Haya tribe, Tanganyika territory. Lon-
       don, published for the International African Institute by P. Lund,
       Humphries, 1945. Out of print; ca. $4.00.

845. Cory, Hans
       The Ntemi; the traditional rites in connection with the burial,
       election, enthronment, and magic powers of a Sukuma chief.
       London, Macmillan, 1951. (Custom and tradition in east Africa.)
       2/-.
       U. S. distributor: St. Martins Press, New York, $0.75.

846. Cory, Hans
       Sukuma law and custom. With a foreword by J. P. Moffett.
       London, New York, published for the International African Insti-
       tute by the Oxford University Press, 1953, $4.00.

847. Coupland, Reginald
       East Africa and its invaders, from the earliest times to the
       death of Seyyid Said in 1856. Oxford, Clarendon Press, 1938
       (reprinted 1956). 45/-.

848. Coupland, Reginald
       The exploitation of East Africa, 1856-1890; the slave trade
       and the scramble. London, Faber & Faber, 1939. Out of print;
       ca. $6.00.

849. Culwick, Arthur Theodore, and G. M. Culwick
       Ubena of the Rivers . . . with a chapter by Mtema Towegale
       Kiwanga, and an introduction by Dr. L. H. Dudley Buxton, London,
       Allen & Unwin, 1935, 16/-.

850. Edel, May (Mandelbaum)
      The Chiga of western Uganda. New York, published for the
International African Institute by Oxford University Press, 1957,
$5.60.

851. Evans-Pritchard, Edward Evan
      The divine kinship of the Shilluk of the Nilotic Sudan. Cam-
bridge, University Press, 1948. (The Frazer Lecture, 1948.)
Out of print? ca. $1.00

852. Evans-Pritchard, Edward Evan
      Kinship and marriage among the Nuer. Oxford, Clarendon
Press, 1951, $2.90.

853. Evans-Pritchard, Edward Evan
      The Nuer, a description of the modes of livelihood and politi-
cal institutions of a Nilotic people. Oxford, Clarendon Press,
1940, $4.80.

854. Evans-Pritchard, Edward Evan
      Nuer religion. Oxford, Clarendon Press, 1956, $6.75.

855. Evans-Pritchard, Edward Evan
      Witchcraft, oracles and magic among the Azande . . . with a
foreword by Professor C. G. Seligman. Oxford, Clarendon Press,
1937 (reprinted 1951), 30/-. In print?

856. Fallers, Lloyd A.
      Bantu bureaucracy; a study of integration and conflict in the
political institutions of an east African people. Cambridge, published for the East African Institute of Social Research by Heffer, 1956, 30/-.

857. Gulliver, Pamela, and P. H. Gulliver
      The central Nilo-Hamites. London, International African Insti-
tute, 1953. (Ethnographic Survey of Africa: east Central Africa,
pt. 7.) 12/-.

858. Gulliver, P. H.
      The family herds; a study of two pastoral tribes in east Africa,
the Jie and Turkana. London, Routledge & Kegan Paul, 1955.
(International Library of Sociology and Social Reconstruction.)
£1/5/-.
      U. S. distributor: New York, Humanities Press, $6.50.

      Howell, Paul Philip
      A manual of Nuer law. See no. 192.

859. Huntingford, George Wynn Brereton
      The Galla of Ethiopia: the Kingdoms of Kafa and Janjero.
London, International African Institute, 1955. (Ethnographic Survey of Africa: north-eastern Africa, pt. 2.) 16/-.

860. Huntingford, George Wynn Brereton
    The Nandi of Kenya; tribal control in a pastoral society. London, Routledge & Kegan Paul, 1953, £1/1/-.
    U. S. distributor: New York, Humanities Press, $4.50.

861. Huntingford, George Wynn Brereton
    The southern Nilo-Hamites. London, International African Institute, 1953. (Ethnographic Survey of Africa: east Africa, pt. 8.) 15/-.

862. Ingrams, William Harold
    Zanzibar, its history and its people. London, Witherby, 1931. Out of print? ca. $8.00.

862a. Kenyatta, Jomo
    Facing Mount Kenya; the tribal life of the Gikuyu, with an introduction by B. Malinowski. London, Secker and Warburg, 1938 (reprinted 1956), 25/-.
    U. S. distributor: New York, British Book Center, $6.00.

863. Lambert, H. E.
    Kikuyu social and political institutions. London, New York, published for the International African Institute by the Oxford University Press, 1956, $2.40.

864. Lawrence, J. C. D.
    The Iteso; fifty years of change in a Nilo-Hamitic tribe of Uganda. With a foreword by Sir Andrew Cohen. London, New York, Oxford University Press, 1957, $5.80.

865. Leakey, Louis Seymour Bazett
    Mau Mau and the Kikuyu. London, Methuen, 1952, 7/6.

866. Leakey, Louis Seymour Bazett
    Olduvai Gorge; a report on the evolution of the hand-axe culture in beds I-IV. With chapters on the geology and fauna by Hans Reck and A. T. Hopwood. Cambridge, University Press, 1951, $9.50.

867. Leakey, Louis Seymour Bazett
    The stone age cultures of Kenya colony . . . with appendices by J. D. Solomon, C. E. P. Brooks, A. T. Hopwood, H. C. Beck and M. Connolly. Cambridge, University Press, 1931, $9.50.

868. Leakey, Louis Seymour Bazett
    The stone age races of Kenya . . . with appendices by T. W. P. Lawrence, Sir Grafton Elliott-Smith, Sir F. Colyer, and L. S. B. Leakey. London, Oxford University Press, H. Milford, 1935. Out of print; ca. $10.00.

869. Lewis, I. M.
    Peoples of the Horn of Africa: Somali, Afar, and Saho. London, International African Institute, 1955. (Ethnographic Survey of Africa: north-eastern Africa, pt. 1.) 21/-.

870. MacMichael, Harold Alfred
         The tribes of the northern and central Kordofan. Cambridge,
      University Press, 1912. Out of print; ca. $5.00.

871. Mair, Lucy Philips
         An African people in the twentieth century. London, Rout-
      ledge, 1934. Out of print; ca. $4.00.

872. Malcolm, Donald Wingfield
         Sukumaland: an African people and their country; a study of
      land use in Tanganyika. London, New York, published for the
      International African Institute by the Oxford University Press,
      1953, $5.20.

873. Middleton, John
         The central tribes of the North-eastern Bantu; the Kikuyu,
      including Embu, Meru, Mbere, Chuka, Mwimbi, Tharaka, and
      the Kamba of Kenya. London, International African Institute, 1953.
      (Ethnographic Survey of Africa: East central Africa, pt. 5.) Out
      of print; ca. $2.00.

      Middleton, John
      Lugbara religion. See no. 222.

874. Nadel, Siegfried Frederick
         The Nuba; an anthropological study of the hill tribes in
      Kordofan. With a foreword by Sir Hubert Huddleston. London,
      New York, Oxford University Press, 1947. Out of print; ca.
      $6.00.

875. O'Brien, Terence Patrick
         The prehistory of Uganda Protectorate. With a chapter on
      the Pleistocene succession, by J. D. Solomon and an appendix
      on the mammalian fossils, by A. Tindell Hopwood. Cambridge,
      University Press, 1939, $10.00.

876. Perham, Margery Freda
         The government of Ethiopia. London, Faber & Faber, 1948, out
      of print; New York, Oxford University Press, 1948, $4.80.

877. Prins, Adriaan Hendrik Johan
         The coastal tribes of the north-eastern Bantu (Pokomo, Nyika,
      and Teita). London, International African Institute, 1952.
      (Ethnographic survey of Africa: east central Africa, pt. 3.)
      10/6.

878. Prins, Adriaan Hendrik Johan
         East African age-class systems; an inquiry into the social
      order of Galla, Kipsigis, and Kikuyu. Groningen, Wolters, 1953,
      Glds. 7.90.
         U. S. distribuotr: Gregory Lounz, New York, $3.50.

879. Raum, Otto Friedrich
        Chaga childhood; a description of indigenous education in an
        east African tribe. With an introduction by W. Bryant Mumford.
        London, New York, published for the International Institute of
        African Languages and Cultures by the Oxford University Press,
        1940. Out of print; ca. $6.00.

880. Richards, Audrey Isabel, ed.
        East African chiefs; a study of political development in some
        Uganda and Tanganyika tribes. London, published for the East
        African Institute of Social Research by Faber & Faber, 1960, 42/-;
        New York, Praeger, 1960, $10.00.

881. Richards, Audrey Isabel, ed.
        Economic development and tribal change; a study of immigrant
        labour in Buganda. Cambridge, published for the East African
        Institute of Social Research by Heffer, 1954, 30/-.

882. Roscoe, John
        The Baganda; an account of their native customs and beliefs.
        London, Macmillan, 1911. Out of print; ca. $8.00.

883. Roscoe, John
        The Bagesu and other tribes of the Uganda protectorate; the third
        part of the report of the Mackie ethnological expedition to central
        Africa. Cambridge, University Press, 1924, $5.50.

884. Roscoe, John
        The Bakitara or Banyoro; the first part of the report of the
        Mackie ethnological expedition to central Africa. Cambridge,
        University Press, 1923, $7.50.

885. Roscoe, John
        The Banyankole; the second part of the report of the Mackie
        ethnological expedition to central Africa. Cambridge, University
        Press, 1923, $5.00.

886. Ruud, Jörgen
        Taboo; a study of the Malagasy fady. (Translated from the
        Norwegian.) Oslo, Oslo University Press, 1959, 27.50 Kr.
        U. S. distributor: New York, Humanities Press, $7.50.

887. Schlippe, Pierre de
        Shifting cultivation in Africa; the Zande system of agriculture.
        London, Routledge & Kegan Paul, 1956, £2/2/-.

888. Seligman, Charles Gabriel, and Brenda Z. Seligman
        Pagan tribes of the Nilotic Sudan. London, Routledge, 1932,
        £2/10/-.

889. Southall, Aidan William
        Alur society: a study in processes and types of domination.
        Cambridge, Heffer, 1956, 30/-.

890. Southall, Aidan William, and Peter C. W. Gutkind
        Townsmen in the making: Kampala and its suburbs. Kampala,
East African Institute of Social Research, 1956. (East African
Studies, no. 9.) 5/-.

891. Trimmingham, John Spencer
        Islam in Ethiopia. London, New York, Oxford University Press,
1952, $4.40.

892. Trimmingham, John Spencer
        Islam in the Sudan. London, New York, Oxford University
Press, 1949. Out of print; ca. $6.00.

893. Ullendorff, Edward
        The Ethiopians; an introduction to country and people. London,
New York, Oxford University Press, 1960, $4.80.

894. Wagner, Günter
        The Bantu of North Kavirondo. London, New York, published
for the International African Institute by the Oxford University
Press, 1949-1956; 2 v.; v. 1, $8.35; v. 2, $5.80. (V. 2, Economic
life, ed. by L. P. Mair.)

895. Wieschhoff, Heinrich Albert
        The Zimbabwe-Monomatapa culture in southeast Africa.
Menasha, Wis., Banta, 1941. (General Series in Anthropology,
no. 8.) Out of print; ca. $3.00.

896. Wilson, Monica (Hunter)
        Communal rituals of the Nyakyusa. London, New York, pub-
lished for the International African Institute by the Oxford University Press, 1959, $5.60.

897. Wilson, Monica (Hunter)
        Good company: a study of Nyakyusa age-villages. London, New
York, published for the International African Institute by the Oxford University Press, 1951. Out of print; ca. $5.00.

898. Wilson, Monica (Hunter)
        Rituals of kinship among the Nyakyusa. London, New York,
published for the International African Institute by the Oxford
University Press, 1957, $5.60.

899. Winter, Edward Henry
        Beyond the mountains of the moon; the lives of four Africans.
Urbana, University of Illinois Press, 1959, $5.50 (on the Amba
of Uganda).

900. Winter, Edward Henry
        Bwamba; a structural-functional analysis of patrilineal society.
Cambridge, published for the East African Institute of Social Research by Heffer, 1956, 30/-.

d. Central

901. Barnes, James Albert
      Politics in a changing society; a political history of the Fort
      Jameson Ngoni. Cape Town, New York, published for the Rhodes-
      Livingstone Institute by Oxford University Press, 1954. Present
      publisher: Manchester University Press, 30/-.
      U. S. distributor: New York, Humanities Press, $6.00.

902. Brelsford, William Vernon
      The tribes of Northern Rhodesia. Lusaka, Northern Rhodesia,
      Govt. Printer, 1956, ca. $3.00.

903. Clark, John Desmond
      The Stone Age cultures of Northern Rhodesia, with particular
      reference to the cultural and climatic succession in the upper
      Zambesi Valley and its tributaries. With a chapter on the geol-
      ogy by F. Dixey and appendixes by H. B. S. Cooke, L. H. Wells
      And Geoffrey Bond. Claremont, Cape, South African Archaeologi-
      cal Society, 1950, 21/-.

904. Colson, Elizabeth
      Marriage and the family among the plateau Tonga of North-
      ern Rhodesia. Manchester, published on behalf of the Rhodes-
      Livingstone Institute, Northern Rhodesia by Manchester University
      Press, 1958, 42/-.
      U. S. distributor: Humanities Press, New York, $8.50.

905. Colson, Elizabeth, and Max Gluckman, eds.
      Seven tribes of British Central Africa. London, New York,
      published on behalf of the Rhodes-Livingstone Institute, Northern
      Rhodesia by Oxford University Press, 1951, 42/-.

906. Colson, Elizabeth
      Social organization of the Gwembe Tonga. Manchester, Man-
      chester University Press, 1960. (Rhodes-Livingstone Institute,
      Northern Rhodesia. Human problems of Kariba series, v. 1.)
      35/-.
      U. S. distributor: New York, Humanities Press, $6.50.

907. Cunnison, Ian George
      Luapula peoples of Northern Rhodesia: custom and history in
      tribal politics. Manchester, published on behalf of the Rhodes-
      Livingstone Institute, Northern Rhodesia, by Manchester Univer-
      sity Press, 1959, 35/-.
      U. S. distributor: Humanities Press, New York, $6.50.

908. Epstein, Arnold Leonard
      Politics in an urban African community. Manchester, published
      on behalf of the Rhodes-Livingstone Institute by Manchester Uni-
      versity Press, 1958, 28/-.
      U. S. distributor: New York, Humanities Press, $5.50.

909. Gann, L. H.
    The birth of a plural society; the development of Northern
    Rhodesia under the British South Africa Company, 1894-1914.
    Manchester, published on behalf of the Rhodes-Livingstone Insti-
    tute, Northern Rhodesia, by Manchester University Press, 1958,
    25/-.
    U. S. distributor: New York, Humanities Press, $5.00.

910. Gelfand, Michael
    Medicine and magic of the Mashona. With a foreword by Rob-
    ert Tredgold. Capetown, Juta, 1956. No price. Estimate: $4.00.

911. Gluckman, Max
    The judicial process among the Barotse of Northern Rhodesia.
    Manchester, Manchester University Press, 1955, 37/6; Glencoe,
    Ill., Free Press, 1955, $7.50.

912. Holleman, J. F.
    Shona customary law, with reference to kinship, marriage, the
    family and the estate. Cape Town, New York, Oxford University
    Press, 1952, $6.75.

913. Merriam, Alan P.
    Congo: background of conflict. Evanston, Ill., Northwestern
    University Press, 1961. (Northwestern University African Studies,
    no. 6.) $6.00.

914. Mitchell, J. Clyde
    The Kalela dance; aspects of social relationships among urban
    Africans in Northern Rhodesia. Manchester, published on behalf
    of the Rhodes-Livingstone Institute by the Manchester University
    Press, 1956. (Rhodes-Livingstone Papers, no. 27.) 7/6.

915. Mitchell, J. Clyde
    The Yao village; a study in the social structure of a Nyasa-
    land tribe. Manchester, published on behalf of the Rhodes-Living-
    stone Institute, by Manchester University Press, 1956, 30/-.
    U. S. distributor: New York, Humanities Press, $6.00.

916. Read, Margaret
    Children of their fathers; growing up among the Ngoni of
    Nyasaland. London, Methuen, 1959, 18/-; New Haven, Yale Uni-
    versity Press, 1960, $4.75.

917. Read, Margaret
    The Ngoni of Nyasaland. London, New York, published for the
    International African Institute by Oxford University Press, 1956,
    $5.60.

918. Richards, Audrey Isabel
    Chisungu; a girls' initiation ceremony among the Bemba of
    Northern Rhodesia. London, Faber & Faber, 1956, 42/-; New York,
    Grove Press, 1956, $6.50.

919. Richards, Audrey Isabel
      Hunger and work in a savage tribe; a functional study of nutri-
      tion among the southern Bantu. With a preface by B. Malinowski.
      Glencoe, Ill., Free Press, 1948, $3.50.

920. Richards, Audrey Isabel
      Land, labour and diet in Northern Rhodesia; an economic study
      of the Bemba tribe. London, New York, published for the Inter-
      national Institute of African Languages and Cultures by the Oxford
      University Press, 1939 (reprinted 1961), 42/-.

921. Shepperson, George, and Thomas Price
      Independent African; John Chilembwe and the origins, setting,
      and significance of the Nyasaland native rising of 1915. Edinburgh,
      University Press, 1958. (Edinburgh University Publications; His-
      tory, Philosophy, and Economics, no. 8.) 50/-.
      U. S. distributor: Chicago, Quadrangle Books, $10.00.

922. Turner, V. W.
      Schism and continuity in an African society; a study of Ndembu
      village life. Manchester, published on behalf of the Rhodes-Living-
      stone Institute, Northern Rhodesia, by Manchester University Press,
      1957, 35/-.
      U. S. distributor: New York, Humanities Press, $6.50.

923. Watson, William
      Tribal cohesion in a money economy; a study of the Mambwe
      people of Northern Rhodesia. Manchester, published on behalf of
      the Rhodes-Livingstone Institute, Northern Rhodesia by Manchester
      University Press, 1958, 30/-.
      U. S. distributor: New York, Humanities Press, $6.00.

      Wilson, Godfrey, and Monica (Hunter) Wilson
      The analysis of social change, based on observations in central
      Africa. See no. 377.

      e. South

924. Ashton, Hugh
      The Basuto. London, New York, published for the International
      African Institute by the Oxford University Press, 1952, $5.60.

925. Bleek, Dorothea F.
      The Naron, a Bushman tribe of the central Kalahari. Cam-
      bridge, University Press, 1928. Out of print? ca. $4.00.

      Broom, Robert, and G. W. H. Schepers
      The South African fossil ape-man, the Australopithecinae. See
      no. 499.

Broom, Robert, J. T. Robinson, and G. W. H. Schepers
Sterkfontein ape-man Plesianthropus. See no. 500.

Broom, Robert, and J. T. Robinson
Swartkrans ape-man, Paranthropus crassidens. See no. 501.

926. Bryant, Alfred T.
The Zulu people, as they were before the white man came.
Pietermaritzburg, Shuter & Shooter, 1949, 35/-.

927. Caton-Thompson, Gertrude
The Zimbabwe culture; ruins and reactions. Oxford, Clarendon
Press, 1931. In print? ca. $10.00.

928. Clark, John Desmond
The prehistory of southern Africa. Harmondsworth, Middlesex,
Penguin, 1959. (Pelican Books, A458.) $1.50.

Dart, Raymond Arthur
The osteodontokeratic culture of Australopithecus prometheus.
See no. 509.

929. Gluckman, Max
Rituals of rebellion in south-east Africa. Manchester, Man-
chester University Press, 1954. (The Frazer Lecture, 1952.)
In print? ca. $1.00.

930. Hellmann, Ellen, ed.
Handbook on race relations in South Africa . . . assisted by
Leah Abrahams. Published for the South African Institute of
Race Relations. Cape Town, New York, Oxford University Press,
1949. Out of print; ca. $10.00.

931. Junod, Henri Alexandre
The life of a South African tribe. 2d ed. rev. and enl. London, Macmillan, 1927. Out of print; ca. $30.00.

932. Krige, Eileen (Jensen), and Jacob Daniel Krige
The realm of a rain-queen, a study of the pattern of Lovedu
society . . . with a foreword by the Rt. Hon. Field-Marshal J. C.
Smuts. London, New York, published for the International African
Institute by the Oxford University Press, 1943, $5.20.

933. Krige, Eileen (Jensen)
The social system of the Zulus. 3d ed. Pietermaritzburg,
Shuter & Shooter, 1957, 42/-.

934. Kuper, Hilda
An African aristocracy; rank among the Swazi of Bechuanaland.
London, New York, published for the International African Institute
by Oxford University Press, 1947 (reprinted 1961), 35/-.

935. Kuper, Hilda
The uniform of colour, a study of white-black relationships
in Swaziland. Johannesburg, Witwatersrand University Press,
1947, 10/-.

936. Kuper, Leo, Hilstan Watts, and Ronald Davies
Durban: a study in racial ecology. With an introd. by Alan
Paton. London, Cape, 1958, 21/-; New York, Columbia Univer-
sity Press, 1958, $3.75.

937. Longmore, Laura
The dispossessed; a study of the sex-life of Bantu women
in urban areas in and around Johannesburg. London, Cape,
1959, 30/-.
U. S. distributor: Humanities Press, New York, $6.00.

938. Marais, Johannes Stephanus
The Cape colored people, 1652-1937. London, New York,
Longmans, Green, 1939, out of print; Johannesburg, Witwaters-
rand University Press, 1957, 22/6.

939. Marwick, Brian Allan
The Swazi; an ethnographic account of the natives of the
Swaziland protectorate. Cambridge, University Press, 1940.
Out of print; ca. $5.00.

940. Patterson, Sheila
Color and culture in South Africa; a study of the status of
the Cape coloured people within the social structure of the
Union of South Africa. London, Routledge & Kegan Paul, 1953.
(International Library of Sociology and Social Reconstruction.)
Out of print; ca. $6.00.

941. Patterson, Sheila
The last trek; a study of the Boer people and the Afrikaner
nation. London, Routledge & Kegan Paul, 1957, £1/8/-.
U. S. distributor: Hillary House, New York, $5.50.

Robinson, John Talbot
The dentition of the Australopithecinae. See no. 530.

942. Robinson, K. R.
Khami Ruins; report on excavations undertaken for the Commission for the Preservation of Natural and Historical Monuments and Relics, Southern Rhodesia, 1947-1955. With reports
by G. Bond and E. Voce. Cambridge, University Press, 1959,
$7.50.

943. Schapera, Isaac, ed.
The Bantu-speaking tribes of South Africa; an ethnographical
survey, edited for the (South African) Inter-university committee
for African studies. Contributors: Raymond A. Dart, Clement

M. Doke, and others. London, Routledge, 1937. £1/15/-.
U. S. distributor: New York, Humanities Press, $7.50.

944. Schapera, Isaac
Government and politics in tribal societies. London, Watts,
1956 (Josiah Mason Lectures). 21/-.
U. S. distributor: New York, Humanities Press, $4.50.

Schapera, Isaac
A handbook of Tswana law and custom. See no. 199.

945. Schapera, Isaac
The Khoisan peoples of South Africa; Bushmen and Hotten-
tots. London, Routledge, 1930, £1/15/-.

946. Schapera, Isaac
Married life in an African tribe . . . with an introduction
by Bronislaw Malinowski. London, Faber & Faber, 1940; New
York, Sheridan House, 1941. Out of print; ca. $4.00.

947. Schapera, Isaac
Migrant labour and tribal life, a study of conditions in the
Bechuanaland Protectorate. London, New York, Oxford Univer-
sity Press, 1947. Out of print; ca. $4.00.

948. Schoeman, Pieter Johannes
Hunters of the desert land; illustrated by E. Toussaint van
Hove. Cape Town, Timmins, 1958, 17/6.

949. Stayt, Hugh Arthur
The Bavenda . . . with an introduction by Mrs. A. W. Hoernlé.
London, published for the International African Institute by
Oxford University Press, H. Milford, 1931. Out of print; ca.
$10.00.

950. Sundkler, Bengt Gustaf Malcolm
Bantu prophets in South Africa. 2d ed. London, New York,
published for the International African Institute by the Oxford
University Press, 1961, $4.80.

951. Thomas, Elizabeth Marshall
The harmless people. 1st ed. New York, Knopf, 1959,
$4.75. (On the Bushmen.)

952. Wilson, Monica (Hunter)
Reaction to conquest; effects of contact with Europeans on
the Pondo of South Africa. With an introduction by General
the Right Hon. J. C. Smuts. 2d ed. London, Oxford University
Press, 1961. $6.75.

D. Asia

a. Siberia

953. Bogoraz, Vladimir Germanovich
     The Chukchee, by Waldemar Bogoras. Leiden, Brill; New York,
     G. E. Stechert, 1904-1909. (Memoir of the American Museum of
     natural history, v. 11.) (Publications of the Jesup north Pacific
     expedition, v. 7.) 3 v. Out of print.

954. Bogoraz, Vladimir Germanovich
     The Eskimo of Siberia, by Waldemar Bogoras. Leiden, Brill;
     New York, Stechert, 1913. (Memoirs of the American Museum of
     Natural History, v. 12.) (Publications of the Jesup north Pacific
     expedition, v. 8, pt. 3.) Out of print.

955. Donner, Kai
     Among the Samoyed in Siberia. Translated by Rinehart Kyler,
     edited by Genevieve A. Highland. New Haven, Human Relations
     Area Files, 1954. (Behavior Science Translations.) $2.50.

956. Jakobson, Roman, Gerta Hüttl-Worth, and John Fred Beebe
     Paleosiberian peoples and languages; a bibliographic guide. New
     Haven, HRAF Press, 1957. (Behavior Science Bibliographies.) $5.50.

957. Jochelson, Vladimir Il'ich
     The Yakut, by Waldemar Jochelson. New York city, The Ameri-
     can Museum of Natural History, 1933. (Anthropological Papers of
     the American Museum of Natural History. v. 33, pt. 2.) Out of print?
     ca. $4.00.

958. Jochelson, Vladimir Il'ich
     The Yukaghir and the Yukaghirized Tungus, by Waldemar Jochel-
     son. Leiden, Brill, New York, Stechert, 1910-1926. 3 v. (Ameri-
     can Museum of Natural History. Memoirs, v. 13, pt. 1-2.) (Jesup
     north Pacific expedition. Publications, v. 9, pt. 1-3.) Pt. 1, out of
     print; pt. 2, Gld. 21.-; pt. 3, Gld. 15.75.

959. Kolarz, Walter
     The peoples of the Soviet Far East. New York, Praeger, 1954,
     out of print; London, Philip, 1954, 15/6.

960. Michael, Henry N.
     The Neolithic age in eastern Siberia. Philadelphia, American
     Philosophical Society, 1958. (Transactions of the American Philo-
     sophical Society, new ser., v. 48, pt. 2.) $2.50.

961. Okladnikov, Aleksei Pavlovich
     Ancient population of Siberia and its cultures. Cambridge, Mass.,
     Peabody Museum, 1959. (Harvard University. Peabody Museum of
     Archaeology and Ethnology. Russian translation Series, v. 1, no. 1.)
     $3.50.

962. Spiridonov, Nikolai
     Snow people (Chukchee) by Taeki Odulok (pseud.). New Haven,
     Human Relations Area Files, 1954. (Behavior Science Transla-
     tions.) $2.00.

     b. Central

963. Aberle, David Friend
     The kinship system of the Kalmuk Mongols. Albuquerque, Uni-
     versity of New Mexico Press, 1953. (University of New Mexico
     Publications in Anthropology, no. 8.) $1.00.

964. Bacon, Elizabeth E.
     Obok, a study of social structure in Eurasia. New York, Wen-
     ner-Gren Foundation for Anthropological Research, 1958. (Viking
     Fund Publications in Anthropology, no. 25.) $4.00.

965. Bunak, Viktor Valerianovich, G. F. Debets, and M. G. Levin
     Contributions to the physical anthropology of the Soviet Union
     . . . with contributions by M. G. Abdushelishvili and others. Cam-
     bridge, Mass., Peabody Museum, 1960. (Harvard University. Pea-
     body Museum of Archaeology and Ethnology. Russian Translation
     Series, v. 1, no. 2.) $4.50.

966. Caroe, Sir Olaf Kirkpatrick
     Soviet empire; the Turks of Central Asia and Stalinism. Lon-
     don, New York, Macmillan, 1953. Out of print; ca. $5.00.

967. Carrasco Pizana, Pedro
     Land and polity in Tibet. Seattle, University of Washington
     Press, 1959. (American Ethnological Society Publication.) $5.75.

968. Czaplicka, Marie Antoinette
     The Turks of Central Asia in history and at the present day,
     an ethnological inquiry into the Pan-Turanian problem, and biblio-
     graphical material relating to the early Turks and the present
     Turks of Central Asia. Oxford, Clarendon Press, 1918. Out of
     print; ca. $7.00.

969. Ekvall, Robert Brainerd
     Cultural relations on the Kansu-Tibetan border. Chicago, Uni-
     versity of Chicago Press, 1939. (University of Chicago Publica-
     tions in Anthropology. Occasional papers, no. 1.) Out of print;
     ca. $3.00.

970. Hudson, Alfred E.
     Kazak social structure. New Haven, published for the Depart-
     ment of Anthropology, Yale University, by the Yale University
     Press; London, H. Milford, Oxford University Press, 1938. (Yale
     University Publications in Anthropology, no. 20.) Out of print;
     ca. $3.00.

971. Jochelson, Vladimir Il'ich
      Peoples of Asiatic Russia. New York, American Museum of
      Natural History, 1928. Out of print; ca. $4.00.

972. Krader, Lawrence, ed.
      Handbook of Central Asia. New Haven, Human Relations Area
      Files, 1956, 3 v. (Human Relations Area Files. Subcontractor's
      monograph, HRAF-49. American U.-1.) No price; ca. $10.00.

973. Rice, Tamara (Abelson) Talbot
      The Scythians. London, Thames and Hudson, 1957, 25/-; New
      York, Praeger, 1957. (Ancient Peoples and Places.) $6.50.

974. Stubel, Hans
      Mewu Fantzu; a Tibetan tribe of Kansu. Translated from the
      German for the Human Relations Area Files by Frieda Schutze.
      New Haven, HRAF Press, 1958. (Behavior Science Translations.)
      $2.75.

975. Vreeland, Herbert Harold
      Mongol community and kinship structure. 2d ed. New Haven,
      Human Relations Area Files, 1957. (Behavior Science Mono-
      graphs.) $3.50.

      c. South

976. Archer, William George
      The vertical man; a study in primitive Indian sculpture. Lon-
      don, Allen & Unwin, 1947, 15/-.
      U. S. distributor: Macmillan, New York, $3.50.

977. Baden-Powell, Baden Henry
      The Indian village community. New Haven, HRAF Press, 1957
      (Behavior Science Reprints.) $3.95.

978. Bailey, Frederick George
      Caste and the economic frontier; a village in highland Orissa.
      Manchester, Manchester University Press, 1957, 35/-.
      U. S. distributor: New York, Humanities Press, $6.50.

979. Bailey, Frederick George
      Tribe, caste, and nation; a study of political activity and poli-
      tical change in highland Orissa. Manchester, Manchester Univer-
      sity Press, 1960, 35/-.
      U. S. distributor: New York, Humanities Press, $6.50.

980. Barth, Fredrik
      Indus and Swat Kohistan; an ethnographic survey. Oslo, Forenede
      Trykkerier, 1956. (Oslo. Universitet. Etnografiske Museum.
      Studies honouring the centennial of Universitetets Etnografiske
      Museum, Oslo, 1857-1957, v. 2.) Estimate: $2.00.

981. Barth, Fredrik
Political leadership among Swat Pathans. London, University
of London, Athlone Press, 1959. (London School of Economics.
Monographs on Social Anthropology, no. 19.) 25/-.
U. S. distributor: New York, Humanities Press, $5.00.

982. Basham, Arthur Llewellyn
The wonder that was India; a survey of the culture of the
Indian sub-continent before the coming of the Muslims. London,
Sidgwick & Jackson, 1954, 45/-.
U. S. distributor: New York, Macmillan, $9.00.
Paper: New York, Grove Press, 1959. (Evergreen Encyclopedia,
v. 1 [E-145].) $3.95.

983. Carstairs, G. Morris
The twice-born; a study of a community of high-caste Hindus.
With a pref. by Margaret Mead. London, Hogarth Press, 1957. Out
of print; Bloomington, Indiana University Press, 1958, $6.50.

984. Chicago. University. College.
Introduction to the civilization of India; changing dimensions of
Indian society and culture. Chicago, Syllabus Division. University
of Chicago Press, 1957. ca. $8.00.

985. Conference on Traditional Cultures, Ceylon University, 1956
Some aspects of traditional Sinhalese culture; a symposium
edited by Ralph Pieris. Peradeniya, 1956. Estimate: $2.00.

986. Culshaw, W. J.
Tribal heritage; a study of the Santals. London, Lutterworth
Press, 1949 (Lutterworth Library, v. 34. Missionary Research
Series, no. 15.) Out of print; ca. $4.00.

987. Davies, Cuthbert Collin
An historical atlas of the Indian peninsula. 2d ed. Madras,
New York, Oxford University Press, 1959, $1.10.

988. Davis, Kingsley
The population of India and Pakistan. Princeton, Princeton
University Press, 1951, $7.50.

989. De Bary, William Theodore, ed.
Sources of Indian tradition. Compiled by Wm. Theodore De
Bary and others. New York, Columbia University Press, 1958.
(Records of civilization: sources and studies, 56. Introduction
to oriental civilizations.) $7.50.

990. Desai, Akshayakumar Ramanlal
Rural sociology in India. Rev. ed. Bombay, Indian society of
agricultural economics, 1959. Estimate: $4.00.

De Terra, H. and T. Thomson
Studies on the ice age in India. See no. 389.

991.   Dube, Shyama Charan
       Indian village. Foreword by Morris Edward Opler. Ithaca,
       N. Y., Cornell University Press, 1955. Out of print; London,
       Routledge & Kegan Paul, 1955. (International Library of Sociology
       and Social Reconstruction.) £1/5/-.
       U. S. distributor: Humanities Press, New York, $5.00.

992.   Dube, Shyama Charan
       India's changing villages; human factors in community devel-
       opment. London, Routledge & Kegan Paul, 1958. (International
       Library of Sociology and Social Reconstruction.) £1/15/-;
       Ithaca, N. Y., Cornell University Press, 1958. $3.50.

993.   Dubois, Jean Antoine
       Hindu manners, customs and ceremonies, by the Abbé J. A.
       Dubois, tr. from the author's later French ms. and ed. with
       notes, corrections, and biography, by Henry K. Beauchamp . . .
       3d ed. Oxford, Clarendon Press, 1924.

994.   Dumont, Louis
       Hierarchy and marriage alliance in South Indian kinship.
       London, Royal Anthropological Institute of Great Britain and
       Ireland, 1957. (Royal Anthropological Institute of Great Britain
       and Ireland. Occasional papers, 12.) 10/-.

995.   Dumont, Louis
       Une sous-caste de l'Inde du Sud; organisation sociale et
       religion des Pramali Kallar. Paris, LaHaye, Mouton & Co.,
       1957, f. 32.- (Le monde d'outre-mer, passé et present.
       Études, 1.)
       U. S. distributor: Humanities Press, New York, $9.75.

996.   Eglar, Zekiye Suleyman
       A Punjabi village in Pakistan. New York, Columbia Univer-
       sity Press, 1960, $6.00.

997.   Elwin, Verrier
       The Baiga; with a foreword by J. H. Hutton. London, Murray,
       1939. Out of print; ca. $6.00.

998.   Elwin, Verrier
       Bondo highlander. Bombay, New York, Oxford University
       Press, 1950, $7.95.

999.   Elwin, Verrier
       Maria murder and suicide. With a foreword by Sir W. V.
       Grigson. 2d ed. Bombay, New York, Indian Branch, Oxford
       University Press, 1950, $3.30.

1000. Elwin, Verrier
       The Muria and their ghotul. Bombay, Oxford University Press,
       1947. Out of print; ca. $6.00.

1001.   Elwin, Verrier
        Myths of middle India. Bombay, New York, Indian Branch,
        Oxford University Press, 1949. (*His* Specimens of the oral
        literature of middle India, 4.) Out of print; ca. $5.00.

1002.   Elwin, Verrier
        The religion of an Indian tribe. Bombay, Oxford University
        Press, 1955, $6.55.

1003.   Fuchs, Stephen
        The children of Hari, a study of the Nimar Balahis in the
        Central Provinces of India. Vienna, Verlag Herold, 1950; New
        York, Praeger, 1951. (Wiener Beiträge zur Kulturgeschichte
        und Linguistik, v. 8.) Out of print? ca. $7.50.

1004.   Fuchs, Stephen
        The Gond and Bhumia of eastern Mandla. Bombay, New York,
        Asia Pub. House, 1960, Rs 28.50 (71/6).
        U. S. distributor: Taplinger, New York, $9.00.

1005.   Fürer-Haimendorf, Christoph von
        Aboriginal tribes of Hyderabad. London, Macmillan, 1943-
        v. 1, The Chenchus, jungle folk of the Deccan, out of print.
        V. 2, The Reddis of the Bison Hills, $8.00. V. 3, book 1, The
        Raj Gonds of Adilabad: myth and ritual, $8.00.
        U. S. distributor: New York, St. Martins Press.

1006.   Fürer-Haimendorf, Christoph von
        Himalayan barbary. London, Murray, 1955, 25/-; New York,
        Abelard-Schuman, 1956, $4.50.

1007.   Fürer-Haimendorf, Christoph von
        The naked Nagas, head-hunters of Assam in peace and war.
        Calcutta, Thacker, Spink, 1946. Out of print? ca. $7.50.

1008.   Fürer-Haimendorf, Elizabeth von, comp.
        An anthropological bibliography of South Asia, together with
        a directory of recent anthropological field work. With a fore-
        word by Christoph von Fürer-Haimendorf. Paris, Mouton, 1958
        (Le Monde d'outre-mer, passé et present. 4. ser.: bibliogra-
        phies, 3.) f. 76.-,
        U. S. distributor: New York, Humanities Press, $22.50.

1009.   Ghurye, Govind Sadashiv
        Caste and class in India. 2d ed. Bombay, Popular Book
        Depot, 1957, Rs. 16.25.
        U. S. distributor: New York, Heinman, $5.00.
        First ed. published in 1932 under title: Caste and race in
        India.

1010.   Gorer, Geoffrey
        Himalayan village; an account of the Lepchas of Sikkim. With
        an introduction by J. H. Hutton. London, Joseph, 1938. Out of
        print; about $9.00.

1011.   Griffiths, Walter G.
        The Kol tribe of central India. With an introduction by B. S.
        Guha. Calcutta, Royal Asiatic Society of Bengal, 1946. (Royal
        Asiatic Society of Bengal. Monograph Series, no. 2.) In print?
        Estimate: $4.00.

1012.   Hocart, Arthur Maurice
        Caste; a comparative study. London, Methuen, 1950, 15/-.

1013.   Honigmann, John Joseph
        Three Pakistan villages. Chapel Hill, Institute for Research
        in Social Science, University of North Carolina, 1958. No price.
        Estimate: $3.00.

1014.   Hutton, John Henry
        The Angami Nagas, with some notes on neighboring tribes.
        Published by direction of the Assam administration. London,
        Macmillan, 1921. Out of print; ca. $15.00.

1015.   Hutton, John Henry
        Caste in India; its nature, function, and origins. 2d ed.
        Bombay, New York, Indian Branch, Oxford University Press,
        1951. Out of print; ca. $6.00.

1016.   Hutton, John Henry
        The Sema Nagas . . . with maps and illustrations and a fore-
        word by Henry Balfour. Published by direction of the Assam
        government. London, Macmillan, 1921. Out of print; $15.00.

1017.   Ikram, Sheikh Mohamad, and Percival Spear, eds.
        The cultural heritage of Pakistan. Karachi, New York, Ox-
        ford University Press, 1955, $4.00.

1018.   Kapadia, Kanailal Motilal
        Marriage and family in India. 2d ed. Bombay, New York,
        Indian Branch, Oxford University Press, 1958, $4.00.

1019.   Karve, Irawati (Karmarkar)
        Kinship organisation in India. 1st ed. Poona, Deccan College
        Post-graduate and Research Institute, 1953. (Deccan College
        Monograph Series, 11.) Rs. 15.

1020.   Lalavihari De
        Bengal peasant life, by the Rev. Lal Behari Day. New ed.
        London, Macmillan, 1920. Out of print; ca. $6.00.
        First published in 1874 with title: Govinda Samanta; or the
        history of a Bengal Raiyat.

1021.   Leach, Edmund Ronald, ed.
        Aspects of caste in south India, Ceylon, and north-west Paki-
        stan. Cambridge, published for the Dept. of Archaeology and
        Anthropology at the University Press, 1960. (Cambridge papers
        in Social Anthropology, 2.) $3.50.

1022.   Leach, Edmund Ronald
        Pul Eliya, a village in Ceylon: a study of land tenure and
        kinship. Cambridge, University Press, 1961, $8.00.

1023.   Lewis, Oscar
        Village life in northern India; studies in a Delhi village with the
        assistance of Victor Barnouw. Urbana, University of Illinois Press,
        1958, $7.50.

1024.   MacKay, Ernest John Henry
        Early Indus civilizations. 2d ed., rev. and enl. by Dorothy
        Mackay. London, Luzac, 1948. Out of print; ca. $3.00. First
        published as The Indus civilization, 1935.

1025.   Majumdar, Dhirendra Nath
        The affairs of a tribe; a study in tribal dynamics. Lucknow,
        published for the Ethnographic and Folk Culture Society, U. P.,
        by Universal Publishers, 1950. In print? ca. $6.00. A new and
        enl. ed. of the author's A tribe in transition.

1026.   Majumdar, Dhirendra Nath
        Caste and communication in an Indian village. Bombay, Asia
        Pub. House, 1958.
        U. S. distributor: Taplinger, New York, $6.50.

1027.   Majumdar, Dhirendra Nath
        Races and cultures of India. 3d ed. Bombay, Asia Pub.
        House, 1958.
        U. S. distributor: Taplinger, New York, $6.95.

1028.   Mandelbaum, David Goodman
        Materials for a bibliography of the ethnology of India. Berkeley,
        Dept. of Anthropology, University of California, 1949. No price.

1029.   Maron, Stanley, ed.
        Pakistan: society and culture. Contributors: John Aird and
        others. New Haven, Human Relations Area Files, 1957. (Behavior
        Science Monographs.) Out of print; ca. $3.50.

1030.   Marriott, McKim
        Caste ranking and community structure in five regions of India
        and Pakistan. Poona, Deccan College Post-Graduate and Research
        Institute, 1960. (Deccan College monograph series, 23). Estimate:
        $2.00.

1031.   Marriott, McKim, ed.
        Village India; studies in the little community, papers by Alan R.
        Beals and others. Chicago, University of Chicago Press, 1955. (Com-
        parative Studies of Cultures and Civilizations) $6.50. (Published also
        as Memoir no. 83 of the American Anthropological Association.)

1032.   Mason, Philip
        Call the next witness, by Philip Woodruff (pseud.). New York,
        Harcourt, Brace, 1946. Out of print; ca. $3.00.

1033.   Mayer, Adrian C.
        Caste and kinship in central India; a village and its region.
London, Routledge & Kegan Paul, 1960. (International Library of
Sociology and Social Reconstruction.) 35/-; Berkeley and Los
Angeles, University of California Press, 1960, $6.00.

1034.   Mayer, Adrian C.
        Land and society in Malabar, with a pref. by Raymond Firth.
Bombay, New York, Indian Branch, Oxford University Press,
1952, $1.85.

1035.   Mills, James Philip
        The Ao Nagas . . . with a foreword by Henry Balfour . . . and
supplementary notes and bibliography by Dr. J. H. Hutton. Published by direction of the government of Assam. London, Macmillan, 1926. Out of print; ca. $6.00.

1036.   Mills, James Philip
        The Lhota Nagas . . . with an introduction and supplementary
notes by J. H. Hutton. Published by direction of the government
of Assam. London, Macmillan, 1922. Out of print; ca. $6.00.

1037.   Mills, James Philip
        The Rengma Nagas. Published by direction of the government
of Assam. London, Macmillan, 1937. Out of print; ca. $6.00.

1038.   Morgan, Kenneth William, ed.
        The religion of the Hindus. Contributors: D. S. Sarma and
others. New York, Ronald Press, 1953, $6.00.

1039.   Naik, T. B.
        The Bhils, a study. Delhi, Bharatiya Adimjati Sevak Sangh,
1956, Rs. 15.

1040.   Nath, V. V. S.
        Bhils of Ratanmals. Baroda, 1960. Estimate: $3.00.

1041.   Pieris, Ralph
        Sinhalese social organization; the Kandyan period. Colombo,
Ceylon University Press, 1956, Rs. 10.

1042.   Piggott, Stuart
        Some ancient cities of India. London, New York, Bombay,
G. Cumberlege, Oxford University Press, 1945, $0.80.

1043.   Prabhu, Pandhari-nath
        Hindu social organization; a study in socio-psychological and
ideological foundations. 3d ed. Bombay, Popular Book Depot,
1958, Rs. 20.00. First ed. published in 1940 under title: Hindu
social institutions.
        U. S. distributors: Heinman, New York, $6.00.

1044.   Radcliffe-Brown, Alfred Reginald
            The Andaman islanders. Glencoe, Ill., Free Press, 1948.
        Out of print; ca. $6.00. First published Cambridge, University
        Press, 1922; reprinted with additions, 1933.

1045.   Radhakrishnan, Sir Sarvepalli, and Charles A. Moore, eds.
            A source book in Indian philosophy. Princeton, N. J., Princeton
        University Press, 1957, $7.50.

1046.   Rivers, William Halse Rivers
            The Todas. London, New York, Macmillan, 1906. Out of print;
        ca. $8.00.

1047.   Roy, Sarat Chandra
            The Birhors: a little-known jungle tribe of Chota Nagpur.
        Ranchi (The author) 1925. In print? ca. $3.00.

1048.   Roy, Sarat Chandra
            The Mundas and their country . . . with an introduction by E. A.
        Gait. Calcutta, Jogendra Nath Sarkar at the City book society, 1912.
            Distributor: "Man in India" office, Ranchi, India; estimate: $4.00.

1049.   Roy, Sarat Chandra
            Oraon religion and customs. With an introduction by Colonel T.
        C. Hodson. Ranchi, "Man in India" office, 1928. In print; estimate:
        $4.00.

1050.   Ryan, Bryce
            Caste in modern Ceylon; the Sinhalese system in transition. New
        Brunswick, Rutgers University Press, 1953. Out of print; ca. $4.50.

1051.   Ryan, Bryce
            Sinhalese village . . . in collaboration with L. D. Jayasena and
        D. C. R. Wickremesinghe. Coral Gables, Fla., University of Miami
        Press, 1958, $3.00.

1052.   Seligman, Charles Gabriel, and Brenda Z. Seligman
            The Veddas. With a chapter by C. S. Myers . . . and an appendix
        by A. Mendis Gunasekara. Cambridge, University Press, 1911. Out
        of print; ca. $20.00.

1053.   Singer, Milton B., ed.
            Traditional India: structure and change. Philadelphia, American
        Folklore Society, 1959. (Publications of the American Folklore So-
        ciety; Bibliographical Series, v. 10.) $5.00. Also published as
        Journal of American Folklore, v. 71, no. 281.

1054.   The Economic Weekly.
            India's villages, edited by M. N. Srinivas. 2nd rev. ed.
        London, Asia Publishing House, 1960, 32/-.
            Essays by D. G. Mandelbaum, M. N. Srinivas, G. M. Car-
        stairs, and others originally published in the Economic Weekly
        of Bombay.

1055.   Srinivas, Mysore Narasimhachar
        Marriage and family in Mysore. Foreword by Rajakarya-
        praveena N. S. Subba Rao. Bombay, New Book, 1942. Out of
        print; ca. $5.00.

1056.   Srinivas, Mysore Narasimhachar
        Religion and society among the Coorgs of South India. Ox-
        ford, Clarendon Press, 1952, $5.60.

1057.   Subbarao, Bendapudi
        The personality of India; pre-and proto-historic foundation
        of India and Pakistan. 2d ed. Baroda, Faculty of Arts, Maha-
        raja Sayajirao University of Baroda, 1958. (M. S. University
        Archaeology Series, no. 3.) Rs. 15.

1058.   Thurston, Edgar
        Castes and tribes of southern India . . . assisted by K. Ranga-
        chari. Madras, Government Press, 1909, 7 v. ca. $60.00.

1059.   Tod, James
        Annals and antiquities of Rajast'han, or the central and west-
        ern Rajpoot states of India. With a pref. by Douglas Sladen.
        London, Routledge & Kegan Paul, 1957, 2 v., £2/10/-. First
        published 1829-1932.
        U. S. distributor: New York, Hillary House, $10.00.

1060.   Useem, John, and Ruth Hill Useem
        The Western-educated man in India; a study of his social
        roles and influence. New York, Dryden Press, 1955, $3.00.

        Weber, Max
        The religion of India. See no. 242.

1061.   Wheeler, Sir Robert Eric Mortimer
        Early India and Pakistan to Ashoka. London, Thames & Hud-
        son, 1959. 25/-; New York, Praeger, 1959, $6.50. (Ancient
        Peoples and Places, v. 12.)

1062.   Wheeler, Sir Robert Eric Mortimer
        The Indus civilization. 2d ed. Cambridge, University Press,
        1960. (Cambridge History of India. Supplementary volume.)
        22/6.

1063.   Wiser, Charlotte Melina (Viall), and William H. Wiser
        Behind mud walls. New York, Smith, 1930; New York, Friend-
        ship Press, 1946. Out of print; ca. $3.00.

1064.   Wiser, William Henricks
        The Hindu jajmani system, a socio-economic system inter-
        relating members of a Hindu village community in services.
        Lucknow, U. P., Lucknow Publishing House, 1936. Out of print?
        ca. $4.00.

d. Southeast, including Indonesia
    and the Philippines

1065.   Arnold, Guy
        Longhouse and jungle, an expedition to Sarawak. London,
        Chatto & Windus, 1959, 21/-.

1066.   Barton, Roy Franklin
        The half-way sun; life among the headhunters of the Philip-
        pines. New York, Brewer & Warren, 1930. Out of print; ca. $8.00.

1067.   Barton, Roy Franklin
        The Kalingas, their institutions and custom law. With an
        introd. by E. Adamson Hoebel. Chicago, University of Chicago
        Press, 1949. Out of print; ca. $4.00.

1068.   Barton, Roy Franklin
        The mythology of the Ifugaos. Philadelphia, American Folklore
        Society, 1955. (Memoirs of the American Folklore Society, v. 46.)
        $4.00.

1069.   Barton, Roy Franklin
        Philippine pagans; the autobiographies of three Ifugaos. Lon-
        don, Routledge, 1938. Out of print; ca. $8.00.

1070.   Barton, Roy Franklin
        The religion of the Ifugaos. Menasha, Wis., American Anthro-
        pological Assn., 1946. (Memoir series of the American Anthro-
        pological Association, no. 65.) $2.75.

1071.   Bateson, Gregory, and Margaret Mead
        Balinese character, a photographic analysis. New York, 1942.
        (New York Academy of Sciences. Special publication, 2.) Out of
        print; ca. $10.00.

1072.   Belo, Jane
        Bali: Rangda and Barong. New York, Augustin, 1949. (Mono-
        graphs of the American Ethnological Society, 16.) $2.75.

1073.   Belo, Jane
        Bali: temple festival. Locust Valley, N. Y., Augustin, 1953.
        (Monographs of the American Ethnological Society, 22.) $2.75.

1074.   Belo, Jane
        Trance in Bali. Pref. by Margaret Mead. New York, Colum-
        bia University Press, 1960, $7.50.

1075.   Benedict, Ruth (Fulton)
        Thai culture and behavior; an unpublished wartime study dated
        September, 1943. Ithaca, N. Y., Southeast Asia Program, Dept.
        of Far Eastern Studies, Cornell University, 1952. (Cornell Uni-
        versity Southeast Asia Program. Data papers, no. 4.) $1.00.

1076. Blanchard, Wendell
      Thailand: its people, its society, its culture . . . in collabora-
tion with Henry C. Ahalt and others. New Haven, HRAF Press,
1958. (Country Survey Series.) $6.50.

1077. Britton, Nancy Pence
      East of the sun. Edinburgh, Blackwood, 1956, 12/6. (On
Malaya.)

1078. Chicago. University. Dept. of Anthropology. Philippine Studies
      Program.
      Selected bibliography of the Philippines, topically arranged
and annotated. Prepared by the Philippine Studies Program . . .
Fred Eggan, director. Preliminary ed. New Haven, Human Relations Area Files, 1956. (Behavior Science Bibliographies.) $3.75.

1079. Cole, Fay Cooper
      The peoples of Malaysia. New York, D. Van Nostrand, 1945,
$6.25.

1080. Conklin, Harold C.
      Hanunóo agriculture; a report on an integral system of shift-
ing cultivation in the Philippines. Rome, Food and Agriculture
Organization of the United Nations, 1957. (FAO Series on Shifting Cultivation, v. 2.) (FAO Forestry Development Paper, no. 12.)
$2.00.

1081. Covarrubias, Miguel
      The Island of Bali; with an album of photographs by Rose
Covarrubias. New York, Knopf, 1937, $12.50.

1082. Cunningham, Clark E.
      The postwar migration of the Toba-Bataks to East Sumatra.
New Haven, Yale University, Southeast Asia Studies, 1958. (Yale
University. Southeast Asia Studies. Cultural Report Series.) $3.50.

1083. deYoung, John E.
      Village life in modern Thailand. Berkeley and Los Angeles,
University of California Press, 1955, $5.50.

1084. Djamour, Judith
      Malay kinship and marriage in Singapore. London, University
of London, Athlone Press, 1959. (London School of Economics.
Monographs on Social Anthropology, no. 21.) 25/-.
      U. S. distributor: Humanities Press, New York, $5.00.

1085. Du Bois, Cora Alice
      The people of Alor; a social-psychological study of an East
Indian island . . .; with analyses by Abram Kardiner and Emil
Oberholzer. Cambridge, Havard University Press, 1960, $10.00.
Reprint of the 1944 ed. (Minneapolis, University of Minnesota
Press) with a new chapter, "Two decades later."
      Paper: New York, Harper, 1961. 2 v. (Harper Torchbooks,
TB 1042-1043.) v. 1, $1.95; v. 2, $1.75.

1086. Du Bois, Cora Alice
       Social forces in southeast Asia. Cambridge, Mass., Harvard
       University Press, 1959, $2.50.
       Three lectures delivered at Smith College in April 1947 (a
       reprinting of the text of the 1949 edition [Minneapolis, Univer-
       sity of Minnesota Press, 1949] with a new preface.)

1087. Elliott, Alan John Anthony
       Chinese spirit-medium cults in Singapore. London, published
       for the Dept. of Anthropology, London School of Economics and
       Political Science by Royal Anthropological Institute, 1955. (Lon-
       don School of Economics. Monographs on social anthropology,
       no. 14.) 18/-.
       U.S. distributor: Humanities Press, New York, $3.00.

1088. Embree, John Fee, and Lillian Ota Dotson
       Bibliography of the peoples and cultures of mainland South-
       east Asia. New Haven, Yale University Southeast Asia Studies,
       1950, $7.50.

1089. Evans, Ivor Hugh Norman
       Among primitive peoples in Borneo; a description of the lives,
       habits, and customs of the piratical head-hunters of North Borneo,
       with an account of interesting objects of prehistoric antiquity
       discovered in the island. London, Seeley, Service, 1922. Out
       of print; ca. $6.00.

1090. Evans, Ivor Hugh Norman
       The Negritos of Malaya. Cambridge, University Press, 1937.
       Out of print; ca. $6.00.

1091. Evans, Ivor Hugh Norman
       Papers on the ethnology and archaeology of the Malay Penin-
       sula. Cambridge, University Press, 1927. Out of print; ca. $7.50.

1092. Evans, Ivor Hugh Norman
       Religion of the Tempasuk Dusuns of North Borneo. Cambridge,
       University Press, 1953, $13.50.

1093. Evans, Ivor Hugh Norman
       Studies in religion, folk-lore, and custom in British North
       Borneo and the Malay Peninsula. Cambridge, University Press,
       1923. Out of print; ca. $5.00.

1094. Firth, Raymond William
       Malay fishermen: their peasant economy. London, Kegan Paul,
       Trench, Trubner, 1946. Out of print; ca. $5.00.

1095. Fraser, Thomas M.
       Rusembilan: a Malay fishing village in southern Thailand.
       Ithaca, N. Y., Cornell University Press, 1960. (Cornell Studies
       in Anthropology.) $5.75.

1096.   Freedman, Maurice
        Chinese family and marriage in Singapore. London, H. M.
        Stationery Office, 1957. (Gt. Brit. Colonial Office. Colonial
        Research Studies, no. 20.) 30/8.

1097.   Freeman, J. D.
        Iban agriculture; a report on the shifting cultivation of hill
        rice by the Iban of Sarawak. London, H. M. Stationery Office,
        1955. (Gt. Brit. Colonial Office. Colonial Research Studies,
        no. 18.) 12/9.

1098.   Geddes, William Robert
        The Land Dayaks of Sarawak; a report on a social economic
        survey of the Land Dayaks of Sarawak presented to the Colonial
        Social Science Research Council. London, published by H. M.
        Stationery Office for the Colonial Office, 1954. (Colonial Re-
        search Studies, no. 14.) 32/6.

1099.   Geddes, William Robert
        Nine Dayak nights. Melbourne, New York, Oxford University
        Press, 1957, $5.50.

1100.   Geertz, Clifford
        The religion of Java. Glencoe, Ill., Free Press, 1960, $7.50.

1101.   Ginsburg, Norton Sydney, and Chester F. Roberts, Jr.
        Malaya. With the collaboration of Leonard Comber and others.
        Seattle, University of Washington Press, 1958. (American Ethno-
        logical Society Publication.) $6.75.

1102.   Gourou, Pierre
        The peasants of the Tonkin delta, a study of human geography.
        Translated by Richard R. Miller. New Haven, Human Relations
        Area Files, 1955, 2 v. (Behavior Science Translations.) $6.00.

1103.   Gullick, J. M.
        Indigenous political systems of western Malaya. London, Uni-
        versity of London, Athlone Press, 1958. (London School of Eco-
        nomics. Monographs on Social Anthropology, no. 17.) 25/-.
        U. S. distributor: New York, Humanities Press, $5.00.

        Haar, Barend ter
        Adat law in Indonesia. See no. 188.

1104.   Harrisson, Thomas Harnett
        World within; a Borneo story. London, Cresset Press,
        1959, 30/-.

1105.   Hart, Donn Vorhis
        The Cebuan Filipino dwelling in Caticugan: its construction
        and cultural aspects. New Haven, Yale University, Southeast
        Asia Studies, 1959. (Yale University. Southeast Asia Studies.
        Cultural Report Series.) $3.00.

1106.   Heekeren, H. R. van
         The bronze-iron age of Indonesia. 's-Gravenhage, Nijhoff,
         1958. (Verhandelingen van het Koniklijk Instituut voor Taal-,
         Land-en Volkenkunde, deel 22.) Cloth, Gld. 18.-; paper, Gld. 15.-.

1107.   Heekeren, H. R. van
         The stone age of Indonesia. 's-Gravenhage, Nijhoff, 1957.
         (Verhandelingen van het Koniklijk Instituut voor Taal-, Land-en
         Volkenkunde, deel 21.) Cloth, Gld. 18.-, paper, Gld. 15.-.

1108.   Human Relations Area Files, inc.
         Laos; its people, its society, its culture, by the staff and
         associates of the Human Relations Area Files. Editors: Frank
         M. LeBar and Adrienne Suddard. New Haven, HRAF Press,
         1960. (Survey of World Cultures, 8.) $6.50.

1109.   Human Relations Area Files, Inc.
         North Borneo, Brunei, Sarawak (British Borneo). New Haven,
         1956. (*Its* Country Survey Series.) Out of print; ca. $6.00.

1110.   Hurgronje, Christian Snouck
         The Achehnese. Tr. by the late A. W. S. O'Sullivan. Leiden,
         Brill; London, Luzac, 1906, 2 v., Gld. 20.-.

1111.   Izikowitz, Karl Gustav
         Lamet: hill peasants in French Indo-China. Goteborg, Elanders
         boktr., 1951. (Etnologiska Studier, 17.) 20 Kr.-.

1112.   Josselin de Jong, Patrick Edward de
         Minangkabau and Negri Sembilan; socio-political structure in
         Indonesia. The Hague, Nijhoff, 1952. Out of print; ca. $4.00.

1113.   Kaufman, Howard Keva
         Bangkhuad; a community study in Thailand. Locust Valley, N. Y.,
         published for the Association for Asian Studies by Augustin, 1960.
         (Monographs of the Association for Asian Studies, 10.) $5.50.

1114.   Kennedy, Raymond
         The ageless Indies. New York, John Day, 1942. Out of print;
         ca. $4.00.

1115.   Kennedy, Raymond
         Bibliography of Indonesian peoples and cultures. Rev. ed.
         Editors of rev. ed.: Thomas W. Maretzki and H. Th. Fischer.
         New Haven, Human Relations Area Files, 1955, 2 v. (Behavior
         Science Bibliographies.) $8.50.

1116.   Kingshill, Konrad
         Ku Daeng, the red tomb; a village study in northern Thailand.
         Chiangmai, Prince Royal's College; distributed by the Siam So-
         ciety, Bangkok, 1960; 35 baht ($1.67).

1116a. Kroeber, Alfred Louis
    Peoples of the Philippines. 2d ed., rev. New York, 1928
    (reprinted 1943). (American Museum of Natural History. Hand-
    book Series, no. 8.) Out of print; ca. $4.00.

1117. Leach, Edmund Ronald
    Political systems of highland Burma; a study of Kachin social
    structure. With a foreword by Raymond Firth. Published for
    the London School of Economics and Political Science. Cam-
    bridge, Harvard University Press, 1954, out of print; London,
    London School of Economics and Political Science, 1954.
    British distributor: London, Bell, 35/-.

1118. Madge, Charles
    Survey before development in Thai villages. New York, United
    Nations Secretariat, 1957. (United Nations Series on Community
    Organization and Development, no. 25.) No price.

1119. Mead, Margaret, and Frances Cooke Macgregor
    Growth and culture; a photographic study of Balinese child-
    hood. Based upon photos. by Gregory Bateson, analyzed in
    Gesell categories. New York, Putnam, 1951, $7.50.

1120. Milne, Mrs. Leslie
    The home of an eastern clan, a study of the Palaungs of the
    Shan estates. Oxford, Clarendon Press, 1924. Out of print; ca.
    $5.00.

1121. Movius, Hallam Leonard
    Early man and Pleistocene stratigraphy in southeast and east-
    ern Asia. Cambridge, Mass., The Museum, 1944. (Harvard Uni-
    versity. Peabody Museum of American Archaeology and Ethnology
    Papers, v. 19, no. 3.) Out of print; ca. $5.00.

1122. Movius, Hallam Leonard
    Lower palaeolithic cultures of southern and eastern Asia.
    Philadelphia, 1949. (American Philosophical Society. Transac-
    tions, new series, v. 38, pt. 4.) Out of print; ca. $3.00.

1123. Murdock, George Peter, ed.
    Social structure in Southeast Asia. Chicago, Quadrangle Books,
    1960. (Wenner-Gren Foundation for Anthropological Research.
    Viking Fund Publications in Anthropology, no. 29.) $5.00.

1124. Scott, Sir James George
    The Burman, his life and notions, by Shway Yoe (pseud?),
    London, Macmillan, 1910. Out of print; ca. $5.00.

1125. Skeat, Walter William
    Malay magic, being an introduction to the folklore and popular
    religion of the Malay peninsula, with a preface by C. O. Blagden.
    London and New York, Macmillan, 1900. Out of print; ca. $8.00.

1126.   Skeat, Walter William, and Charles Otto Blagden
        Pagan races of the Malay Peninsula. London, Macmillan,
        1906. 2 v. Out of print; ca. $10.00.

1127.   Skinner, George William
        Chinese society in Thailand: an analytical history. Ithaca,
        N. Y., Cornell University Press, 1957, $6.50.

1128.   Skinner, George William
        Leadership and power in the Chinese community of Thailand.
        Ithaca, N. Y., published for the Association for Asian Studies
        by Cornell University Press, 1958. (Monographs of the Asso-
        ciation for Asian Studies, 3.) $6.50.

1129.   Skinner, George William, ed.
        Local, ethnic, and national loyalties in village Indonesia; a
        symposium. New Haven, Yale University, Southeast Asia Studies,
        distributed in coöperation with the Institute of Pacific Relations,
        New York, 1959. (Yale University Southeast Asia Studies. Cul-
        tural Report Series, 8.) $2.00.

1130.   Steinberg, David J.
        Cambodia: its people, its society, its culture . . . in collab-
        oration with Chester A. Bain and others. Rev. for 1959 by Her-
        bert H. Vreeland. New Haven, HRAF Press, 1959. (Survey of
        World Cultures.) $7.00.

1131.   T'ien, Ju-k'ang
        The Chinese of Sarawak; a study of social structure. London,
        Dept. of Anthropology, London School of Economics and Political
        Science, 1953. (London School of Economics. Monographs on
        Social Anthropology, no. 12.) 18/-.
        U. S. distributor: New York, Humanities Press, $3.50.

1132.   Tirabutana, Prajuab
        A simple one, the story of a Siamese girlhood. Ithaca, N. Y.,
        Southeast Asia Program, Dept. of Far Eastern Studies, Cornell
        University, 1958. (Cornell University. Dept. of Far Eastern
        Studies. Southeast Asia Program. Data papers, no. 30.) $2.00.

1133.   Tweedie, Michael Willmer Forbes
        Prehistoric Malaya, Singapore, Donald Moore, 1957. (Back-
        ground to Malaya series, no. 6.) Estimate: $2.00.

1134.   Wells, Kenneth E.
        Thai Buddhism, its rites and activities. Bangkok, Thailand,
        Distributors: Christian Bookstore, 1960. Estimate: $3.00.

1135.   Wertheim, William Frederik
        Indonesian society in transition, a study of social change.
        2d, rev. ed. The Hague, van Hoeve, 1959, c1956, Gld. 15.-.
        (An extension of the author's The effects of western civiliza-
        tion on Indonesian society, 1950.)
        U. S. distributor: Institute of Pacific Relations, New York, $6.00.

1136.   Willmott, Donald Earl
        The Chinese of Semarang: a changing minority community in
        Indonesia. Ithaca, N. Y., Cornell University Press, 1960, $5.75.

        e. East

1137.   Abegglen, James C.
        The Japanese factory; aspects of its social organization.
        Glencoe, Ill., Free Press, 1958, $3.50.

1138.   Anesaki, Masaharu
        History of Japanese religion with special reference to the
        social and moral life of the nation. London, Kegan Paul, Trench,
        Trubner, 1930. Out of print; ca. $4.00.

1139.   Anesaki, Masaharu
        Nichiren, the Buddhist prophet. Cambridge, Harvard Univer-
        sity Press; London, H. Milford, Oxford University Press, 1916.
        Reprinted by Harvard, 1949. Out of print; ca. $3.50.

1140.   Ashton, William George
        Shinto (the way of the gods). London, New York, Longmans,
        Green, 1905. Out of print; ca. $2.00.

1141.   Batchelor, John
        Ainu life and lore; echoes of a departing race. Tokyo, Kyo-
        bunkwan, 1927; ca. $10.00.

1142.   Beardsley, Richard King
        Field guide to Japan. Washington, National Academy of Sci-
        ences, National Research Council, 1959. (National Research Coun-
        cil. Committee on International Anthropology. Field guide series,
        no. 3.) (National Research Council. Publication 716.) $1.25.

1143.   Beardsley, Richard King, John W. Hall, and Robert E. Ward
        Village Japan. Chicago, University of Chicago Press, 1959,
        $8.75.

1144.   Bellah, Robert Neelly
        Tokugawa religion; the values of pre-industrial Japan. Glencoe,
        Ill., Free Press, 1957, $5.00.

1145.   Benedict, Ruth (Fulton)
        The chrysanthemum and the sword; patterns of Japanese
        culture. Boston, Houghton Mifflin, 1946, $4.50.

1146.   Borton, Hugh, ed.
        Japan. Ithaca, Cornell University Press, 1951. Out of print;
        ca. $4.00. Articles first published in the 1951 ed. of the Encyclo-
        pedia Americana.

1147. Borton, Hugh
Peasant uprisings in Japan of the Tokugawa period. Tokyo, 1938. (Asiatic Society of Japan. Transactions, ser. 2, v. 16.) Out of print? estimate: $4.00.

Carter, Dagny (Olsen)
Four thousand years of China's art. See no. 251.

1148. Chang, Chung-li
The Chinese gentry; studies on their role in nineteenth-century Chinese society. Introd. by Franz Michael. Seattle, University of Washington Press, 1955, $5.75. (University of Washington Publications on Asia.)

1149. Cheng, Tê-k'un
Archaeological studies in Szechwan, conducted under the auspices of the Harvard-Yenching Institute and the West China Union University. Cambridge, University Press, 1957, $13.50.

1150. Cheng, Tê-k'un
Archaeology in China. Cambridge, Eng., Heffer, 1959- v. 1, Prehistoric China, 42/-; v. 2, Shang China, 84/-. vols. 1-2 of a projected 8 vol. work.

1151. Cohen, Jerome Bernard
Japan's economy in war and reconstruction; with a foreword by George Sansom. Issued under the auspices of the International Secretariat, Institute of Pacific Relations. Minneapolis, University of Minnesota Press, 1949, $7.50.

1152. Cornell, John Bilheimer, and Robert J. Smith
Two Japanese villages: Matsunagi, a Japanese mountain community; by John B. Cornell; Kurusu, a Japanese agricultural community, by Robert J. Smith. Ann Arbor, University of Michigan Press, 1956. (Center for Japanese Studies. Occasional papers, no. 5.) $6.00.

1153. Creel, Herrlee Glessner
The birth of China; a study of the formative period of Chinese civilization. London, Cape, 1936. Out of print; New York, Ungar, 1954, c1937, $7.50.

1154. Crook, Isabel, and David Crook
Revolution in a Chinese village, Ten Mile Inn. London, Routledge and Kegan Paul, 1959. (International Library of Sociology and Social Reconstruction.) £1/1/-.
U. S. distributor: New York, Humanities Press, $4.50.

1155. De Bary, William Theodore, ed.
Sources of Chinese tradition, compiled by Wm. Theodore de Bary, Wing-tsit Chan and Burton Watson. With contributions by Yi-pao Mei and others. New York, Columbia University Press, 1960. (Records of Civilization; Sources and Studies, 55. Introduction to oriental civilizations.) $7.50.

1156.   Dore, Ronald Philip
        City life in Japan; a study of a Tokyo ward. Berkeley and
        Los Angeles, University of California Press, 1958, $8.00. Lon-
        don, Routledge & Kegan Paul, 1958. (International Library of
        Sociology and Social Reconstruction.) £2/5/-.

1157.   Dore, Ronald Philip
        Land reform in Japan. London, New York, Oxford University
        Press, 1959, $8.80.

1158.   Eliot, Sir Charles Norton Edgecumbe
        Japanese Buddhism. London, Arnold, 1935; 42/-.
        Japanese Buddhism, with a memoir of the author by Harold
        Parlett. New York, Barnes & Noble, 1959, $7.00.

1159.   Embree, John Fee
        The Japanese nation, a social survey. New York, Farrar &
        Rinehart, 1945, $4.00.

1160.   Embree, John Fee
        Suye Mura, a Japanese village. Chicago, University of Chi-
        cago Press, 1939, $6.00; London, Kegan Paul, Trench, Trubner,
        1946. (International Library of Sociology and Social Reconstruc-
        tion.) £1/1/-. London ed. has title: A Japanese village, Suye
        Mura.

1161.   Fairbank, John King, ed.
        Chinese thought and institutions. With contributions by T'ung-
        tsu Ch'u and others. Chicago, University of Chicago Press, 1957.
        (Comparative studies of cultures and civilizations.) $8.50.

1162.   Fairbank, John King
        The United States and China. New ed., completely rev. and
        enl. Cambridge, Harvard University Press, 1958. (The Ameri-
        can Foreign Policy Library.) $5.50.

1163.   Fairservis, Walter Ashlin
        The origins of oriental civilization. New York, New Ameri-
        can Library, 1959. (Mentor: Ancient civilizations; Mentor Books,
        MD 251.) $0.50.

1164.   Fei, Hsiao-t'ung
        China's gentry; essays in rural-urban relations. Revised
        and edited by Margaret Park Redfield, with six life-histories
        of Chinese gentry families collected by Yung-teh Chow, and an
        introd. by Robert Redfield. Chicago, University of Chicago
        Press, 1953. Out of print; ca. $5.00.

1165.   Fei, Hsiao-t'ung, and Chih-i Chang
        Earthbound China; a study of rural economy in Yunnan. Rev.
        English ed. prepared in collaboration with Paul Cooper and
        Margaret Park Redfield. London, Routledge & Kegan Paul, 1949,
        £1; Chicago, University of Chicago Press, 1945. Out of print.

1166.   Fei, Hsiao-t'ung
            Peasant life in China; a field study of country life in the
        Yangtze valley. With a preface by Bronislaw Malinowski. New
        York, Dutton, 1939; London, Routledge, 1943. (International
        Library of Sociology and Social Reconstruction.) Out of print;
        ca. $5.00.

1167.   Fox, Richard Michael
            China diary. London, Hale, 1959, 18/-.
            U. S. distributor: International Publications Service, New
        York, $5.25.

        Frankfort, Henri
            The art and architecture of the ancient Orient. See no.
        257.

1168.   Freedman, Maurice
            Lineage organization in southeastern China. London, Univer-
        sity of London, Athlone Press, 1958. (London School of Eco-
        nomics. Monographs on Social Anthropology, no. 18.) 25/-.
            U. S. distributor: New York, Humanities Press, $5.00.

1169.   Fried, Morton Herbert
            Fabric of Chinese society; a study of the social life of a
        Chinese county seat. London, Atlantic Press, 1956, 21/-; New
        York, Praeger, 1953. Out of print.

1170.   Gamble, Sidney David
            Ting Hsien, a North China rural community. Foreword by
        Y. C. James Yen. Field work directed by Franklin Ching-han
        Lee. New York, International Secretariat, Institute of Pacific
        Relations, 1954, $6.50.

1171.   Glacken, Clarence J.
            The Great Loochoo; a study of Okinawan village life. Berkeley
        and Los Angeles, University of California Press, 1955, $6.00.

1172.   Holtom, Daniel Clarence
            Modern Japan and Shinto nationalism; a study of present-day
        trends in Japanese religions. Rev. ed. Chicago, University of
        Chicago Press, 1947. (The Haskell Lectures in Comparative
        Religion.) Out of print; ca. $4.00.

1173.   Holtom, Daniel Clarence
            The national faith of Japan; a study in modern Shinto. London,
        Kegan Paul, Trench, Trubner, 1938, out of print; New York, Dut-
        ton, 1938. Out of print; ca. $5.00.

1174.   Holtom, Daniel Clarence
            The political philosophy of modern Shinto, a study of the state
        religion of Japan. Tokyo, The Asiatic Society of Japan, 1922.
        (Asiatic Society of Japan. Transactions, v. 49, pt. 2.) Out of
        print? ca. $5.00.

1175. Hommel, Rudolf P.
       China at work; an illustrated record of the primitive
       industries of China's masses, whose life is toil, and thus
       an account of Chinese civilization. New York, published for
       Bucks County Historical Society, Doylestown, Pa., by John Day,
       1937. Available from Bucks County Historical Society, $7.50.

1176. Hsu, Francis L. K.
       Americans and Chinese: two ways of life. New York,
       Schuman, 1953, $6.00.

1177. Hsu, Francis L. K.
       Religion, science and human crises; a study on China in
       transition and its implications for the West. London, Rout-
       ledge & Kegan Paul, 1952. (International Library of Sociology
       and Social Reconstruction.) 14/-.
       U. S. distributor: New York, Humanities Press, $3.50.

1178. Hsu, Francis L. K.
       Under the ancestor's shadow; Chinese culture and person-
       ality. N. Y., Columbia University Press, 1948, $4.00; London,
       Routledge & Kegan Paul, 1949. (International Library of Soci-
       ology and Social Reconstruction.) £1/1/-.

1179. Hu, Chang-tu
       China: its people, its society, its culture. In collaboration
       with Samuel C. Chu and others. Editor: Hsiao Hsia. New Haven,
       HRAF Press, 1960. (Survey of World Cultures, 6.) $10.00.

1180. Hu, Hsien-chin
       The common descent group in China and its functions. New
       York, 1948. (Viking Fund Publication in Anthropology, no. 10.)
       Out of print; ca. $2.50.

1181. Japan. Mombusho. Nihon Yunesuko Kokunai Iinkai.
       Japan: its land, people, and culture, compiled by Japanese
       National Commission for UNESCO. Tokyo, Print. Bureau,
       Ministry of Finance, 1958.
       U. S. distributor: International Document Service, Columbia
       University Press, $12.00.

1182. Kang, Younghill
       The grass roof. New York, London, Scribner's, 1931. Out
       of print; ca. $4.00. (On Korea.)

1183. Kano, Tadao, and Kokichi Segawa
       An illustrated ethnography of Formosan aborigines. Rev. ed.
       Tokyo, Maruzen, 1956-   v. 1, The Yami, $10.00.

1184. Keene, Donald
       Living Japan. Garden City, N. Y., Doubleday, 1959, $7.95.

1185. Kerr, George H.
       Okinawa, the history of an island people. 1st ed. Rutland,
       Vt., Tuttle, 1958, $6.75.

1186. Kidder, Jonathan Edward
       Japan before Buddhism. London, Thames & Hudson, 1959,
       25/-; New York, Praeger, 1959, $6.50. (Ancient Peoples and
       Places, v. 10.)

1187. Lang, Olga
       Chinese family and society. Published under the auspices of
       the International secretariat, Institute of Pacific Relations, and
       the Institute of Social Research. New Haven, Yale University
       Press; London, G. Cumberlege, Oxford University Press, 1946.
       Out of print; ca. $5.00.

1188. Lattimore, Owen
       Inner Asian frontiers of China. 2d ed. Irvington-on-Hudson,
       N. Y., Capitol, and American Geographical Society, New York,
       1951. (American Geographical Society of New York. Research
       Series no. 21.) $7.50.

1189. Levy, Marion Joseph
       The family revolution in modern China. Issued in coöperation
       with the Institute of Pacific Relations. Cambridge, Harvard Uni-
       versity Press, 1949. Out of print; ca. $6.00.

1190. Li, Chi
       The beginnings of Chinese civilization; three lectures illus-
       trated with finds at Anyang. Seattle, University of Washington
       Press, 1957, $6.50.

1191. Lin, Yao-hua
       The golden wing, a sociological study of Chinese familism,
       by Lin Yueh-hwa. Issued under the auspices of the International
       Secretariat, Institute of Pacific Relations. London, Kegan Paul,
       Trench, Trubner, 1948. (International Library of Sociology and
       Social Reconstruction.) 18/-.

1192. Matsumoto, Yoshiharu Scott
       Contemporary Japan: the individual and the group. Philadel-
       phia, American Philosophical Society, 1960. (American Philo-
       sophical Society. Transactions, new ser., v. 50, pt. 1.) $2.00.

1193. Norbeck, Edward
       Takashima, a Japanese fishing community. Salt Lake City,
       University of Utah Press, 1954. $3.00.

1194. Osgood, Cornelius
       The Koreans and their culture. New York, Ronald Press,
       1951, $6.50.

1195. Redesdale, Algernon Bertram Freeman-Mitford, baron
      Tales of old Japan. By A. B. Mitford. With illustrations
      drawn and cut on wood by Japanese artists. London, Macmillan,
      1871. 2 v. Reprinted in one vol., 1893. Out of print.

1196. Reischauer, Edwin Oldfather
      Japan, past and present. Foreword by Sir George Sansom.
      2d ed., rev. and enl. New York, Knopf, 1953, $4.00; text ed.,
      $3.00.

1197. Sansom, Sir George Bailey
      A history of Japan. Stanford, Calif., Stanford University
      Press, 1958- (Stanford Studies in the Civilizations of Eastern
      Asia.)
      Vol. 1, A history of Japan to 1334, $8.50. Vol. 2, A history of
      Japan, 1334-1615, $8.25. Vols. 1-2 of a projected 3 vol. work.

1198. Sansom, Sir George Bailey
      Japan: a short cultural history. Rev. ed. New York, Appleton,
      1962, $10.00.

1199. Sansom, Sir George Bailey
      The Western world and Japan, a study in the interaction of
      European and Asiatic cultures. New York, Knopf, 1950, $7.50.

1200. Shirokogorov, Sergiei Mikhailovich
      Anthropology of northern China, by S. M. Shirokogoroff.
      Shanghai, 1923. (Royal Asiatic Society. North China branch.
      Publications. Extra vol. 2.) Out of print?

1201. Shirokogorov, Sergiei Mikhailovich
      Social organization of the Manchus. A study of the Manchu
      clan organization. By S. M. Shirokogoroff. Shanghai, 1924
      (Royal Asiatic Society. North China branch. Publications.
      Extra vol. 3.) Out of print?

1202. Shirokogorov, Sergiei Mikhailovich
      Social organization of the northern Tungus, with introductory
      chapters concerning geographical distribution and history of
      these groups, by S. M. Shirokogoroff. Shanghai, China, The
      Commercial Press, 1929. Out of print? ca. $6.00.

1203. Smith, Allan H.
      The culture of Kabira, southern Ryukyu Islands. Philadelphia,
      American Philosophical Society, 1960. (American Philosophical
      Society. Proceedings. V. 104, no. 2, April 19, 1960, pp. 134-
      171.) $1.00.

1204. Smith, Thomas Carlyle
      The agrarian origins of modern Japan. Stanford, Calif.,
      Stanford University Press, 1959. (Stanford Studies in the Civili-
      zation of Eastern Asia.) $5.00.

1205. Stoetzel, Jean
       Without the chrysanthemum and the sword; a study of the
       attitudes of youth in post-war Japan. New York, Columbia Uni-
       versity Press, 1955 (A UNESCO publication).
       U. S. distributor: International Document Service, Columbia
       University Press, $4.00.

1206. Taeuber, Irene Barnes
       The population of Japan. Princeton, Princeton University
       Press, 1958, $15.00.

1207. Takakura, Shin'ichiro
       Ainu of northern Japan; a study in conquest and accultura-
       tion. Translated and annotated by John A. Harrison. Philadel-
       phia, American Philosophical Society, 1960. (Transactions of
       the American Philosophical Society, new ser., v. 50, pt. 4.) $2.00.

1208. Trewartha, Glenn Thomas
       Japan, a physical, cultural and regional geography. Madison,
       University of Wisconsin Press, 1945, $7.50.

1209. Tsunoda, Ryusaku, William Theodore De Bary, and Donald
       William Keene, Comps.
       Sources of the Japanese tradition. New York, Columbia Uni-
       versity Press, 1958. (Records of Civilization: Sources and
       Studies, 54. Introduction to Oriental Civilizations, 1.) $7.50.

       Weber, Max
       The religion of China. See no. 241.

1210. Williams, Edward Thomas
       China yesterday and today. 5th ed. rev. New York, Crowell,
       1932; London, Harrap, 1933. Out of print; ca. $4.00.

1211. Wittfogel, Karl August
       Oriental despotism; a comparative study of total power. New
       Haven, Yale University Press, 1957, $8.50.

1212. Wright, Arthur F., ed.
       Studies in Chinese thought. With contributions by Derk Bodde
       and others. Chicago, University of Chicago Press, 1953. (Com-
       parative Studies in Cultures and Civilizations.) $4.50. (Also
       published as Memoir no. 75 of The American Anthropological
       Association.)

1213. Yanagida, Kunio, ed.
       Japanese manners and customs in the Meiji era; translated
       and adapted by Charles S. Terry. Tokyo, Obunsha, 1957. (Cen-
       tenary culture council series. Japanese culture in the Meiji
       era, v. 4.)
       U. S. distributor: Tuttle, Rutland, Vermont, $10.00.

1214. Yang, Ch'ing-k'un
       The Chinese family in the Communist revolution. With a
       foreword by Talcott Parsons. Cambridge, Mass., Technology
       Press, Massachusetts Institute of Technology; distributed by
       Harvard University Press, 1959, $6.00.

1215. Yang, Ch'ing-k'un
       A Chinese village in early Communist transition. Cambridge,
       Mass., Technology Press, Massachusetts Institute of Technology;
       distributed by Harvard University Press, 1959, $6.50.

1216. Yang, Mou-Ch'un
       A Chinese village: Taitou, Shantung province, by Martin C.
       Yang. New York, Columbia University Press, 1945, $4.50; Lon-
       don, Routledge & Kegan Paul, 1948. (International Library of
       Sociology and Social Reconstruction.) £1/3/-.

1217. Zabilka, Gladys
       Customs and culture of Okinawa. Rev. (2d) ed. Tokyo, Rut-
       land, Vt., Bridgeway Press, 1959, $2.75.

       E. Oceania

1218. Barnett, Homer Garner
       Being a Palauan. New York, Holt, 1960. (Case Studies in
       Cultural Anthropology.) $1.75; text ed., $1.25.

1219. Bateson, Gregory
       Naven, a survey of the problems suggested by a composite
       picture of the culture of a New Guinea tribe drawn from three
       points of view. 2d ed. Stanford, Calif., Stanford University
       Press, 1958, $6.00.

1220. Beaglehole, Ernest
       Social change in the South Pacific; Rarotonga and Aitutaki.
       New York, Macmillan, 1957, $6.50.

1221. Beaglehole, Ernest, and Pearl Beaglehole
       Some modern Maoris. Wellington, New Zealand council for
       educational research, 1946. (Educational Research Series, no.
       25.) Out of print; ca. $3.00.

1222. Berndt, Ronald Murray, and Catherine H. Berndt
       Arnhem land, its history and its people. Melbourne, Cheshire,
       1954. Out of print? ca. $4.00.

1223. Berndt, Ronald Murray, and Catherine H. Berndt
       The first Australians. Sydney, Smith, 1952; New York, Philo-
       sophical Library, 1954. Out of print; ca. $3.00.

1224.   Berndt, Ronald Murray, and Catherine H. Berndt
        From black to white in South Australia. With an introd. by
        A. P. Elkin. Melbourne, Cheshire, 1951, 37/6.

1225.   Berndt, Ronald Murray
        Kunapipi; a study of an Australian aboriginal religious cult.
        Melbourne, Cheshire, 1951, 39/6.
        U. S. distributor: New York, International Universities Press,
        $7.50.

1226.   Best, Elsdon
        The Maori. Wellington, N. Z., printed by H. H. Tombs, ltd.,
        1924. (Polynesian Society. Memoirs, v. 5.) Out of print? ca.
        $6.00.

1227.   Best, Elsdon
        The Maori as he was; a brief account of Maori life as it was
        in pre-European days. Wellington, N. Z., R. E. Owen, Govt.
        printer, 1952, 20/-.

1228.   Blackwood, Beatrice
        Both sides of Buka passage; an ethnographic study of social,
        sexual, and economic questions in the north-western Solomon
        Islands. Oxford, Clarendon Press, 1935. Out of print? ca.
        $10.00.

1229.   Buck, Sir Peter Henry
        The coming of the Maori, by Te Rangi Hiroa. 2d ed. Well-
        ington, Maori Purposes Fund Board; distributed by Whitcombe
        and Tombs, 1950, 35/-.

1230.   Buck, Sir Peter Henry
        Vikings of the sunrise. Christchurch, N. Z., Whitcombe and
        Tombs, 1954, 35/-.
        Paper: Vikings of the Pacific. Chicago, University of Chi-
        cago Press, 1959. (Phoenix Books, P31.) $1.95.

1231.   Burrows, Edwin Grant, and Melford E. Spiro
        An atoll culture; ethnography of Ifaluk in the central Carolines.
        2d ed. New Haven, Human Relations Area Files, 1957. (Behavior
        Science Monographs.) $4.50.

1232.   Codrington, Robert Henry
        The Melanesians: studies in their anthropology and folklore.
        New Haven. HRAF Press, 1957. (Behavior Science Reprints.) $3.95.

1233.   Condliffe, John Bell
        New Zealand in the making; a study of economic and social
        development. 2d rev. ed. London, Allen & Unwin, 1959, 30/-.
        U. S. distributor: New York, Macmillan, $6.75.

        Elkin, Adolphus Peter, Catherine Berndt, and Ronald Berndt
            Art in Arnhem Land. See no. 256.

1234.   Elkin, Adolphus Peter
        The Australian aborigines; how to understand them. 3rd ed.
        Sydney, Angus & Robertson, 1954, 30/-.

1235.   Elkin, Adolphus Peter
        Marriage and the family in Australia. Sydney, Angus & Robert-
        son, 1957, 27/6.

1236.   Elkin, Adolphus Peter
        Social anthropology in Melanesia; a review of research. Pub-
        lished under the auspices of the South Pacific Commission.
        London, New York, Oxford University Press, 1953, $4.75.

1237.   Firth, Raymond William
        Economics of the New Zealand Maori. With a pref. by R. H.
        Tawney. Being the 2d ed. of Primitive economics of New Zeal-
        and Maori. Wellington, N. Z., R. E. Owen, Govt. printer, 1959,
        £2/10/-.

1238.   Firth, Raymond William
        Primitive Polynesian economy. London, Routledge, 1939. Out
        of print; ca. $5.00.

1239.   Firth, Raymond William
        Social change in Tikopia; restudy of a Polynesian community
        after a generation. London, Allen & Unwin, 1959, 45/-; New York,
        Macmillan, 1959, $8.00.

1240.   Firth, Raymond William
        We, the Tikopia; a sociological study of kinship in primitive
        Polynesia. With a pref. by Bronislaw Malinowski. 2d ed. Lon-
        don, Allen & Unwin, 1957, 50/-.
        U. S. distributor: New York, Macmillan, $7.50.

1241.   Fischer, John L.
        The eastern Carolines . . . with the assistance of Ann M.
        Fischer. New Haven, Pacific Science Board, National Academy
        of Sciences, National Research Council, in association with Human
        Relations Area Files, 1957. (Behavior Science Monographs.) $6.50.

1242.   Force, Roland W.
        Leadership and cultural change in Palau. Chicago, Chicago
        Natural History Museum, 1960. (Fieldiana: Anthropology, v. 50.)
        $5.00.

        Fortune, Reo Franklin
        Manus religion. See no. 206.

1243.   Fortune, Reo Franklin
        Sorcerers of Dobu; the social anthropology of the Dobu
        islanders of the western Pacific . . . with an introduction by
        B. Malinowski. London, Routledge, 1932; New York, Dutton,
        1932. Out of print; ca. $8.00.

1244. Gifford, Edward Winslow
       Tongan society. Honolulu, Hawaii, The Museum, 1929.
       (Bernice P. Bishop Museum. Bulletin 61.) Out of print; ca.
       $5.00.

1245. Gladwin, Thomas, and Seymour B. Sarason
       Truk: man in paradise. New York, Wenner-Gren Foundation
       for Anthropological Research, 1953. (Viking Fund Publications
       in Anthropology, no. 20.) $6.50.

       Goodenough, Ward H.
       Property, kin, and community on Truk. See no. 167.

1246. Grey, Sir George
       Polynesian mythology, and ancient traditional history of the
       Maori as told by their priests and chiefs. Edited by W. W.
       Bird. Illustrated by Russell Clark. Illus. New Zealand ed.
       Christchurch, Whitcombe and Tombs, 1956, 17/6.

1247. Haddon, Alfred Cort, ed.
       Reports of the Cambridge Anthropological expedition to
       Torres straits. Cambridge, University Press, 1901-1935. 6 v.
       v. 1, $12.50; v. 2, pt. 1, $6.50; pt. 2, $6.50; v. 3, $12.50; v. 4, $12.50;
       v. 5, $12.50; v. 6, $12.50.

1248. Handy, Edward Smith Craighill
       The native culture in the Marquesas. Honolulu, Hawaii, The
       Museum, 1923. (Bernice P. Bishop Museum. Bulletin 9.) Out
       of print; ca. $5.00.

       Handy, Edward Smith Craighill
       Polynesian religion. See no. 209.

1249. Hart, Charles William Merton, and Arnold R. Pilling
       The Tiwi of north Australia. New York, Holt, 1960. (Case
       Studies in Cultural Anthropology.) $1.75; text ed., $1.25.

1250. Hogbin, Herbert Ian
       Experiments in civilization; the effects of European culture
       on a native community of the Solomon islands. London, Rout-
       ledge, 1939. Out of print; ca. $5.00.

1251. Hogbin, Herbert Ian
       Law and order in Polynesia; a study of primitive legal insti-
       tutions . . . with an introduction by B. Malinowski. New York,
       Harcourt, Brace, 1934. Out of print; ca. $5.00.

1252. Hogbin, Herbert Ian
       Transformation scene; the changing culture of a New Guinea
       village. London, Routledge & Kegan Paul, 1951. (International
       library of sociology and social reconstruction.) £1/10/-.
       U. S. distributor: New York, Humanities Press, $6.00.

1253. Kaberry, Phyllis Mary
       Aboriginal woman, sacred and profane . . . introduction by
       Professor A. P. Elkin. Philadelphia, Blakiston, 1939, out of
       print; London, Routledge, 1939, £1/1/-.
       U. S. distributor: New York, Humanities Press, $6.00.

1254. Keesing, Felix Maxwell, and Marie M. Keesing
       Elite communication in Samoa; a study of leadership. Stan-
       ford, Calif., Stanford University Press, 1956. (Stanford Anthro-
       pological Series, no. 3.) $4.75.

1255. Keesing, Felix Maxwell
       Field guide to Oceania. Washington, National Academy of
       Sciences, National Research Council, 1959. (National Research
       Council. Committee on International Anthropology. Field guide
       series no. 1.) (National Research Council. Publication 701.) $1.25.

1256. Keesing, Felix Maxwell
       Social anthropology in Polynesia; a review of research. Pub-
       lished under the auspices of the South Pacific Commission. Lon-
       don, New York, Oxford University Press, 1953, $3.60.

1257. Keesing, Felix Maxwell
       The South Seas in the modern world . . . with a foreword by
       J. B. Condliffe. New York, Day, 1941. Out of print; ca. $4.00.

       Linton, Ralph, and Paul S. Wingert
       Arts of the South Seas. See no. 266.

1258. McCarthy, Frederick David
       Australia's aborigines: their life and culture. 1st limited ed.
       Melbourne, Colorgravure Publication, 1957, £5/5/-.
       U. S. distributors: Heinman, New York, $20.00; International
       Publications Service, New York, $16.50.

1259. Malinowski, Bronislaw
       Argonauts of the western Pacific; an account of native enter-
       prise and adventure in the archipelagoes of Melanesian New
       Guinea . . . with a preface by Sir James George Frazer. Lon-
       don, Routledge, 50/-; New York, Dutton, 1922, $10.00.
       Paper: New York, Dutton, 1961. (A Dutton Everyman Paper-
       back.) $2.45.

1260. Malinowski, Bronislaw
       Coral gardens and their magic; a study of the methods of tilling
       the soil and of agricultural rites in the Trobriand islands. London,
       Allen & Unwin, 1935, out of print; New York, American Book, 1935,
       2 v. Out of print; ca. $10.00.

1261. Malinowski, Bronislaw
       The sexual life of savages in north-western Melanesia; an ethno-
       graphic account of courtship, marriage, and family life among the
       natives of the Trobriand Islands, British New Guinea . . . with a
       preface by Havelock Ellis. London, Routledge, 1929, £2/2/-.

1262.   Mead, Margaret
        Coming of age in Samoa; a psychological study of primitive
youth for western civilization . . . foreword by Franz Boas.
New York, Morrow, 1928. Out of print.
        Paper: New York, New American Library, 1949. (Mentor,
MD 153.) $0.50; New York, Morrow, 1961. (Apollo Editions.) $1.95.

1263.   Mead, Margaret
        From the South Seas; studies of adolescence and sex in
primitive societies. New York, Morrow, 1939, $5.00.
Contents: Coming of age in Samoa; Growing up in New Guinea;
Sex and temperament in three primitive societies.

1264.   Mead, Margaret
        Growing up in New Guinea; a comparative study of primitive
education. New York, Morrow, 1930. Out of print.
        Paper: With a new pref. by the author. New York, New
American Library, 1953. (Mentor MD 255.) $0.50.

1265.   Mead, Margaret
        An inquiry into the question of cultural stability in Polynesia.
New York, Columbia University Press, 1928. (Columbia University Contributions to Anthropology, v. 9.) $2.00.

1266.   Mead, Margaret
        New lives for old; cultural transformation—Manus, 1928-1953.
New York, Morrow, 1956, $6.75.
        Paper: New York, New American Library, 1961.   (Mentor
Books.) $0.75.

1267.   Mead, Margaret
        Sex and temperament in three primitive societies. New York,
Morrow, 1935, out of print; London, Routledge & Kegan Paul,
1935, £1/1/-.
        Paper: New York, New American Library, 1950. (A Mentor
Book, MD 133.) $0.50.

1268.   Metraux, Alfred
        Easter Island; a stone-age civilization of the Pacific. Trans-
lated from the French by Michael Bullock. New York, Oxford
University Press, 1957, $5.00.

1269.   Norbeck, Edward
        Pineapple town, Hawaii. Berkeley and Los Angeles, Univer-
sity of California Press, 1959, $4.00.

1270.   Oliver, Douglas Llewellyn
        The Pacific Islands. Decorations and maps by Shelia Mitchell
Oliver. Cambridge, Mass., Harvard University Press, 1951, $6.00.

1271.   Oliver, Douglas Llewellyn
        A Solomon Island society; kinship and leadership among the
Siuai of Bougainville. Cambridge, Mass., Harvard University
Press, 1955, $11.00.

Pospisil, Leopold
Kapauku Papuans and their law. See no. 198.

1272. Powdermaker, Hortense
Life in Lesu; the study of a Melanesian society in New Ire-
land. Foreword by Dr. Clark Wissler. New York, Norton, 1933.
Out of print; ca. $8.00.

1273. Radcliffe-Brown, Alfred Reginald
Social organization of Australian tribes. Melbourne, London,
Macmillan, 1931. ("Oceania" Monographs, no. 1.) Out of print;
scarce.

1274. Reay, Marie
The Kuma; freedom and conformity in the New Guinea High-
lands. Carlton, Melbourne University Press on behalf of the
Australian National University, 1959, 45/-.
U. S. distributor: Cambridge University Press, $8.50.

1275. Rivers, William Halse Rivers
The history of Melanesian society. Cambridge, University
Press, 1914, 2 vols. Out of print; ca. $12.00.

1276. Sahlins, Marshall David
Social Stratification in Polynesia. Seattle, University of Washington Press, 1958. (An American Ethnological Society Publication.) $4.50.

1277. Sharp, Andrew
Ancient voyagers in the Pacific. Harmondsworth, Middlesex,
Penguin, 1957. (A Pelican Book, A 404.) $0.95. Also published
as Polynesian Society Memoir no. 32, Wellington, 1956.

1278. Sinclair, Keith
A history of New Zealand. Harmondsworth, Middlesex; Baltimore, Penguin, 1959. (Pelican Books, A 344.) $0.95.

1279. Sinclair, Keith
The origins of the Maori wars. Wellington, New Zealand
University Press, 1957, 26/6.
U. S. distributor: Cambridge University Press, $5.00.

1280. Spencer, Sir Baldwin, and Francis James Gillin
The Arunta: a study of a stone age people. London, Macmillan,
1927, 2 vols. Out of print; ca. $12.00.

1281. Spencer, Sir Baldwin, and Francis James Gillin
The native tribes of central Australia. London, Macmillan,
1899. Out of print; ca. $8.00.

1282. Spencer, Sir Baldwin
Native tribes of the Northern territory of Australia. London,
Macmillan, 1914. Out of print; ca. $10.00.

1283. Spencer, Sir Baldwin, and Francis James Gillin
       Northern tribes of central Australia. London, Macmillan,
       1904. Out of print; ca. $8.00.

1284. Suggs, Robert Carl
       The island civilizations of Polynesia. New York, New Ameri-
       can Library, 1960. (Mentor Books, MD 304.) $0.50.

1285. Sutherland, Ivan Lorin George, ed.
       The Maori people today; a general survey . . . issued under
       the auspices of the New Zealand institute of international affairs
       and the New Zealand council for educational research. London,
       New York, Oxford University Press, 1940. Out of print; ca. $4.00.

1286. Taylor, Clyde Romer Hughes
       A Pacific bibliography; printed matter relating to the native
       peoples of Polynesia, Melanesia, and Micronesia. Wellington,
       N. Z., Polynesian Society, 1951. (Memoirs of the Polynesian
       Society, v. 24.) Out of print? 42/-.

1287. Thompson, Laura
       Guam and its people. With a village journal by Jesse C.
       Barcinas. Rev. 3d ed. Princeton, Princeton University Press,
       1947. Out of print; ca. $5.00.

1288. Warner, William Lloyd
       A black civilization; a social study of an Australian tribe.
       Rev. ed. New York, Harper, 1958, $6.50.

       Whiting, John W. M.
       Becoming a Kwoma. See no. 356.

1289. Williams, Francis Edgar
       Drama of Orokolo; the social and ceremonial life of the Elema.
       Oxford, Clarendon Press, 1940. (Papua. Government Anthropolo-
       gist. Reports. 18.) 59/3.

1290. Williams, Francis Edgar
       Orokaiva magic. With a foreword by R. R. Marett. London,
       Oxford University Press, H. Milford, 1928. (Papua. Government
       Anthropologist. Reports 6-8.) Out of print; ca. $6.00.

1291. Williams, Francis Edgar
       Orokaiva society. With an introduction by Sir Henry Murray.
       London, Oxford University Press, H. Milford, 1930. (Papua.
       Government Anthropologist. Reports. 10.) 54/-.

1292. Williams, Francis Edgar
       Papuans of the Trans-Fly. Oxford, Clarendon Press, 1936.
       (Papua. Government Anthropologist. Reports. 15.) Out of print;
       ca. $6.00.

1293. Williamson, Robert Wood
       Essays in Polynesian ethnology. Edited by Ralph Piddington.
       With an analysis of recent studies in Polynesian history by
       the editor. Cambridge, University Press, 1939. Out of print;
       ca. $5.00.

1294. Williamson, Robert Wood
       Religion and social organization in central Polynesia. Edited
       by Ralph Piddington. . . with a preface by Raymond Firth. Cam-
       bridge, University Press, 1937. Out of print; ca. $10.00.

1295. Williamson, Robert Wood
       Religious and cosmic beliefs of central Polynesia. Cambridge,
       University Press, 1933, 2 v., $16.50.

1296. Williamson, Robert Wood
       Social and political systems of central Polynesia. Cambridge,
       University Press, 1924, 3 v. Out of print; ca. $20.00.

1297. Worsley, Peter
       The trumpet shall sound; a study of "cargo" cults in Mela-
       nesia. London, MacGibbon & Kee, 1957, 25/-.
       U. S. distributor: New York, Humanities Press, $5.00.

       F. Americas

       1. Aboriginal

       a. General

1298. Anthropological Society of Washington, Washington, D. C.
       New interpretations of aboriginal American culture history.
       75th anniversary volume. Washington, 1955. Out of print?
       ca. $3.00. (Ed. by Betty J. Meggers.)

1299. Bliss, Robert Woods
       Pre-Columbian art. Text and critical analyses by S. K.
       Lothrop, W. F. Foshag, and Joy Mahler. New York, Phaidon
       Publishers; distributed by Garden City Books, 1957, $30.00.

1300. Comas, Juan
       Bibliografia selectiva de las culturas indígenas de América.
       Mexico, Instituto Panamericano de Geografía e Historia, Comisión
       de Historia, 1953. (Instituto Panamericano de Geografía e Historia.
       Comisión de Historia. Bibliografias, 1.) (Instituto Panamericano

de Geografía e Historia. Comisión de Historia. Publicación 64.)
(Instituto Panamericano de Geografía e Historia. Publicación núm.
166.) No price. Estimate: $3.00.

1301. Hibben, Frank Cummings
        Digging up America. 1st ed. New York, Hill & Wang, 1960,
        $5.00.

1302. Martin, Paul Sidney, George I. Quimby, and Donald Collier
        Indians before Columbus; twenty thousand years of North
        American history revealed by archeology. Chicago, University
        of Chicago Press, 1947, $8.50.

        Meggers, Betty J., ed.
        New interpretations of aboriginal American culture history.
        See no. 1298.

1303. Sellards, Elias Howard
        Early man in America; a study in prehistory. Illus. by Hal
        Story. Austin, University of Texas Press, 1952. Out of print;
        ca. $4.00.

        Tax, Sol, ed.
        Acculturation in the Americas. See no. 375.

1304. Tax, Sol, ed.
        The civilizations of ancient America. With an introd. by
        Wendell C. Bennett. Chicago, University of Chicago Press,
        1951. (International Congress of Americanists. 29th, New York,
        1949. Selected papers, v. 1.) Out of print; ca. $7.50.

1305. Tax, Sol, ed.
        Indian tribes of aboriginal America. Chicago, University of
        Chicago Press, 1952. (International Congress of Americanists.
        29th, New York, 1949. Selected papers, v. 3.) $7.50.

1306. Wenner-Gren Foundation for Anthropological Research, New York
        Papers on the physical anthropology of the American Indian,
        delivered at the fourth Viking Fund summer seminar in physi-
        cal anthropology, held at the Viking Fund, September, 1949.
        Edited by William S. Laughlin. New York, 1951. Out of print?
        ca. $3.00.

1307. Willey, Gordon Randolph, ed.
        Prehistoric settlement patterns in the New World. New York,
        Wenner-Gren Foundation for Anthropological Research, 1956.
        (Viking Fund Publications in Anthropology, no. 23.) $5.00.

1308. Wissler, Clark
        The American Indian, an introduction to the anthropology of
        the New World. 3d ed. New York, Smith, 1950, $5.50.
        3d ed. originally published by Oxford University Press, 1938.

b. North America

(1). General

1309. Covarrubias, Miguel
       The eagle, the jaguar, and the serpent; Indian art of the
       Americas. New York, Knopf, 1954, $15.00.

1310. Driver, Harold Edson, and William C. Massey
       Comparative studies of North American Indians. Philadelphia,
       American Philosophical Society, 1957. (Transactions of the
       American Philosophical Society, new ser., v. 47, pt. 2.) $5.00.

1311. Driver, Harold Edson
       Indians of North America. Chicago, University of Chicago
       Press, 1961, $12.50; paper, $7.50.

1312. Edmonson, Munro S.
       Status terminology and the social structure of North Ameri-
       can Indians. Seattle, University of Washington Press, 1958.
       (American Ethnological Society Publication.) $3.00.

       Eggan, Frederick R., ed.
       Social anthropology of North American tribes. See no. 1322.

       Fey, Harold Edward, and D'Arcy McNickle
       Indians and other Americans. See no. 1601.

1313. Griffin, James Bennett, ed.
       Archeology of eastern United States. Chicago, University of
       Chicago Press, 1952, $11.50.

1314. Hodge, Frederick Webb
       Handbook of American Indians north of Mexico. New York,
       Pageant Books, 1959, $27.50. (Reprint of U. S. Bureau of Ameri-
       can Ethnology. Bulletin 30, first published 1907-1910.)

1315. Kroeber, Alfred Louis
       Cultural and natural areas of native North America. Berkeley,
       University of California Press, 1939, $5.00.
       Also issued as: University of California Publications in Ameri-
       can Archaeology and Ethnology, v. 38.

1316. La Farge, Oliver, ed.
       The changing Indian, edited by Oliver La Farge, from a
       symposium arranged by the American Association on Indian
       Affairs, Inc. Norman, University of Oklahoma Press, 1942.
       (Civilization of the American Indian, 23.) Out of print; ca.
       $4.00.

1317. La Farge, Oliver
       Pictorial history of the American Indian. New York, Crown
       Publishers, 1956, $7.50.

       Linton, Ralph, ed.
       Acculturation in seven American Indian tribes. See no. 368.

1318. Murdock, George Peter
       Ethnographic bibliography of North America. 3d ed. New
       Haven, published by Human Relations Area Files, 1960. (Beha-
       vior Science Bibliographies.) $6.75.

1319. Radin, Paul
       The story of the American Indian. Enl. ed. New York,
       Liveright, 1944, $3.50.

       Radin, Paul
       The trickster; a study in American Indian mythology. See
       no. 296.

1320. Slotkin, James Sydney
       The Peyote religion; a study in Indian-white relations. Glen-
       goe, Ill., Free Press, 1956, $4.00.

1321. Smithsonian institution
       Essays in historical anthropology of North America. Published
       in honor of John R. Swanton in celebration of his fortieth year
       with the Smithsonian institution. Washington, Smithsonian institu-
       tion, 1940. (Smithsonian miscellaneous collections, v. 100.) Out
       of print; ca. $10.00.

1322. Social anthropology of North American tribes, by Fred Eggan
          and others. Fred Eggan, editor. Enl. (i.e., 2d) ed. Chicago,
          University of Chicago Press, 1955, $8.00.

1323. Swanton, John Reed
       The Indian tribes of North America. Washington, U. S. Govt.
       Print. Office, 1952. (U. S. Bureau of American Ethnology. Bulle-
       tin 145.) Out of print; ca. $6.00.

       Thompson, Stith
       Tales of the North American Indians. See no. 302.

1324. Underhill, Ruth Murray
       Red Man's America; a history of Indians in the United States.
       Illus. by Marianne Stoller. Chicago, University of Chicago Press,
       1953, $7.50.

1325. Wissler, Clark
       Indians of the United States; four centuries of their history
       and culture. New York, Doubleday, Doran, 1940, $4.50.

234   REXFORD S. BECKHAM

1326. Wormington, Hannah Marie
       Ancient man in North America. 4th ed., rev. Denver, Denver
Museum of Natural History, 1957. (Colorado Museum of Natural
History. Popular Series, no. 4.) $5.20; paper, $3.65.

       (2). Arctic Coast

1327. Birket-Smith, Kaj
       The Chugach Eskimo. Kφbenhavn, Nationalmuseets publikations-
fond, 1953. (Nationalmuseets skrifter. Etnografisk raekke, 6.)
Estimate: $5.00.

1328. Birket-Smith, Kaj
       The Eskimos. Transl. from the Danish by W. E. Calvert, re-
vised by C. Daryll Forde. Foreword by C. Daryll Forde. Enl.
and rev. ed. London, Methuen, 1959, 32/6.
       U. S. distributor: New York, Humanities Press, $6.50.

1329. Birket-Smith, Kaj, and Frederica de Laguna
       The Eyak Indians of the Copper river delta, Alaska. Kφbenhavn,
Levin & Munksgaard, Munksgaard, 1938. Out of print; ca. $7.00.

1330. Boas, Franz
       The central Eskimo. Washington, 1888. (In U. S. Bureau of
American ethnology. Annual Report, 6th, 1884-1885, pp. 399-669.)
Out of print; ca. $10.00.

1331. Boas, Franz
       The Eskimo of Baffin Land and Hudson Bay. New York, 1901-
1907, 2 v. (American Museum of Natural History. Bulletin, v.
15.) Out of print; ca. $10.00.

1332. Collins, Henry Bascom
       Arctic area. Mexico, 1954. (Instituto Panamericano de Geo-
grafia e Historia. Comisión de Historia. Publicaciones, 68.
Program of the history of America. 1: Indigenous period, 2.)
Out of print? ca. $1.00.

1333. de Laguna, Frederica
       Chugach prehistory; the archaeology of Prince William Sound,
Alaska. Seattle, University of Washington Press, 1956. (University of Washington Publications in Anthropology, v. 13.) $7.50.

1334. Freuchen, Peter
       Eskimo . . .; translated by A. Paul Maerker-Branden and Elsa
Branden. New York, Liveright, 1931. Out of print; ca. $4.00.

1335. Giddings, James Louis
       The Arctic woodland culture of the Kobuk River. Philadelphia,
University Museum, University of Pennsylvania, 1952. (Pennsylvania. University. University Museum. Museum monographs.)
$2.50.

1336.   Lantis, Margaret
        Eskimo childhood and interpersonal relationship; Nunivak
        biographies and genealogies. Seattle, University of Washington
        Press, 1960. (American Ethnological Society Publication.) $4.75.

1337.   Lantis, Margaret
        The social culture of the Nunivak Eskimo. Philadelphia, 1946.
        (American Philosophical Society. Transactions, new ser., v. 35,
        pt. 3.) Out of print; ca. $3.75.

1338.   Hrdlička, Aleš
        The Aleutian and Commander islands and their inhabitants.
        Philadelphia, The Wistar Institute of Anatomy and Biology, 1945.
        Out of print; ca. $5.00.

1339.   Hrdlička, Aleš
        The anthropology of Kodiak island. Philadelphia, The Wistar
        Institute of Anatomy and Biology, 1944. Out of print; ca. $5.00.

1340.   Jenness, Diamond
        People of the twilight. Chicago, University of Chicago Press,
        1959. (Phoenix Books, P32.) $1.50.

1341.   Malaurie, Jean
        The last kings of Thule; a year among the polar Eskimos of
        Greenland. Translated by Gwendolen Freeman. With a pref. by
        G. de Poncins. London, Allen & Unwin, 1956, 21/-; New York,
        Crowell, 1956, out of print.

1342.   Spencer, Robert F.
        The North Alaskan Eskimo; a study in ecology and society.
        Washington, U. S. Govt. Print. Office, 1959. (U. S. Bureau of
        American Ethnology. Bulletin 171.) $2.50.

1343.   Thule expedition, 5th, 1921-1924.
        Report of the fifth Thule Expedition, 1921-1924; the Danish
        expedition to arctic North America in charge of Knud Rasmussen.
        Copenhagen, Glydendal, 1927-1952.
        Contents. V. 3. No. 1. Skeletal remains of the Central Eski-
        mos, by K. Fischer-Møller, 1937, Kr. 5.00. No. 2. Anthropolo-
        gical observations on the Central Eskimos, by Kaj Birket-Smith,
        1940, Kr. 10.00. No. 3. Five hundred Eskimo words; a compara-
        tive vocabulary from Greenland and Central Eskimo dialects, by
        Kaj Birket-Smith, 1928, Kr. 3.50. No. 4. Alaskan Eskimo words
        compiled by Knud Rasmussen, ed. by H. Ostermann, 1941, Kr. 5.00.
        V. 4. Archaeology of the Central Eskimos I-II, by Therkel
        Mathiassen, 1927, Kr. 18.00.
        V. 5. The Caribou Eskimos I-II: Material and social life and
        their cultural position, by Kaj Birket-Smith, 1929, Kr. 22.00.
        V. 6. No. 1. Material culture of the Iglulik Eskimos, by
        Therkel Mathiassen, 1928, Kr. 8.50. No. 2. Ethnographical col-
        lections from the North-West Passage, by Kaj Birket-Smith,

1945, Kr. 20.00. No. 3. Contributions to Chipewyan ethnology, by Kaj Birket-Smith, 1930, Kr. 5.00.

V. 7. No. 1. Intellectual culture of the Iglulik Eskimos, by Knud Rasmussen, 1929, Kr. 12.00. No. 2-3. Observations on the intellectual culture of the Caribou Eskimos, by Knud Rasmussen. Igluik and Caribou Eskimo texts, by Knud Rasmussen, 1930, Kr. 12.00.

V. 8. No. 1-2. The Netsilik Eskimos; social life and spiritual culture, by Knud Rasmussen, 1931, Kr. 15.00.

V. 9. Intellectual culture of the Copper Eskimos, by Knud Rasmussen, 1932, Kr. 12.00.

V. 10. No. 1. Archaeological collections from the Western Eskimos, by Therkel Mathiassen, 1930, Kr. 5.00. No. 2. The Mackenzie Eskimos; after Knud Rasmussen's posthumous notes, ed. by H. Ostermann, 1942, Kr. 10.00. No. 3. The Alaskan Eskimos; as described in the posthumous notes of Dr. Knud Rasmussen, by H. Ostermann, 1952, Kr. 25.00.

1344.   Weyer, Edward Moffat
        The Eskimos; their environment and folkways. Hamden, Conn., Archon Books, 1962, $12.50. First published Yale University Press, 1932.

        (3). Mackenzie-Yukon

1345.   Honigmann, John Joseph
        Culture and ethos of Kaska society. New Haven, University Press, 1949. (Yale University Publications in Anthropology, no. 40.) $4.00.

1346.   Honigmann, John Joseph
        Ethnography and acculturation of the Fort Nelson Slave. New Haven, published for the Department of Anthropology, Yale University, Yale University Press; London, H. Milford, Oxford University Press, 1946. (Yale University Publications in Anthropology, no. 33.) $2.50.
        Bound with J. A. Mason's Notes on the Indians of the Great Slave Lake area. (Yale University Publications in Anthropology, no. 34.)

1347.   Honigmann, John Joseph
        The Kaska Indians: an ethnographic reconstruction. New Haven, published for the Dept. of Anthropology, Yale University, by the Yale University Press, 1954. (Yale University Publications in Anthropology, no. 51.) $2.00.

1348.   Jenness, Diamond
        The Indians of Canada. 4th ed. Ottawa, National Museum of Canada, 1958. (Canada. National Museum, Ottawa. Bulletin 65. Anthropological Series, no. 15.) Estimate: $5.00.

1349. McKennan, Robert Addison
       The Upper Tanana Indians. New Haven, Dept. of Anthropology,
       Yale University, 1959. (Yale University Publications in Anthro-
       pology, no. 55.) $3.00.

1350. Osgood, Cornelius
       Contributions to the ethnography of the Kutchin. New Haven,
       published for the Section of anthropology, Department of the
       Social Sciences, Yale University, by the Yale University Press;
       London, H. Milford, Oxford University Press, 1936. (Yale Uni-
       versity Publications in Anthropology, no. 14.) $2.50.

1351. Osgood, Cornelius
       The ethnography of the Tanaina. New Haven, published for the
       Section of Anthropology, Department of the Social Sciences, Yale
       University, by the Yale University Press; London, H. Milford,
       Oxford University Press, 1937. (Yale University Publications
       in Anthropology, no. 16.) $3.00.

1352. Osgood, Cornelius
       Ingalik material culture. New Haven, published for the Dept.
       of Anthropology, Yale University, by the Yale University Press;
       London, H. Milford, Oxford University Press, 1940. (Yale Uni-
       versity Publications in Anthropology, no. 22.) $4.00.

1353. Osgood, Cornelius
       Ingalik mental culture. New Haven, Dept. of Anthropology,
       Yale University, 1959. (Yale University Publications in Anthro-
       pology, no. 56.) $2.50.

1354. Osgood, Cornelius
       Ingalik social structure. New Haven, published for the Dept.
       of Anthropology, Yale University by the Yale University Press,
       1958. (Yale University Publications in Anthropology, no. 53.)
       $4.00.

       (4). Northwest Coast

1355. Barnett, Homer Garner
       The Coast Salish of British Columbia. Eugene, University of
       Oregon, 1955. (University of Oregon Monographs. Studies in
       Anthropology, no. 4.) $3.50; cloth, $5.00.

1356. Barnett, Homer Garner
       Indian shakers: a messianic cult of the Pacific Northwest.
       Carbondale, Southern Illinois University Press, 1957, $5.75.

1357. Boas, Franz
       Ethnology of the Kwakiutl, based on data collected by George
       Hunt. Washington, 1921. (*In* U. S. Bureau of American Ethnology.
       Annual report, 35th, 1913-1914, pp. 795-1481.) In print 1956;
       no price.

1358. Boas, Franz
        The religion of the Kwakiutl Indians. New York, Columbia Uni-
        versity Press, 1930. (Columbia University Contributions to Anthro-
        pology, v. 10.) Out of print; ca. $7.00.

1359. Codere, Helen
        Fighting property; a study of Kwakiutl potlatching and warfare,
        1792-1930. With tribal and linguistic map of Vancouver Island and
        adjacent territory drawn and compiled by Vincent F. Kotschar.
        New York, Augustin, 1950. (Monographs of the American Ethno-
        logical Society, 18.)

1360. Colson, Elizabeth
        The Makah Indians; a study of an Indian tribe in modern Ameri-
        can society. Minneapolis, University of Minnesota Press, 1953,
        $4.75.

1361. de Laguna, Frederica
        The story of a Tlingit community: a problem in the relationship
        between archeological, ethnological, and historical methods. Wash-
        ington, U. S. Govt. Print. Office, 1960. (U. S. Bureau of American
        Ethnology. Bulletin 172.) $2.00.

1362. Drucker, Philip
        Indians of the Northwest coast. New York, published for the
        American Museum of Natural History by McGraw-Hill, 1955.
        (American Museum of Natural History, New York. Anthropological
        Handbook no. 10.) $5.75.

1363. Elmendorf, William W.
        The structure of Twana culture. With comparative notes on the
        structure of Yurok culture, by A. L. Kroeber. Pullman, Washing-
        ton, Washington State University, 1960. (Washington State Univer-
        sity. Research Studies, v. 28, no. 3; Monograph Supplement no. 2.)
        $6.00.

1364. Ford, Clellan Stearns
        Smoke from their fires; the life of a Kwakiutl chief. New Haven,
        published for the Institute of Human Relations by Yale University
        Press; London, H. Milford, Oxford University Press, 1941. Out
        of print; ca. $5.00.

1365. Garfield, Viola Edmundson
        Tsimshian clan and society. Seattle, Washington, University of
        Washington, 1939. (Washington. University. Publications in
        Anthropology, v. 7, no. 3.) $3.50.

1366. Garfield, Viola Edmundson, and Linn A. Forrest
        The wolf and the raven. Seattle, University of Washington Press,
        1948, $3.50.

1367. Hawthorn, Harry Bertram, C. S. Belshaw, and S. M. Jamieson
        The Indians of British Columbia; a study of contemporary social
        adjustment. Berkeley and Los Angeles, University of California
        Press, 1958, $12.50.

Inverarity, Robert Bruce
Art of the Northwest Coast Indians. See no. 263.

1368.   Krause, Aurel
The Tlingit Indians; results of a trip to the northwest coast of
America and the Bering Straits. Translated by Erna Gunther.
Seattle, published for the American Ethnological Society by the
University of Washington Press, 1956, $4.50.

1369.   McIlwraith, Thomas Forsyth
The Bella-Coola Indians. Toronto, University of Toronto Press,
1948, 2 v., $15.00.

Park, Willard Z.
Shamanism in western North America. See no. 226.

1370.   Smith, Marian Wesley, ed.
Indians of the urban Northwest. New York, Columbia University
Press, 1949. (Columbia University Contributions to Anthropology,
no. 36.) Out of print; ca. $6.00.

1371.   Smith, Marian Wesley
The Puyallup-Nisqually. New York, Columbia University Press,
1940. (Columbia University Contributions to Anthropology, v. 32.)
$5.00.

1372.   Underhill, Ruth Murray
Indians of the Pacific Northwest. Riverside, Calif., Sherman
Institute Press, 1945. (U. S. Office of Indian affairs. Indian life
and customs, 5.) Out of print? ca. $4.00.

(5). California

1373.   The Archaeology of central California.
Berkeley and Los Angeles, University of California Press, 1949.
(Anthropological Records, 12: 1-2).
Contents: 1. The early horizons, by Robert F. Heizer. 2. A com-
parative analysis of human bone from nine sites, by Robert F.
Heizer and Sherburne F. Cook. Pt. 1, out of print; pt. 2, $0.50.

1374.   Cressman, Luther Sheeleigh
Klamath prehistory; the prehistory of the culture of the Klamath
Lake area, Oregon. With appendices by William G. Haag and
William S. Laughlin. Philadelphia, American Philosophical Society,
1956. (Transactions of the American Philosophical Society, new
ser., v. 46, pt. 4.) $2.00.

1375.   Du Bois, Cora Alice
Wintu ethnography. Berkeley, University of California Press,
1935. (University of California Publications in American Archaeology and Ethnology, v. 36, no. 1.) Out of print; ca. $3.00.

1376. Harrington, Mark Raymond
    Ancient life among the southern California Indians. Illus. by
Clarence Ellsworth. Los Angeles, Southwest Museum, 1955.
(Los Angeles. Southwest Museum. Leaflets, no. 26.) $0.50.

1377. Heizer, Robert Fleming, and Mary Anne Whipple, eds.
    The California Indians; a source book. Berkeley and Los
Angeles, University of California Press, 1951, $6.50.

1378. Heizer, Robert Fleming, and John E. Mills, eds.
    The four ages of Tsurai; a documentary history of the Indian
village on Trinidad Bay. Translation of Spanish documents by
Donald C. Cutter. Berkeley and Los Angeles, University of California Press, 1952, $3.75.

1379. Kroeber, Alfred Louis
    Handbook of the Indians of California. Berkeley, California
Book Company, 1953, $15.00. (Reprint of U. S. Bureau of American
Ethnology. Bulletin 78, first published 1925.)

1380. Merriam, Clinton Hart
    Studies of California Indians; edited by the Staff of the Dept. of
Anthropology of the University of California. Berkeley and Los
Angeles University of California Press, 1955, $5.00.

1381. Spier, Leslie
    Klamath ethnography. Berkeley, University of California Press,
1930. (University of California Publications in American Archaeology and Ethnology, v. 30.) Out of print; ca. $4.00.

(6). Basin

1382. Barrett, Samuel Alfred
    The Washo Indians. Milwaukee, Wis., published by order of the
Trustees, 1917. (Bulletin of the Public Museum of the City of Mil-
waukee, v. 2, no. 1.) $0.50.

1383. Brew, John Otis
    Archaeology of Alkali Ridge, southeastern Utah, with a review
of the prehistory of the Mesa Verde division of the San Juan and
some observations on archaeological systematics. Appendices by
Alice Brues and Volney H. Jones. Cambridge, Mass., The Museum,
1946. (Harvard University. Peabody Museum of American Archaeology and Ethnology. Papers, v. 21.) Out of print; ca. $7.50.

1384. Burgh, Robert Frederic, and Charles R. Scoggin
    The Archaeology of Castle Park, Dinosaur National Monument
. . . with appendices by Edgar Anderson, Richard E. Pillmore, and
Volney H. Jones. Boulder, University of Colorado Press, 1948.
Colorado. University. Studies: Series in Anthropology, no. 2.)
$1.50.

1385. Cressman, Luther Sheeleigh
Archaeological researches in the northern Great Basin . . .
with the collaboration of Frank C. Baker, Paul S. Conger,
Henry P. Hansen, and Robert F. Heizer. Washington, D. C.,
1942. (Carnegie Institution of Washington. Publication 538.)
Out of print; ca. $5.00.

1386. Heizer, Robert Fleming, and Alex D. Krieger
The archaeology of Humboldt Cave, Churchill County, Nevada.
Berkeley and Los Angeles, University of California Press, 1956.
(University of California Publications in American Archaeology
and Ethnology, v. 47, no. 1.)

1387. Jennings, Jesse David
Danger Cave. With a chapter on textiles by Sara Sue Rudy,
and six appendices by Charles B. Hunt and others. Salt Lake
City, University of Utah Press, 1957. (Memoirs of the Society
for American Archaeology, no. 14.) (Utah. University. Dept.
of Anthropology. Anthropological papers, 27.) $6.00.

1388. Morss, Noel
The ancient culture of the Fremont River in Utah; report on
the explorations under the Claflin-Emerson fund, 1928-1929.
Cambridge, 1931. (Harvard University. Peabody Museum of
Archaeology and Ethnology. Papers, v. 12, no. 3.) $2.80.

1389. Nusbaum, Jesse Logan
A basket-maker cave in Kane County, Utah . . . with notes
on the artifacts, by A. V. Kidder and S. J. Guernsey. New
York, 1922. (Museum of the American Indian. Indian notes
and monographs, Miscellaneous Series, no. 29.) Out of print;
ca. $4.00.

1390. Steward, Julian Haynes
Basin-plateau aboriginal sociopolitical groups. Washington,
U. S. Govt. print. office, 1938. (U. S. Bureau of American
Ethnology. Bulletin 120.) Out of print; ca. $5.00.

Whiting, Beatrice B.
Paiute sorcery. See no. 243.

(7). Plateau

1391. Haines, Francis
The Nez Percés: tribesmen of the Columbia Plateau. 1st
ed. Norman, University of Oklahoma Press, 1955. (Civilization
of the American Indian Series, 42.) Out of print; ca. $5.00.

(8). Plains

1392.   Bowers, Alfred W.
          Mandan social and ceremonial organization. Chicago, Univer-
        sity of Chicago Press, 1950. Out of print; ca. $4.00.

        Devereux, George
          Reality and dream; psychotherapy of a Plains Indian. See
        no. 321.

1393.   Ewers, John Canfield
          The Blackfeet; raiders of the Northwestern Plains. 1st ed.
        Norman, University of Oklahoma Press, 1958. (Civilization of
        the American Indian Series, 49.) $5.75.

1394.   Ewers, John Canfield
          The horse in Blackfoot Indian culture, with comparative
        material from other western tribes. Washington, U. S. Govt.
        Print. Office, 1955. (U. S. Bureau of American Ethnology.
        Bulletin 159.) $2.75.

1395.   Fortune, Reo Franklin
          Omaha secret societies. New York, Columbia University
        Press, 1932. (Columbia University Contributions to Anthro-
        pology, v. 14.) Out of print; ca. $3.50.

1396.   Grinnell, George Bird
          The Cheyenne Indians, their history and ways of life . . .
        photographs by Elizabeth C. Grinnell and Mrs. J. E. Tuell.
        New Haven, Yale University Press, 1923, 2 v. Out of print;
        ca. $12.00.

1397.   Grinnell, George Bird
          The fighting Cheyennes. Norman, University of Oklahoma
        Press, 1956, c1915. (Civilization of the American Indian series,
        44.) $5.00.
          (First published New York, Scribner's, 1915.)

1398.   Hanks, Lucien Mason, and Jane R. Hanks
          Tribe under trust; a study of the Blackfoot reserve of Alberta.
        Photos. by F. Gully. Toronto, University of Toronto Press, 1950,
        $4.00.

1399.   Hoebel, Edward Adamson
          The Cheyennes; Indians of the Great Plains. New York, Holt,
        1960. (Case studies in Cultural Anthropology.) $1.75; text ed., $1.25.

1400.   Hyde, George E.
          Indians of the High Plains: from the prehistoric period to the
        coming of Europeans. 1st ed. Norman, University of Oklahoma
        Press, 1959. (Civilization of the American Indian series, 54.)
        $4.00.

1401. Hyde, George E.
      Red Cloud's folk; a history of the Oglala Sioux Indians.
Norman, University of Oklahoma Press, 1957. (The Civilization
of the American Indian, 15.) $5.00.

1402. Hyde, George E.
      A Sioux chronicle. 1st ed. Norman, University of Oklahoma
Press, 1956. (Civilization of the American Indian Series, 45.)
$5.00.

1403. Lewis, Oscar
      The effects of white contact upon Blackfoot culture, with
special reference to the role of the fur trade. New York,
Augustin, 1942. (American Ethnological Society. Monographs,
6.) Out of print; ca. $3.00.

Llewellyn, Karl Nickerson, and Edward Adamson Hoebel
The Cheyenne way. See no. 193.

1404. Lowie, Robert Harry
      The Crow Indians. New York, Rinehart, 1956, c1935, $3.00.

1405. Lowie, Robert Harry
      Indians of the Plains. New York, published for the American
Museum of Natural History by McGraw-Hill, 1954. (American
Museum of Natural History, New York. Anthropological handbook
no. 1.) Out of print; ca. $4.75.

Lowie, Robert Harry
Religion of the Crow Indians. See no. 219.

Macgregor, Gordon
Warriors without weapons. See no. 345.

1406. Mead, Margaret
      The changing culture of an Indian tribe. New York, Columbia
University Press, 1932. (Columbia University Contributions to
Anthropology, v. 15.) Out of print; ca. $5.00.

1407. Mishkin, Bernard
      Rank and warfare among the plains Indians. New York, J. J.
Augustin, 1940. (Monographs of the American Ethnological Society,
3.) Out of print; ca. $3.00.

1408. Strong, William Duncan
      An introduction to Nebraska archeology. Washington, The
Smithsonian Institution, 1935. (Smithsonian Miscellaneous Collections, v. 93, no. 10.) Out of print; ca. $5.00.

1409. Wallace, Ernest, and Edward Adamson Hoebel
      The Comanches, lords of the south plains. 1st ed. Norman,
University of Oklahoma Press, 1952. (Civilization of the American Indian, 34.) $5.00.

1410.   Wendorf, Fred
        Midland discovery; a report on the Pleistocene human remains
        from Midland, Texas . . . with a description of the skull by T. D.
        Stewart. Austin, University of Texas Press, 1955, $3.50.

        (9). Midwest

1411.   Blowsnake, Sam
        Autobiography of a Winnebago Indian, by Paul Radin. New
        York, Dover, 1960, $1.25.
        First published as University of California Publications in
        American Archaeology and Ethnology, v. 16, no. 7, 1920. Part I
        published also in 1920 under title: Crashing Thunder; the auto-
        biography of an American Indian.

1412.   Cole, Fay-Cooper
        Kincaid, a prehistoric Illinois metropolis. Chicago, Univer-
        sity of Chicago Press, 1951. Out of print; ca. $6.00.

        Gearing, F. O., R. M. Netting, and L. R. Peattie, eds.
        Documentary history of the Fox project, 1948-1959. See no.
        363.

1413.   Keesing, Felix Maxwell
        The Menomini Indians of Wisconsin; a study of three centuries
        of cultural contact and change. Philadelphia, American Philosophi-
        cal Society, 1939. (American Philosophical Society. Memoirs,
        v. 10.) Out of print; ca. $3.00.

1414.   McGregor, John Charles
        The Pool and Irving villages; a study of Hopewell occupation
        in the Illinois River Valley. Urbana, University of Illinois Press,
        1958, $3.50.

1415.   Radin, Paul
        The Winnebago tribe. Washington, 1923. (U. S. Bureau of
        American Ethnology. Annual report, 37th, 1915-1916, Washing-
        ton, 1923, pp. 35-560.) Out of print; ca. $6.00.

        Spindler, George D.
        Sociocultural and psychological process in Menomini accul-
        turation. See no. 373.

        (10). Eastern Canada

1416.   Dunning, Robert William
        Social and economic change among the northern Ojibwa.
        Toronto, University of Toronto Press, 1959, $5.50.

1417. Hallowell, Alfred Irving
    The role of conjuring in Saulteaux society. Philadelphia,
University of Pennsylvania Press; London, H. Milford, Oxford
University Press, 1942. (Publications of the Philadelphia Anthro-
pological Society, v. 2.) Out of print; ca. $3.00.

1418. Mandelbaum, David Goodman
    The Plains Cree. New York, American Museum of Natural
History, 1940. (Anthropological Papers of the American Museum
of Natural History, v. 37, pt. 2.) In print? ca. $2.00.

1419. Quimby, George Irving
    Indian life in the Upper Great Lakes, 11,000 B. C. to A. D.
1800. Chicago, University of Chicago Press, 1960, $5.95.

1420. Speck, Frank Gouldsmith
    Naskapi, the savage hunters of the Labrador peninsula. Nor-
man, University of Oklahoma Press, 1935. (Civilization of the
American Indian, 10.) Out of print; ca. $3.00.

1421. Speck, Frank Gouldsmith
    Penobscot man; the life history of a forest tribe in Maine.
Philadelphia, University of Pennsylvania Press; London, H. Milford, Oxford University Press, 1940. Out of print; ca. $4.00.

1422. Wallis, Wilson Dallam, and Ruth Sawtell Wallis
    The Micmac Indians of eastern Canada. Minneapolis, Univer-
sity of Minnesota Press, 1955, $7.50.

    (11). Northeast

1423. Archaeology of New Jersey. v. 1-
    Trenton, N. J., published by the Archaeological Society of
New Jersey and the New Jersey State Museum, 1941-
    (v. 1-2 by Dorothy Cross and others) v. 1, $3.00; paper,
$2.50; deluxe ed. $5.00; v. 2 (1956) $7.00 cloth; $8.00 deluxe.

1424. Morgan, Lewis Henry
    League of the Ho-dé-no-sau-nee, or Iroquois. New Haven,
Reprinted by Human Relations Area Files, 1954, 2 v. (Behavior
Science Reprints.) $7.50.

    Noon, John A.
    Law and government of the Grand River Iroquois. See no. 197.

1425. Rouse, Irving, and John M. Goggin
    An anthropological bibliography of the eastern seaboard. New
Haven, The Federation, 1947. (Eastern States Archaeological
Federation. Research Publication no. 1.) Out of print? ca. $4.00.

1426.   Speck, Frank Gouldsmith
        The Iroquois, a study in cultural evolution. Bloomfield Hills,
Mich., Cranbrook Institute of Science, 1945. (Cranbrook Institute
of Science. Bulletin no. 23. October, 1945.) $1.00.

(12). Southeast

1427.   Debo, Angie
        The road to disappearance. Norman, University of Oklahoma
Press, 1941. (Civilization of the American Indian series, 22.)
Out of print; ca. $4.00.

1428.   Fundaburk, Emma Lila, ed.
        Sun circles and human hands; the southeastern Indians art
and industries. Luverne, Ala., the Author, 1957, $7.50.

1429.   Lewis, Thomas M. N., and Madeline Kneberg
        Hiwassee island, an archaeological account of four Tennessee
Indian peoples . . . partially based on field reports by Charles H.
Nash. Knoxville, Tenn., University of Tennessee Press, 1946,
$5.50.

1430.   Lewis, Thomas M. N., and Madeline Kneberg
        Tribes that slumber; Indian times in the Tennessee region.
Knoxville, University of Tennessee Press, 1958, $4.75; paper
ed., $3.25.

1431.   Swanton, John Reed
        The Indians of the southeastern United States. Washington,
U. S. Govt. Print. Office, 1946. (U. S. Bureau of American
Ethnology. Bulletin 137.) Out of print; ca. $6.00.

1432.   Willey, Gordon Randolph
        Archaeology of the Florida Culf Coast. Washington, Smith-
sonian institution, 1949. (Smithsonian Miscellaneous Collections,
v. 113.) $4.00.

(13). Southwest

        Aberle, David F.
        The psychosocial analysis of a Hopi life-history. See no.
317.

1433.   Amsden, Charles Avery
        Prehistoric Southwesterners from Basketmaker to Pueblo.
With an introd. by Alfred V. Kidder. Los Angeles, Southwest
Museum, 1949, $3.50.

Bellah, Robert N.
Apache kinship systems. See no. 161.

Benedict, Ruth
Zuni mythology. See no. 286.

1434. Brandt, Richard Booker
Hopi ethics; a theoretical analysis. Chicago, University of
Chicago Press, 1954, $7.50.

Bunzel, Ruth Leah
The Pueblo potter. See no. 306.

1435. Castetter, Edward Franklin, and Willis H. Bell
Pima and Papago Indian agriculture. Albuquerque, N. M.,
The University of New Mexico Press, 1942. (New Mexico.
University. School of Inter-American Affairs. Inter-Americana
Series. Studies, 1.) $3.50.

1436. Castetter, Edward Franklin, and Willis H. Bell
Yuman Indian agriculture; primitive subsistence on the lower
Colorado and Gila rivers. Albuquerque, University of New
Mexico Press, 1951, $4.00.

1437. Chicago. Natural History Museum
Mogollon cultural continuity and change; the stratigraphic
analysis of Tularosa and Cordova caves, by Paul S. Martin and
others. Chicago, 1952. (Fieldiana: Anthropology, v. 40.) $8.00.

1438. Collier, John
Patterns and ceremonials of the Indians of the Southwest,
with over 100 lithographs and drawings by Ira Moskowitz, text
by John Collier, with an introd. by John Sloan. 1st ed. New
York, Dutton, 1949. Out of print; ca. $12.00.

1439. Cosgrove, Cornelius Burton
Caves in the Upper Gila and Hueco areas in New Mexico and
Texas. Cambridge, 1947. (Harvard University. Peabody Museum
of Archaeology and Ethnology. Papers, v. 24, no. 2.) $6.25.

1440. Cummings, Byron
First inhabitants of Arizona and the Southwest. Tucson, Cum-
mings Publication Council, 1953.
Distributor: Southwestern Monuments Association, Globe,
Arizona, $6.00.

1441. Dale, Edward Everett
The Indians of the Southwest; a century of development under
the United States. 1st ed. Norman, published in coöperation
with the Huntington Library, San Marino, Calif., by the University of Oklahoma Press, 1949. (The Civilization of the American
Indian, 28.) Out of print; ca. $4.00.

1442. Di Peso, Charles Corradino
       The Reeve ruin of southeastern Arizona; a study of a prehistoric
western Pueblo migration into the Middle San Pedro Valley. Col-
laborator: Hugh C. Cutler. Dragoon, Ariz., Amerind Foundation,
1958. (Amerind Foundation. Publication, no. 8.) No price.

1443. Di Peso, Charles Corradino
       The Sobaipuri Indians of the Upper San Pedro River Valley,
southeastern Arizona. Collaborators: Arthur Woodward, Rex E.
and M. Virginia Gerald. Dragoon, Amerind Foundation, 1953.
(Amerind Foundation. Publication, no. 6.) No price.

1444. Di Peso, Charles Corradino
       The Upper Pima of San Cayetano del Tumacacori; an archaeo-
historical reconstruction of the Ootam of Pimeria Alta. Collaborators: David A. Breternitz and others. Dragoon, Ariz.,
Amerind Foundation, 1956. (Amerind Foundation. Publication,
no. 7.) No price.

1445. Eggan, Frederick Russell
       Social organization of the western pueblos. Chicago, Univer-
sity of Chicago Press, 1950, $6.00.

1446. Gladwin, Harold Sterling, Emil W. Haury, E. B. Sayles, and
          Nora Gladwin
       Excavations at Snaketown. Globe, Ariz., privately printed for
Gila Pueblo, 1937-1948. 4 v. (Medallion Papers, no. 25-26, 30,
38.) Out of print? ca. $25.00.

1447. Gladwin, Harold Sterling
       A history of the ancient Southwest. Portland, Me., Bond
Wheelwright, 1957, $8.50.

1448. Goodwin, Grenville
       The social organization of the western Apache. Chicago, Uni-
versity of Chicago Press, 1942. Out of print; ca. $5.00.

1449. Guernsey, Samuel James, and Alfred V. Kidder
       Basket maker caves of northeastern Arizona; report on the
explorations, 1916-1917. Cambridge, 1921. (Harvard University.
Peabody Museum of Archaeology and Ethnology. Papers, v. 8,
no. 2.) Out of print; ca. $4.00.

1450. Haury, Emil Walter
       Painted cave, northeastern Arizona . . . with an appendix,
The maize collections from Painted cave, by Edgar Anderson.
Dragoon, Ariz., The Amerind Foundation, 1945. (The Amerind
Foundation. Publications, no. 3.) No price.

1451. Haury, Emil Walter
       The stratigraphy and archaeology of Ventana Cave, Arizona.
Albuquerque, Univ. of New Mexico Press; Tucson, University
of Arizona Press, 1950, $15.00.

1452.   Hewett, Edgar Lee, and Bertha P. Dutton
        The Pueblo Indian world; studies on the natural history of
        the Rio Grande valley in relation to Pueblo Indian culture,
        edited, adapted, and amplified by Edgar L. Hewett and Bertha
        P. Dutton; with appendices: The southwest Indian languages and
        The sounds and structure of the Aztecan language, by John P.
        Harrington. Albuquerque, The University of New Mexico and
        the School of American Research, 1945. Out of print; ca. $5.00.

1453.   Joseph, Alice, Rosamond B. Spicer, and Jane Chesky
        The desert people; a study of the Papago Indians. Chicago,
        University of Chicago Press, 1949. (Indian Education Research
        Series, no. 4.) Out of print; ca. $6.00.

1454.   Judd, Neil Merton
        The material culture of Pueblo Bonito. With appendix, Candid
        remains from Pueblo Bonito and Pueblo de Arroyo, by Glover
        M. Allen. Washington, Smithsonian Institution, 1954. (Smithsonian
        Miscellaneous Collections, v. 124.) $5.00.

1455.   Kidder, Alfred Vincent, and Samuel J. Guernsey
        Archeological explorations in northeastern Arizona. Washing-
        ton, Govt. Print. Office, 1919. (U. S. Bureau of American Eth-
        nology, Bulletin 65.) Out of print; ca. $5.00.

1456.   Kidder, Alfred Vincent
        Pecos, New Mexico: archaeological notes. Andover, Mass.,
        Phillips Academy, the Foundation, 1958. (Phillips Academy,
        Andover, Mass., Robert S. Peabody Foundation for Archaeology.
        Papers, v. 5.) $7.50.

1457.   Kluckhohn, Clyde, and Dorothea (Cross) Leighton
        The Navaho. Cambridge, Mass., Harvard University Press;
        London, G. Cumberledge, Oxford University Press, 1946, $5.00;
        text ed., $3.75.

        Kluckhohn, Clyde
        Navaho witchcraft. See no. 212.

1458.   Ladd, John
        The structure of a moral code; a philosophical analysis of
        ethical discourse applied to the ethics of the Navaho Indians.
        Cambridge, Mass., Harvard University Press, 1957, $9.00.

1459.   Lange, Charles H.
        Cochiti: a New Mexico pueblo, past and present. Austin,
        University of Texas Press, 1960, $10.00.

        Left Handed, Navajo Indian
        Son of Old Man Hat; a Navaho autobiography recorded by
        Walter Dyk. See no. 343.

1460.   Leighton, Dorothea (Cross), and Clyde Kluckhohn
        Children of the people; the Navaho individual and his develop-
        ment. Cambridge, Mass., Harvard University Press, 1947. Out
        of print; ca. $4.00.

1461.   Leighton, Alexander Hamilton, and Dorothea (Cross) Leighton
        The Navaho door; an introduction to Navaho life. Foreword by
        John Collier. Cambridge, Mass., Harvard University Press, 1944.
        Out of print; ca. $5.00.

1462.   Lockett, H. Claiborne, and Lyndon L. Hargrave
        Woodchuck cave, a Basketmaker II site in Tsegi Canyon, Ariz.
        Edited by Harold S. Colton and Robert C. Euler. Flagstaff, 1953.
        (Museum of Northern Arizona. Bulletin 26.) No price.

        McAllester, David P.
        Enemy way music; a study of social and esthetic values as seen
        in Navaho music. See no. 279.

1463.   McCombe, Leonard, Evon Z. Vogt, and Clyde Kluckhohn
        Navaho means people; photos. by Leonard McCombe, text by
        Evon Z. Vogt and Clyde Kluckhohn. Cambridge, Mass., Harvard
        University Press, 1951, $5.00.

1464.   McGregor, John Charles
        The Cohonia culture of northwestern Arizona. Urbana, Univer-
        sity of Illinois Press, 1951. Out of print; ca. $2.00.

1465.   McGregor, John Charles
        Southwestern archaeology. New York, Wiley; London, Chapman
        & Hall, 1941. Out of print; ca. $7.50.

1466.   Martin, Paul Sidney, John B. Rinaldo, and Elaine Bluhm
        Caves of the Reserve area. Chicago, Chicago Natural History
        Museum, 1954. (Fieldiana: Anthropology, v. 42.) $5.00.

1467.   Martin, Paul Sidney, John B. Rinaldo, and Ernest Antevs
        Cochise and Mogollon sites, Pine Lawn Valley, western New
        Mexico. Chicago, Chicago Natural History Museum, 1949.
        (Fieldiana: Anthropology, v. 38, no. 1.) $3.50.

        Martin, Paul Sidney
        Digging into history; a brief account of fifteen years of archaeo-
        logical work in New Mexico. See no. 426.

1468.   Martin, Paul Sidney
        Excavations in the upper little Colorado drainage, eastern
        Arizona. Chicago, Chicago Natural History Museum, 1960.
        (Fieldiana: Anthropology, v. 51, no. 1.) $4.00.

1469.   Martin, Paul Sidney
        Higgins Flat Pueblo, western New Mexico, by Paul S. Martin
        and others. Chicago, Chicago Natural History Museum, 1956.
        (Fieldiana: Anthropology, v. 45.) $4.50.

1470.   Martin, Paul Sidney, John B. Rinaldo, and Eloise R. Barter
        Late Mogollon communities; four sites of the Tularosa phase,
        western New Mexico. Chicago, Chicago Natural History Museum,
        1957. (Fieldiana: Anthropology, v. 49, no. 1.) $4.00.

1471.   Martin, Paul Sidney
        The SU site excavations at a Mogollon village, western New
        Mexico, 1939 . . . with reports on pottery and artifacts, by
        John Rinaldo, and appendix on skeletal material, by Marjorie
        Kelly. Chicago, Field Museum of Natural History, 1940.
        (Fieldiana: Anthropology, v. 32, no. 1.) $2.00.

1472.   Martin, Paul Sidney
        The SU site excavations at a Mogollon village, western New
        Mexico, second season, 1941. Chicago, Field Museum of Natural
        History, 1943. (Fieldiana: Anthropology, v. 32, no. 2.) Out of
        print; ca. $4.00.

1473.   Martin, Paul Sidney, and John B. Rinaldo
        The SU site excavation at a Mogollon village, western New
        Mexico, third season, 1946. Chicago, Field Museum of Natural
        History, 1947. (Fieldiana: Anthropology, v. 32, no. 3.) Out of
        print; ca. $4.00.

1474.   Martin, Paul Sidney, and John B. Rinaldo
        Table rock pueblo, Arizona. Chicago, Chicago Natural History
        Museum, 1960. (Fieldiana: Anthropology, v. 51, no. 2.) $5.50.

1475.   Martin, Paul Sidney, and John B. Rinaldo
        Turkey Foot Ridge site; a Mogollon village, Pine Lawn Valley,
        western New Mexico. Chicago, Chicago Natural History Museum,
        1950. (Fieldiana: Anthropology, v. 38, no. 2.) $2.75.

1476.   Opler, Morris Edward
        An Apache life-way; the economic, social, and religious insti-
        tutions of the Chiricahua Indians. Chicago, University of Chicago
        Press, 1941. Out of print; ca. $5.00.

1477.   Opler, Morris Edward
        Childhood and youth in Jicarilla Apache society. Los Angeles,
        The Southwest Museum, 1946. (Publications of the Frederick Webb
        Hodge Anniversary Publication Fund, v. 5.) $3.00.

        Parsons, Elsie Worthington (Clews)
        Pueblo Indian religion. See no. 227.

        Reichard, Gladys Amanda
        Navaho religion. See no. 230.

1478.   Spier, Leslie
        Havasupai ethnography. New York, 1928. (American Museum
        of Natural History. Anthropological Papers, v. 29, pt. 3.) Out of
        print? ca. $4.00.

1479. Spier, Leslie
        Yuman tribes of the Gila river. Chicago, University of
        Chicago Press, 1933. Out of print; ca. $4.00.

        Talayesva, Don C.
        Sun chief. See no. 354.

1480. Thompson, Laura
        Culture in crisis; a study of the Hopi Indians. With a fore-
        word by John Collier, and a chapter from the writings of Ben-
        jamin Lee Whorf. New York, Harper, 1950. Out of print; ca.
        $4.00.

1481. Thompson, Laura, and Alice Joseph
        The Hopi way . . . with a foreword by John Collier, com-
        missioner of Indian affairs. Chicago, Ill., University of Chi-
        cago Press, 1945. Out of print; ca. $4.00.

1482. Titiev, Mischa
        Old Oraibi, a study of the Hopi Indians of third mesa. Cam-
        bridge, Mass., The Museum, 1944. (Papers of the Peabody
        Museum of American Archaeology and Ethnology, Harvard Uni-
        versity, v. 22, no. 1.) Out of print; ca. $5.50.

1483. Underhill, Ruth Murray
        The Navajos. Norman, University of Oklahoma Press, 1956.
        (Civilization of the American Indian Series, 43.) $4.50.

        Underhill, Ruth Murray
        Papago Indian religion. See no. 236.

1484. Vogt, Evon Zartman
        Navaho veterans; a study of changing values. Cambridge,
        Mass., The Museum, 1951. (Reports of the Rimrock Project.
        Values Series, no. 1.) (Papers of the Peabody Museum of Ameri-
        can Archaoelogy and Ethnology, Harvard University, v. 41, no. 1.)
        $3.00.

1485. White, Leslie A.
        The Acoma Indians. (In U. S. Bureau of American Ethnology.
        Forty-seventh Annual Report, 1929-1930. Washington, 1932.
        pp. 17-192.) Out of print; ca. $6.00.

1486. White, Leslie A.
        The Pueblo of Santa Ana, New Mexico. Menasha, Wis., 1942.
        (American Anthropological Association. Memoirs, no. 60.) $3.75.

1487. Wormington, Hannah Marie
        Prehistoric Indians of the Southwest; appendix: Outstanding
        exhibit-sites, modern pueblos, local museums, by Erik K.
        Reed. 3d ed. Denver, Colo., Denver Museum of Natural His-

tory, 1956. (Denver, Colo., Museum of Natural History. Popular Ser., no. 7.) $3.20; paper, $2.20.

C. Central America and Mexico

1488. Barlow, Robert Hayward
The extent of the empire of the Culhua Mexica. Berkeley and Los Angeles, University of California Press, 1949. (Ibero-Americana: 28.) $2.50.

1489. Beals, Ralph Leon
The aboriginal culture of the Cáhita Indians. Berkeley and Los Angeles, University of California Press, 1943. (Ibero-Americana: 19.) $1.25.

1490. Beals, Ralph Leon
The comparative ethnology of northern Mexico before 1750. Berkeley, University of California Press, 1932. (Ibero-Americana: 2.) $1.50.

1491. Beals, Ralph Leon
Contemporary culture of the Cáhita Indians. Washington, U. S. Govt. Printing Office, 1945. (U. S. Bureau of American Ethnology. Bulletin 142.) In print 1956; no price.

1492. Beals, Ralph Leon
Ethnology of the western Mixe. Berkeley and Los Angeles, University of California Press, 1945. (University of California Publications in American Archaeology and Ethnology, v. 42, no. 1.) $2.25.

1493. Borah, Woodrow Wilson
New Spain's century of depression. Berkeley and Los Angeles, University of California Press, 1951. (Ibero-Americana: 35.) Out of print.

1494. Borah, Woodrow Wilson, and Sherburne Friend Cook
Price trends of some basic commodities in central Mexico, 1531-1570. Berkeley and Los Angeles, University of California Press, 1958. (Ibero-Americana: 40.) $2.00.

1495. Brainerd, George Walton
The archaeological ceramics of Yucatan. Berkeley and Los Angeles, University of California Press, 1958, $8.00.
Also published as: University of California Anthropological Records, v. 19.

1496. Brainerd, George Walton
The Maya civilization. Los Angeles, Southwest Museum, 1954, $2.50.

1497.   Caso, Alfonso
        The Aztecs; people of the sun. Illus. by Miguel Covarrubias;
        translated by Lowell Dunham. 1st ed. Norman, University of
        Oklahoma Press, 1958. (Civilization of the American Indian
        series, 50.) $7.95.

1498.   Cook, Sherburne Friend, and Lesley Byrd Simpson
        The population of central Mexico in the sixteenth century.
        Berkeley and Los Angeles, University of California Press, 1948.
        (Ibero-Americana: 31.) $3.75.

1499.   Cook, Sherburne Friend
        Santa María Ixcatlán: habitat, population, subsistence. Berkeley
        and Los Angeles, University of California Press, 1958. (Ibero-
        Americana: 41.) $1.50.

1500.   Cortés, Hernando
        Five letters, 1519-1526, translated by J. Bayard Morris,
        with an introduction. London, Routledge, 1928; New York,
        McBride, 1929. Out of print; ca. $6.00.

1501.   Covarrubias, Miguel
        Indian art of Mexico and Central America. Color plates and
        line drawings by the author. 1st ed. New York, Knopf, 1957,
        $17.50.

1502.   Covarrubias, Miguel
        Mexico south, the isthmus of Tehuantepec. Paintings and
        drawings by the author, photographs by Rose Covarrubias, the
        author, and others. New York, Knopf, 1947, $12.50.

1503.   De Terra, Helmut
        Man and mammoth in Mexico; translated from the German
        by Alan Houghton Brodrick. London, Hutchinson, 1957, 25/-.

1504.   Diaz del Castillo, Bernal
        Discovery and conquest of Mexico, 1517-1521. Edited from
        the only exact copy of the original ms. (and published in Mexi-
        co) by Genaro García. Translated with an introd. and notes by
        A. P. Maudslay. Introd. to the American ed. by Irving A. Leon-
        ard. New York, Farrar, Straus and Cudahy, 1956, $6.50.

1505.   Drucker, Philip, Robert F. Heizer, and Robert J. Squier
        Excavations at La Venta, Tabasco, 1955. With appendixes
        by Jonas E. Gullberg, Garniss H. Curtis and A. Starker Leopold.
        Washington, U. S. Govt. Print. Office, 1959. (U. S. Bureau of
        American Ethnology. Bulletin 170.) $4.00.

        Foster, George M.
        Empire's children. See no. 1641.
        A primitive Mexican economy. See no. 1642.

1506.   Gallenkamp, Charles
        Maya; the riddle and rediscovery of a lost civilization.
        Drawings by John Skolle. New York, McKay, 1959, $5.50.

1507.   Gibson, Charles
        Tlaxcala in the sixteenth century. New Haven, Yale University
        Press, 1952. (Yale Historical Publications. Miscellany, 56) $7.50.

1508.   Kidder, Alfred Vincent, Jesse D. Jennings, and Edwin M. Shook
        Excavations at Kaminaljuyu . . . with technological notes by
        Anna O. Shepard. Washington, 1946. (Carnegie Institution of
        Washington. Publication 561.) Out of print; ca. $8.00.

1509.   Landa, Diego de
        Landa's relación de las cosas de Yucatan, a translation,
        edited with notes by Alfred M. Tozzer. Cambridge, Mass., 1941.
        (Harvard University. Peabody Museum of American Archaeology
        and Ethnology. Papers, v. 18.) $5.85; bound in cloth, $8.85.

        Lewis, Oscar
        Life in a Mexican village: Tepoztlan restudied. See no. 1647.

1510.   Linné, Sigvald
        Archaeological researches at Teotihuacan, Mexico. Stockholm,
        Petterson, 1934. (The Ethnographical Museum of Sweden. [Riks-
        museets etnografiska avdelning] New series. Publication no. 1.)
        Out of print? ca. $10.00.

1511.   Linné, Sigvald
        Mexican highland cultures; archaeological researches at
        Teotihuacan, Calpulalpan and Chalchicomula in 1934/35. Stock-
        holm, 1942. (Ethnographical Museum of Sweden, Stockholm.
        New series. Publications no. 7.) 36 Kr.-.
        U. S. distributor: Humanities Press, New York, $10.00.

        Linné, Sigvald
        Treasures of Mexican art. See no. 265.

1512.   Linné, Sigvald
        El Valle y la ciudad de Mexico en 1550; relación histórica
        fundada sobre un mapa geográfico, que se conserva en la
        Biblioteca de la Universidad de Uppsala, Suecia. Stockholm,
        Esselte, 1948. (Statens Etnografiska Museum, Stockholm. New
        series. Publication no. 9.)
        U. S. distributor: Humanities Press, New York, $20.00.

1513.   Linné, Sigvald
        Zapotecan antiquities and the Paulson collection in the Ethno-
        graphical Museum of Sweden. With 27 text figures and 32 plates.
        Stockholm, Sweden, Bokförlags aktiebolaget Thule, 1938. [The
        Ethnographical Museum of Sweden, Stockholm (Statens Etnogra-
        fiska Museum) new series. Publication no. 4.] 30 Kr.-.
        U. S. distributor: New York, Humanities Press, $7.50.

256 REXFORD S. BECKHAM

1514. McBryde, Felix Webster
        Cultural and historical geography of southwest Guatemala.
        Prepared in coöperation with the United States Department of
        State as a project of the Interdepartmental Committee on
        Scientific and Cultural Coöperation. Washington, U. S. Govt.
        Print. Office, 1947. (Smithsonian Institution. Institute of Social
        Anthropology. Publication no. 4.) Out of print; estimate: $3.00.

1515. Marquina, Ignacio
        Arquitectura prehispánica. México, Instituto Nacional de
        Antropología e Historia, Secretaría de Educación Pública, 1951.
        (Memorias del Instituto Nacional de Antropología e Historia, 1.)
        Estimate: $8.00.

1516. The Maya and their neighbors. Limited ed. New York, London,
        Appleton-Century, c1940. Out of print; rare. Reprint announced
        for 1962 by University of Utah Press. No price.

1517. Morley, Sylvanus Griswold
        The ancient Maya. Revised by George W. Brainerd. 3d ed.
        Stanford, Calif., Stanford University Press, 1956, $10.00; text
        ed., $8.50.

        Nash, Manning
        Machine age Maya. See no. 1650.

1518. Peterson, Frederick A.
        Ancient Mexico; an introduction to pre-Hispanic cultures. Maps
        and drawings by José Luis Franco. New York, Putnam, 1959, $7.95.

1519. Proskouriakoff, Tatiana Avenirovna
        An album of Maya architecture. Washington, D. C., 1946.
        (Carnegie Institution of Washington. Publication 558.) Out of
        print.
        1961 reprint available from Mrs. Frances Swadener, Manager,
        Hacienda Uxmal, Uxmal, Yucatan, Mexico, $12.00.

        Redfield, Robert
        Folk culture of Yucatan. See no. 1653.
        Tepoztlan. See no. 1654.

1520. Rivet, Paul
        Maya cities. Translated from the French by Miriam and
        Lionel Kochan. London, Elek Books, 1960, 35/-; New York,
        Putnam, 1960, $5.95.

1521. Ruppert, Karl, J. Eric S. Thompson, and Tatiana Proskouriakoff
        Bonampak Chiapas, Mexico. Copies of the mural paintings
        by Antonio Tejeda F. Identification of pigments in the mural
        paintings by Rutherford J. Gettens. Washington, 1955. (Carnegie
        Institution of Washington. Publication 602.) $3.00.

1522. Sahagún, Bernardino de
General history of the things of New Spain; Florentine codex, translated from the Aztec into English, with notes and translations, by Arthur J. O. Anderson and Charles E. Dibble. Santa Fe, New Mexico, School of American Research, 1950- (Monographs of the School of American Research, no. 14.) In progress. Nine parts have been published. Book I, $4.00; II, $8.00; III, $4.00; IV-V, $8.00; VII, $4.00; VIII, $4.50; IX, $6.50; XII, $6.50.

1523. Sauer, Carl Ortwin
Colima of New Spain in the sixteenth century. Berkeley and Los Angeles, University of California Press, 1948. (Ibero-Americana: 29.) $2.00.

1524. Séjourné, Laurette
Burning water; thought and religion in ancient Mexico. With 82 drawings by Abel Mendoza and 22 photographs. Translated by Irene Nicholson. New York, Thames & Hudson, 1957. (Myth and man.)
U. S. distributor: Vanguard Press, $6.00.
Paper: New York, Grove Press, 1960 (Myth and Man series: Evergreen ed. E241.) $1.95.

1525. Simpson, Leslie Byrd
Many Mexicos. 3d ed., rev. and enl. Berkeley and Los Angeles, University of California Press, 1952, $6.50.
Paper: Berkeley and Los Angeles, University of California Press, 1959, $1.95.

1526. Spicer, Edward Holland
Pascua, a Yaqui village in Arizona. Chicago, The University of Chicago Press, 1940. Out of print; ca. $4.00.

1527. Spicer, Edward Holland
Potam, a Yaqui village in Sonora. Menasha, Wis., 1954. (American Anthropological Association. Memoir no. 77.) $3.00.

1528. Spinden, Herbert Joseph
Maya art and civilization. Rev. and enl. with added illus. Indian Hills, Colo., Falcon's Wing Press, 1957, $10.00.
First published in 1913 under title: A study of Maya art.

1529. Stone, Doris (Zemurray)
The archaeology of central and southern Honduras. Cambridge, Mass., Peabody Museum, 1957. (Papers of the Peabody Museum of Archaeology and Ethnology, Harvard University, v. 49, no. 3.) $5.85.

1530. Stone, Doris (Zemurray)
Introduction to the archaeology of Costa Rica. San Jose, Costa Rica, Museo Nacional, 1958. No price; estimate: $1.00.

Tax, Sol
  Heritage of conquest. See no. 1657.
  Penny capitalism. See no. 1658.

1531. Taylor, Douglas MacRae
  The Black Carib of British Honduras. New York, Wenner-
Gren Foundation for Anthropological Research, 1951. (Viking
Fund Publications in Anthropology, no. 17.) Out of print; ca.
$3.00.

1532. Thompson, John Eric Sidney
  Maya hieroglyphic writing; an introduction. 2d ed. Norman,
University of Oklahoma Press, 1960. (Civilization of the Ameri-
can Indian Series, no. 56.) $10.00.

1533. Thompson, John Eric Sidney
  Mexico before Cortez; an account of the daily life, religion,
and ritual of the Aztecs and kindred peoples. New York, London, Scribner's, 1940. Out of print; ca. $6.00.

1534. Thompson, John Eric Sidney
  The rise and fall of Maya civilization. 1st ed. Norman,
University of Oklahoma Press, 1954. (Civilization of the Ameri-
can Indian, 39.) $5.00.

1535. Vaillant, George Clapp
  The Aztecs of Mexico; origin, rise and fall of the Aztec
nation. Garden City, N. Y., Doubleday, Doran, 1941. (American
Museum of Natural History. Science Series, v. 2.) Out of print;
ca. $5.00.
  Paper ed: With a postscript by C. A. Burland. Harmondsworth, Middlesex, Penguin, 1950. (Pelican Books, A200.) $1.45.

Wagley, Charles
  Economics of the Guatemalan village. See no. 1660.
  The social and religious life in a Guatemalan village. See
no. 1661.

1536. Wolf, Eric Robert
  Sons of the shaking earth. Chicago, University of Chicago
Press, 1959. $5.00.

d. South America

1537. Acosta Saignes, Miguel
  Estudios de etnología antigua de Venezuela. Prólogo de Fer-
nando Ortiz. Caracas, Instituto de Antropología y Geografía,
Facultad de Humanidades y Educación, Universidad Central de
Venezuela, 1954. (Antropología, 1.) No price. Estimate: $3.00.

1538. Antiguo Perú; espacio y tiempo; trabajos presentados a la
Semana de arqueología peruana (9-14 de noviembre de 1959)
Lima, Librería-Editorial Juan Mejía Baca, 1960. Estimate:
$3.00.

1539. Baldus, Herbert
Bibliografia crítica de etnologia brasileira. Sao Paulo, Co-
missão do IV Centenário da Cidade de São Paulo Serviço de
Comemoracões Culturais, 1954. No price. Estimate: $10.00.

Bennett, Wendell Clark
Ancient arts of the Andes. See no. 248.

1540. Bennett, Wendell Clark, and Junius B. Bird
Andean culture history. 2d and rev. ed. New York, 1960. (American Museum of Natural History. Handbook Series, no. 15.) $5.00.

1541. Bennett, Wendell Clark
Archaeological regions of Colombia: a ceramic survey. New
Haven, published for the Dept. of Anthropology, Yale University,
by the Yale University Press; London, H. Milford, Oxford University Press, 1944. (Yale University Publications in Anthropology,
no. 30.) $2.50.

1542. Bennett, Wendell Clark, comp.
A reappraisal of Peruvian archaeology. Menasha, Wis., Published jointly by the Society for American Archaeology and the
Institute for Andean Research, 1948. (Memoirs of the Society
for American Archaeology, no. 4.) $2.00.

1543. Bushnell, Geoffrey Hext Sutherland
The archaeology of the Santa Elena Peninsula in southwest
Ecuador. Cambridge, University Press, 1951. (Occasional publications of the Cambridge University Museum of Archaeology
and Ethnology, 1.) $9.50.

1544. Bushnell, Geoffrey Hext Sutherland
Peru. London, Thames & Hudson, 1957; New York, Praeger,
1957, $6.50 (Ancient Peoples and Places, v. 1.)

1545. Caspar, Franz
Tupari. Translated by Eric Northcott. London, Bell, 1956,
18/6.

1546. Chile. Universidad, Santiago. Centro de Estudios Antropológicos.
Arqueología chilena; contribuciónes al estudio de la región
comprendida entre Arica y la Serena. Richard P. Schaedel,
editor. Santiago de Chile, 1957-
Contents: 1. Informe general sobre la expedición a la zona
comprendida entre Arica y la Serena, por R. P. Schaedel.
Secuencias culturales de la zona de Arica, por C. Munizaga
A. Apéndices al trabajo no. 1, por A. A. Toro, et al. Estimate: $3.00.

1547. Cieza de León, Pedro de
       The Incas. Translated by Harriet de Onis. Edited, with an
       introd. by Victor Wolfgang von Hagen. 1st ed. Norman, Uni-
       versity of Oklahoma Press, 1959. (Civilization of the American
       Indian Series, v. 53.) $5.95.

1548. Cornely, Francisco L.
       Cultura diaguita chilena, y Cultura de El Molle. Santiago de
       Chile, Editorial del Pacífico, 1956. Estimate: $4.00.

1549. Cruxent, José María, and Irving Rouse
       An archeological chronology of Venezuela. Washington, Pan
       American Union, 1958-1959, 2 v. (Pan American Union. Social
       Science Monographs, no. 6.) $1.00 per vol.

1550. Evans, Clifford, and Betty Jane Meggers
       Archeological investigations in British Guiana. Washington,
       U. S. Govt. Print. Office, 1960. (U. S. Bureau of American
       Ethnology. Bulletin 177.) $4.00.

1551. Fejos, Pál
       Ethnography of the Yagua, by Paul Fejos. New York, The
       Viking Fund, inc., 1943. (Viking Fund Publications in Anthro-
       pology, no. 1.) Out of print; ca. $3.50.

1552. Hilger, Inez
       Araucanian child life and its cultural background. Washing-
       ton, Smithsonian Institution, 1957. (Smithsonian Miscellaneous
       Collections, v. 133.) $7.00.

1553. Holmberg, Allan R.
       Nomads of the long bow; the Siriono of eastern Bolivia. Pre-
       pared in coöperation with the U. S. Dept. of State as a project
       of the Interdepartmental Committee on Scientific and Cultural
       Cooperation. Washington, U. S. Govt. Print. Office, 1950. (Smith-
       sonian Institution. Institute of Social Anthropology. Publication
       no. 10.) $0.65.

1554. Huxley, Francis
       Affable savages; an anthropologist among the Urubu Indians
       of Brazil. London, Hart-Davis, 1956, 25/-; New York, Viking,
       1957, $4.75.

1555. Kahn, Morton Charles
       Djuka, the bush Negroes of Dutch Guiana . . . with an intro-
       duction by Blair Niles, and a foreword by Clark Wissler. New
       York, Viking, 1931. Out of print; ca. $4.00.

1556. Karsten, Rafael
       The head-hunters of Western Amazonas; the life and culture
       of the Jibaro Indians of eastern Ecuador and Peru. Helsingfors,
       1935. (Finska vetenskaps-societeten, Helsingfors. Commentationes
       humanarum litterarum. VII. 1.) Out of print; ca. $7.50.

1557. Lévi-Strauss, Claude
       Tristes tropiques. Translated by John Russell. New York, Cri-
       terion Books, 1961, $12.50. London, Hutchinson, 1961, 42/-. Brit-
       ish ed. has title: A world on the wane.
       A translation of the French work (Paris, Plon, 1955) omitting
       chapters 14-16 and 39.

1558. Lima. Universidad de San Marcos. Instituto de Etnología y
       Arqueología.
       La actuales comunidades de indígenas: Huarochirí en 1955,
       por José Matos, Teresa Guillén de Boluarte, Julio Cotler, Edu-
       ardo Soler, Francisco Boluarte. Lima, 1958. (Universidad
       Nacional Mayor de San Marcos. Serie monografías etnológicas,
       v. 1.) Estimate: $3.00.

1559. Lothrop, Samuel Kirkland
       Indians of the Paraná delta, Argentina. New York, 1932. (New
       York Academy of Sciences. Annals, v. 33, art. 3, pp. 77-232.) $2.00.

1560. Mason, John Alden
       Ancient civilization of Peru. Harmondsworth, Middlesex.
       Penguin, 1957. (Pelican Books, A395.) $1.45.

1561. Meggers, Betty Jane, and Clifford Evans
       Archaeological investigations at the mouth of the Amazon.
       Washington, U. S. Govt. Printing Office, 1957. (U. S. Bureau of
       American Ethnology. Bulletin 167.) $5.00.

1562. Moore, Sally Falk
       Power and property in Inca Peru. New York, Columbia Uni-
       versity Press, 1958, $5.00.

1563. Nimuendajú, Curt
       The Apinaye . . . translated by Robert H. Lowie, edited by
       Robert H. Lowie and John M. Cooper. Washington, D. C., The
       Catholic University of America Press, 1939. (Catholic Univer-
       sity of America. Anthropological Series, no. 8.) $2.50.

1564. Nimuendajú, Curt
       The eastern Timbira. Translated and edited by Robert H.
       Lowie. Berkeley and Los Angeles, University of California
       Press, 1946. Out of print.
       Also published as University of California Publications in
       American Archaeology and Ethnology, v. 41.

1565. Nimeundajú, Curt
       The Serente . . . translated from the manuscript by Robert
       H. Lowie, Los Angeles, The Southwest Museum, 1942. (Publi-
       cations of the Frederick Webb Hodge Anniversary Publication
       Fund, v. 4.) $1.75.

1566. Oberg, Kalervo
       Indian tribes of northern Mato Grosso, Brazil. With appen-
       dix: Anthropometry of the Umotina, Nambicuara, and Iranxe,
       with comparative data from other northern Mato Grosso tribes

by Marshall T. Newman. Washington, U. S. Govt. Print. Office, 1953. (Smithsonian Institution. Institute of Social Anthropology. Publication no. 15.) $1.00.

1567.   Osgood, Cornelius, and George D. Howard
An archeological survey of Venezuela. New Haven, published for the Dept. of Anthropology, Yale University by the Yale University Press; London, H. Milford, Oxford University Press, 1943. (Yale University Publications in Anthropology, no. 27.) $3.50.

1568.   Rydén, Stig
Andean excavations. I: the Tiahuanaco era east of Lake Titicaca. II: Tupuraya and Cayhuasi; 2 Tiahuanaco sites. Stockholm, 1957-1959. (Stockholm. Statens Etnografiska Museum. Monograph series. Publication, 4 & 6.) I, 52 Kr.; II, ca. $10.50.

1569.   Rydén, Stig
Archaeological researches in the highlands of Bolivia. Göteborg. (The author, Museum, Göteborg, Sweden.) 1947. In print? 50 Kr.

1570.   Rydén, Stig
Contributions to the archaeology of the Rio Loa region; with five colour plates, 132 illustrations, and two appendices by Carl-Herman Hjortsjö and Bengt Kjerrman. Göteborg, Elanders boktryckeri aktiebolag, 1944. ca. $4.00.

1571.   Schmidt, Max
Kunst and Kultur von Peru. Berlin, Propyläen-Verlag, 1929.

1572.   Squier, Ephraim George
Peru; incidents of travel and exploration in the land of the Incas. New York, Harper, 1877; London, Macmillan, 1877. Out of print.

1573.   Steward, Julian Haynes, ed.
Handbook of South American Indians. Prepared in coöperation with the United States Department of State as a project of the Interdepartmental Committee on Cultural and Scientific Coöperation. Washington, U. S. Govt. Print. Office, 1946-1959, 7 v. (U. S. Bureau of American Ethnology. Bulletin 143.) v. 1-6, out of print; ca. $75.00; v. 7 (Index) $2.00.

1574.   Steward, Julian Haynes, and Louis C. Faron
Native peoples of South America. New York, McGraw-Hill, 1959, $11.50; text ed., $8.50.

1575.   Strong, William Duncan, Gordon R. Willey, and John M. Corbett
Archaeological studies in Peru, 1941-1942. New York, Columbia University Press, 1943. (Columbia Studies in Archeology and Ethnology, v. 1.) $4.75.

1576. Strong, William Duncan, and Clifford Evans
       Cultural stratigraphy in the Virú Valley, northern Peru; the
       formative and florescent epochs. New York, Columbia Univer-
       sity Press, 1952. (Columbia Studies in Archeology and Eth-
       nology, v. 4.) $8.50.

1577. Ubbelohde-Doering, Heinrich
       The art of ancient Peru. New York, Praeger, 1952. (Books
       That Matter.) Out of print; ca. $9.00.

1578. United Nations Educational, Scientific and Cultural Organization
       Cuzco, reconstruction of the town and restoration of its monu-
       ments. Report of the UNESCO mission of 1951, by George Kubler.
       Paris, 1952. (Museums and Monuments, 3.) $1.50.

1579. Verger, Pierre
       Indians of Peru; photography by Pierre Verger, with a text
       by Luis E. Valcárcel. Lake Forest, Ill., Pocahontas Press;
       distributed by Pantheon, New York, 1950. Out of print? ca.
       $7.50.

1580. Walter, H. V.
       The pre-history of the Lagoa Santa region, Minas Gerais.
       Guajajaras, 1948. Estimate: $4.00.

1581. Willey, Gordon Randolph, and John M. Corbett
       Early Ancón and Early Supe culture, Chavín horizon sites of
       the Central Peruvian coast. With special sections by Lila M.
       O'Neale and others. New York, Columbia University Press,
       1954. (Columbia Studies in Archeology and Ethnology, v. 3) $5.00.

1582. Willey, Gordon Randolph
       Prehistoric settlement patterns in the Virú Valley, Perú.
       Washington, U. S. Govt. Print. Office, 1953. (U. S. Bureau of
       American Ethnology. Bulletin 155.) $4.00.

       e. West Indies

1583. Harrington, Mark Raymond
       Cuba before Columbus. New York, 1921. (New York. Mu-
       seum of the American Indian, Heye Foundation. Indian notes and
       monographs. Miscellaneous series, no. 17.) 2 v. In print? ca.
       $8.00.

1584. Krieger, Herbert William
       Archaeological and historical investigations in Samaná, Do-
       minican Republic. Washington, U. S. Govt. Print. Office, 1929.
       (U. S. National museum. Bulletin, no. 147.) Out of print? ca.
       $5.00.

1585. Lovén, Sven
       Origins of the Tainan culture, West Indies . . . with nineteen
       plates and one map. Göteborg, Elanders boktryckeri aktiebolag,
       1935. Out of print? ca. $10.00.

1586. Mason, John Alden
       A large archaeological site at Capa, Utuado, with notes on
       other Porto Rico sites visited in 1914-1915, with numerous
       illustrations, by J. Alden Mason; Appendix—an analysis of the
       artifacts of the 1914-1915 Porto Rican Survey, with many illus-
       trations, by Irving Rouse. New York, 1941. (New York Academy
       of Sciences. Scientific survey of Porto Rico and the Virgin
       Islands, v. 18, pt. 2.) $2.00.

1587. Osgood, Cornelius, and Irving Rouse
       The Ciboney culture of Cayo Redondo, Cuba, by Cornelius
       Osgood; Archeology of the Maniabón Hills, Cuba, by Irving Rouse.
       New Haven, published for the Department of Anthropology, Yale
       University by the Yale University Press; London, H. Milford,
       Oxford University Press, 1942. (Yale University Publications
       in Anthropology, no. 25-26.) $3.50.

1588. Rainey, Froelich Gladstone, and Irving Rouse
       Excavations in the Ft. Liberté region, Haiti, by F. G. Rainey;
       Culture of the Ft. Liberté region, Haiti, by Irving Rouse. New
       Haven, published for the Dept. of Anthropology, Yale University,
       Yale University Press; London, H. Milford, Oxford University
       Press, 1941. (Yale University Publications in Anthropology,
       no. 23-24.) $3.50.

1589. Rainey, Froelich Gladstone
       Porto Rican archaeology. New York, 1940. (New York Aca-
       demy of Sciences. Scientific survey of Porto Rico and the Vir-
       gin Islands, v. 18, pt. 1.) $2.00.

1590. Rouse, Irving
       Porto Rican prehistory: excavations in the interior, south,
       and east; chronological implications. New York, 1952. (New
       York Academy of Sciences. Scientific Survey of Porto Rico and
       the Virgin Islands, v. 18, pt. 4.) $2.00.

1591. Rouse, Irving
       Porto Rican prehistory: introduction; excavations in the West
       and North, illustrated. New York, 1952. (New York Academy
       of Sciences. Scientific Survey of Porto Rico and the Virgin
       Islands, v. 18, pt. 3.) $2.00.

1592. Rouse, Irving
       Prehistory in Haiti; a study in method. New Haven, published
       for the Department of Anthropology, Yale University, by the Yale
       University Press; London, H. Milford, Oxford University Press,
       1939. (Yale University Publications in Anthropology, no. 21.)
       $2.50.

2. Contemporary

a. North America

1593. Barnard, Chester Irving
   The functions of the executive. Cambridge, Mass., Harvard
   University Press, 1938, $5.50.

1594. Berle, Beatrice (Bishop)
   80 Puerto Rican families in New York City; health and
   disease studied in context. New York, Columbia University
   Press, 1958, $6.00.

1595. Burrows, Edwin Grant
   Hawaiian Americans, an account of the mingling of Japanese,
   Chinese, Polynesian, and American cultures. New Haven, Yale
   University Press, 1947. Out of print; ca. $4.00.

1596. Caudill, William A.
   Japanese-American personality and acculturation. Province-
   town, Mass., Journal Press, 1952. (Genetic Psychology Monographs, v. 45, 1st half.) In print? ca. $5.00.

1597. Davis, Allison, and John Dollard
   Children of bondage; the personality development of Negro
   youth in the urban South . . . prepared for the American youth
   Commission. Washington, D. C., American Council on Education,
   1940, $2.00.

1598. Davis, Allison, Burleigh B. Gardner, and Mary R. Gardner
   Deep south; a social anthropological study of caste and class
   . . . directed by W. Lloyd Warner. Chicago, University of
   Chicago Press, 1941, $8.00.

1599. Dollard, John
   Caste and class in a Southern town. 2d ed. New York, Harper,
   1949. Out of print.
   Paper: New York, Doubleday, 1957 (Anchor books, A95) $1.45.

1600. Drake, St. Clair, and Horace R. Cayton
   Black metropolis; a study of Negro life in a northern city
   . . . with an introduction by Richard Wright. New York, Harcourt,
   Brace, 1945, $6.75.

1601. Fey, Harold Edward, and D'Arcy McNickle
   Indians and other Americans; two ways of life meet. 1st ed.
   New York, Harper, 1959, $3.75.

1602. Gorer, Geoffrey
   The American people, a study in national character. London,
   Cresset Press, 1946, 12/6; New York, Norton, 1948, $3.95.
   London edition has title: The Americans.

1603.   Herskovits, Melville Jean
        The American Negro; a study in racial crossing. New York,
        Knopf, 1928. Out of print; ca. $4.00.

1604.   Herskovits, Melville Jean
        The myth of the Negro past. New York, London, Harper,
        1941. Out of print.
        Paper: Boston, Beacon Press, 1958. (Beacon Paperback no.
        69.) $2.25.

        Hsu, Francis L. K.
        Americans and Chinese: two ways of life. See no. 1176.

1605.   Hughes, Charles Campbell
        People of cove and woodlot; communities from the viewpoint
        of social psychiatry, by Charles C. Hughes and others. New
        York, Basic Books, 1960. (The Stirling County study of psychi-
        atric disorder and sociocultural environment, v. 2.) $10.00.

1606.   Junek, Oscar Waldemar
        Isolated communities; a study of a Labrador fishing village
        . . . foreword by Clark Wissler. New York, Cincinnati, Ameri-
        can Book, 1937. Out of print; ca. $5.00.

1607.   Kibbe, Pauline Rochester
        Latin Americans in Texas. Albuquerque, University of New
        Mexico Press, 1946. (New Mexico. University. School of Inter-
        American affairs. Inter-Americana Series. Studies, 3.) $1.75.

1608.   Kimball, Solon Toothaker, and Marion Pearsall
        The Talladega story; a study in community process. Univer-
        sity, University of Alabama Press, 1954, $3.50.

1609.   Leighton, Alexander Hamilton
        My name is legion; foundations for a theory of man in rela-
        tion to culture. New York, Basic Books, 1959. (The Stirling
        County study of psychiatric disorder and sociocultural environ-
        ment, v. 1.) $7.50.

1610.   Lewis, Hylan
        Blackways of Kent. Chapel Hill, University of North Carolina
        Press, 1955. (Field studies in the modern culture of the South.)
        $5.00.

1611.   Lynd, Robert Staughton, and Helen Merrell Lynd
        Middletown, a study in contemporary American culture . . .
        foreword by Clark Wissler. New York, Harcourt, Brace, 1929.
        Out of print.
        Paper: Middletown, a study in American culture. New York,
        Harcourt, Brace, 1959, c1956. (Harvest Books, HB-27.) $2.25.

1612.   Lynd, Robert Staughton, and Helen Merrell Lynd
        Middletown in transition; a study in cultural conflicts. New
        York, Harcourt, Brace, 1937, $6.00; text ed., $4.50.

Mandelbaum, David G.
Soldier groups and Negro soldiers. See no. 574.

1613.   Mead, Margaret
And keep your powder dry; an anthropologist looks at
America. New York, Morrow, 1942, $3.50.

Merton, Robert King
Social theory and social structure. See no. 174.

1614.   Miner, Horace Mitchell
Culture and agriculture; an anthropological study of corn-
belt country. Ann Arbor, University of Michigan Press, 1949.
(Michigan. University. Museum of Anthropology. Occasional
Contributions, no. 14.) $1.50.

1615.   Miner, Horace Mitchell
St. Denis; a French-Canadian parish. Chicago, University
of Chicago Press, 1939. Out of print; ca. $6.00.

1616.   Morland, John Kenneth
Millways of Kent. Chapel Hill, University of North Carolina
Press, 1958. (Field studies in the modern culture of the South.)
$5.00.

Parsons, Talcott
Essays in sociological theory. See no. 114.
The social system. See no. 115.

1617.   Parsons, Talcott
Structure and process in modern societies. Glencoe, Ill.,
Free Press, 1960, $6.00.

1618.   Pearsall, Marion
Little Smoky Ridge; the natural history of a southern Appala-
chian neighborhood. University, University of Alabama Press,
1959, $4.00.

1619.   Powdermaker, Hortense
After freedom; a cultural study in the Deep South. New
York, Viking, 1939. Out of print; ca. $5.00.

1620.   Powdermaker, Hortense
Hollywood, the dream factory; an anthropologist looks at the
movie-makers. Boston, Little, Brown, 1950. Out of print;
ca. $3.50.

Rohrer, John Harrison, and Munro S. Edmonson, eds.
The eighth generation: cultures and personalities of New
Orleans Negroes. See no. 353.

268

1621. Sasaki, Tom Taketo
       Fruitland, New Mexico: a Navaho community in transition.
       Ithaca, N. Y., Cornell University Press, 1960. (Cornell Studies
       in Anthropology.) $4.75.

1622. Veblen, Thorstein
       The theory of the leisure class; an economic study of insti-
       tutions . . . with a foreword by Stuart Chase. New York, The
       Modern Library, 1934. (The Modern Library of the World's
       Best Books, 63.) $1.95.
       Paper: New York, New American Library, 1954. (A Mentor
       Book, MD 93.) $0.50.

1623. Vidich, Arthur J., and Joseph Bensman
       Small town in mass society; class, power, and religion in a
       rural community. Princeton, Princeton University Press, 1958.
       Out of print; ca. $6.00.
       Paper: Garden City, N. Y., Doubleday, 1960 (A Doubleday
       Anchor Book, A216.) $1.45.

1624. Vogt, Evon Zartman
       Modern homesteaders; the life of a twentieth-century frontier
       community. Cambridge, Mass., Belknap Press of Harvard Uni-
       versity Press, 1955, $4.25.

1625. Warner, William Lloyd
       Democracy in Jonesville; a study in quality and inequality
       . . . with the collaboration of Wilfrid C. Bailey and others.
       New York, Harper, 1949, $4.50.

1626. Warner, William Lloyd
       The living and the dead; a study of the symbolic life of
       Americans. New Haven, Yale University Press, 1959. (Yankee
       City series, v. 5.) $7.50.

1627. Warner, William Lloyd, Marcia Meeker, and Kenneth Eells
       Social class in America, a manual of procedure for the
       measurement of social status. Chicago, Science Research
       Associates, 1949. Out of print; ca. $4.00.
       Paper: With a new essay, Theory and method for the com-
       parative study of social stratification, by W. Lloyd Warner.
       New York, Harper, 1960. (Harper Torchbooks, TB1013. The
       Academy library.) $1.60.

1628. Warner, William Lloyd, and Paul S. Lunt
       The social life of a modern community. New Haven, Yale
       University Press; London, H. Milford, Oxford University Press,
       1941. (Yankee City Series, v. 1.) $7.50.

1629. Warner, William Lloyd, and J. O. Low
       The social system of the modern factory. The strike: a social
       analysis. New Haven, Yale University Press, London, G. Cumber-
       lege, Oxford University Press, 1947. (Yankee City Series, v. 4.)
       $5.00.

1630. Warner, William Lloyd, and Leo Srole
       The social systems of American ethnic groups. New Haven,
Yale University Press; London, H. Milford, Oxford University
Press, 1945. (Yankee City Series, v. 3.) $6.00.

       Weber, Max
       From Max Weber: Essays in sociology. See no. 139.
       Protestant ethic and the spirit of capitalism. See no. 240.
       Theory of social and economic organization. See no. 140.

1631. Whyte, William Foote
       Street corner society; the social structure of an Italian slum.
Enl. (2d) ed. Chicago, University of Chicago Press, 1955, $5.00.
       Paper: Chicago, University of Chicago Press, 1961. (Phoenix
Books.) $1.95.

1632. Withers, Carl
       Plainville, U. S. A., by James West (pseud.) New York,
Columbia University Press, 1945, $3.75.

       b. Central America and Mexico

1633. Adams, Richard N.
       Cultural surveys of Panama—Nicaragua—Guatemala—El Salva-
dor—Honduras. Washington, Pan American Sanitary Bureau,
1957. (Pan American Sanitary Bureau. Scientific Publications,
no. 33.) $8.00.

1634. Bailey, Helen Miller
       Santa Cruz of the Etla Hills. Gainesville, University of
Florida Press, 1958, $6.00.

1635. Beals, Ralph Leon
       Cherán: a Sierra Tarascan village; prepared in coöperation
with the United States Department of State as a project of the Interdepartmental Committee on Cultural and Scientific Coöperation.
Washington, U. S. Govt. Print. Office, 1946. (Smithsonian Institution. Institute of Social Anthropology. Publication no. 2.) $0.70.

1636. Bennett, Wendell Clark, and Robert M. Zingg
       The Tarahumara, an Indian tribe of northern Mexico. Chicago,
University of Chicago Press, 1935. Out of print; ca. $6.00.

1637. Biesanz, John Berry, and Mavis Biesanz
       Costa Rican life. New York, Columbia University Press,
1944, $3.75.

1638. Biesanz, John Berry, and Mavis Biesanz
       The people of Panama. New York, Columbia University Press,
1955, $6.75.

1639.   Brand, Donald Dilworth
        Quiroga, a Mexican municipio . . . assisted by José Corona
Nuñez, prepared in coöperation with the U. S. Dept. of State as
a project of the Interdepartmental Committee on Scientific and
Cultural Coöperation. Washington, U. S. Govt. Print. Office,
1951. (Smithsonian Institution. Institute of Social Anthropology.
Publication no. 11.) $1.75.

1640.   Bunzel, Ruth Leah
        Chichicastenango; a Guatemalan village. Locust Valley, N. Y.,
Augustin, 1952. (Publications of the American Ethnological
Society, 22.) $7.00.

        Foster, George McClelland
        Culture and conquest: America's Spanish heritage.   See no.
362.

1641.   Foster, George McClelland
        Empire's children; the people of Tzintzuntzan . . . assisted
by Gabriel Ospina. Mexico, Impr. Nuevo Mundo, 1948. (Smithsonian Institution. Institute of Social Anthropology. Publication
no. 6.) No price; ca. $2.00.

1642.   Foster, George McClelland
        A primitive Mexican economy. New York, Augustin, 1942.
(Monographs of the American Ethnological Society, 5.) Out of
print; ca. $3.00.

1643.   Gillin, John Philip
        The culture of security in San Carlos; a study of a Guate-
malan community of Indians and Ladinos. New Orleans, 1951.
(Tulane University of Louisiana. Middle American Research
Institute. Publication no. 16.) $4.00.

1644.   La Farge, Oliver
        Santa Eulalia: the religion of a Cuchumatán Indian town.
Chicago, University of Chicago Press, 1947. Out of print; ca.
$4.00.

1645.   Leslie, Charles M.
        Now we are civilized; a study of the world view of the Zapo-
tec Indians of Mitla, Oaxaca. Detroit, Wayne State University
Press, 1960, $3.95.

1646.   Lewis, Oscar
        Five families; Mexican case studies in the culture of poverty.
With a foreword by Oliver La Farge. New York, Basic Books,
1959, $5.50.

1647.   Lewis, Oscar
        Life in a Mexican village: Tepoztlan restudied; with drawings
by Alberto Beltran. Urbana, University of Illinois Press, 1951,
$7.50.

1648. Lewis, Oscar
       Tepoztlán, village in Mexico. New York, Holt, 1960. (Case
       Studies in Cultural Anthropology.) $1.75; text ed., $1.25.

1649. Madsen, William
       The Virgin's children; life in an Aztec village today. Austin,
       University of Texas Press, 1960, $4.50.

1650. Nash, Manning
       Machine age Maya: the industrialization of a Guatemalan
       community. Glencoe, Ill., Free Press, 1958, $5.00.
       Also published as American Anthropological Association
       Memoir, no. 87.

1651. Parra, Manuel Germán, and Wigberto Jiménez Moreno
       Bibliografía indígenista de México y Centroamérica (1850-
       1950). México, Instituto Nacional Indígenista, 1954. (Memorias
       del Instituto Nacional Indígenista, v. 4.) Estimate: $4.00.

1652. Parsons, Mrs. Elsie Worthington (Clews)
       Mitla, town of souls, and other Zapoteco-speaking pueblos of
       Oaxaca, Mexico. Chicago, University of Chicago Press, 1936.
       Out of print; ca. $5.00.

1653. Redfield, Robert
       The folk culture of Yucatan. Chicago, University of Chicago
       Press, 1941, $7.50.

1654. Redfield, Robert
       Tepoztlan, a Mexican village; a study of folk life. Chicago,
       University of Chicago Press, 1930, $6.50.

1655. Redfield, Robert
       A village that chose progress; Chan Kom revisited. Chicago,
       University of Chicago Press, 1950, $4.00.

1656. Stanislawski, Dan
       The anatomy of eleven towns in Michoacán. Austin, Univer-
       sity of Texas Press, 1950. (Latin-American Studies, 10.) No
       price; estimate: $2.00.

1657. Tax, Sol
       Heritage of conquest; the ethnology of Middle America, by
       Sol Tax and members of the Viking Fund seminar on Middle
       American Ethnology held in New York City, Aug. 28 through
       Sept. 3, 1949. Glencoe, Ill., Free Press, 1952, $5.00.

1658. Tax, Sol
       Penny capitalism: a Guatemalan Indian economy. Washington,
       U. S. Govt. Print. Office, 1953. (Smithsonian Institution. Institute
       of Social Anthropology. Publication no. 16.) $1.75.

Toor, Frances
A treasury of Mexican folkways. See no. 303.

1659. Tumin, Melvin Marvin
Caste in a peasant society; a case study in the dynamics of caste. Princeton, Princeton University Press, 1952, $5.00.

1660. Wagley, Charles
Economics of the Guatemalan village. Menasha, Wis., American Anthropological Association, 1941. (American Anthropological Association. Memoirs, no. 58.) Out of print; ca. $3.00.

1661. Wagley, Charles
The social and religious life in a Guatemalan village. Menasha, Wis., 1959. (American Anthropological Association. Memoirs, no. 71.) $2.25.

1662. West, Robert Cooper
Cultural geography of the modern Tarascan area. Prepared in coöperation with the United States Dept. of State as a project of the Interdepartmental Committee on Scientific and Cultural Coöperation. Washington, U. S. Govt. Print. Office, 1948. (Smithsonian Institution. Institute of Social Anthropology. Publication no. 7.) $0.75.

1663. Whetten, Nathan Laselle
Rural Mexico; with a foreword by Manuel Gamio. Chicago, University of Chicago Press, 1948, $11.50.

1664. Wisdom, Charles
The Chorti Indians of Guatemala. Chicago, University of Chicago Press, 1940. Out of print; ca. $6.00.

c. South America

1665. Adams, Richard N.
A community in the Andes; problems and progress in Muquiyauyo. Seattle, University of Washington Press, 1959. (American Ethnological Society Publication.) $4.75.

1666. Azevedo, Fernando de
Brazilian culture; an introduction to the study of culture in Brazil; translated by William Rex Crawford. New York, Macmillan, 1950, $15.00.

1667. Bolinder, Gustaf
Indians on horseback. London, Dobson, 1957, 25/-.

1668. Collier, John, and Aníbal Buitrón
The awakening valley. Chicago, University of Chicago Press,
1949. Out of print; ca. $6.00.
(A photographic record of the Indians of the Otavalo Valley
in Ecuador.)

1669. Eduardo, Octavio da Costa
The Negro in northern Brazil; a study in acculturation. New
York, Augustin, 1948. (American Ethnological Society. Mono-
graphs, 15.) $2.75.

1670. Fals-Borda, Orlando
Peasant society in the Colombian Andes: a sociological study
of Saucío. Gainesville, University of Florida Press, 1955, $5.00.

1671. Ford, Thomas R.
Man and land in Peru. Gainesville, University of Florida
Press, 1955, $4.00.

1672. Freyre, Gilberto
New world in the tropics; the culture of modern Brazil.
New York, Knopf, 1959, $5.00.
Expanded and completely rewritten version of the author's
Brazil: an interpretation.

1673. Fujii, Yukio, and T. Lynn Smith
The acculturation of the Japanese immigrants in Brazil.
Gainesville, University of Florida Press, 1959. (Latin American
Monographs, 8.) No price.

1674. Gillin, John Philip
Moche; a Peruvian coastal community. Washington, U. S.
Govt. Print. Office, 1947. (Smithsonian Institution. Institute of
Social Anthropology. Publication no. 3.) $1.00.

1675. Harris, Marvin
Town and country in Brazil. New York, Columbia University
Press, 1956. (Columbia University Contributions to Anthropology,
no. 37.) $4.50.

1676. Henry, Jules
Jungle people, a Kaingáng tribe of the highlands of Brazil.
New York, Augustin, 1941. Out of print; ca. $4.00.

1677. Herskovits, Melville Jean, and Frances S. Herskovits
Rebel destiny; among the bush Negroes of Dutch Guiana.
New York and London, Whittlesey House, McGraw-Hill, 1934.
Out of print; ca. $4.00.

1678. Hutchinson, Harry William
Village and plantation life in northeastern Brazil. Seattle,
University of Washington Press, 1957. (American Ethnological
Society Publication.) $3.50.

1679. La Barre, Weston
        The Aymara Indians of the Lake Titicaca Plateau, Bolivia.
Menasha, Wis., 1948. (American Anthropological Association.
Memoirs, no. 68.) Out of print; ca. $3.50.

1680. Leonard, Olen Earl
        Bolivia; land, people, and institutions. Washington, Scare-
crow Press, 1952. Out of print; ca. $5.00.

1681. Leonard, Olen E., and Charles P. Loomis, eds.
        Readings in Latin American social organization and institu-
tions. East Lansing, Area Research Center, Michigan State
College Press, 1953, $5.00.

1682. Murphy, Robert Francis
        Headhunter's heritage; social and economic change among the
Mundurucú Indians. Berkeley and Los Angeles, University of
California Press, 1960, $5.00.

        Murphy, Robert Francis
        Mundurucú religion. See no. 223.

1683. Osborne, Harold
        Indians of the Andes; Aymaras and Quechas. London, Rout-
ledge & Kegan Paul, 1952. (International Library of Sociology
and Social Reconstruction.) £1/15/-; Cambridge, Mass., Harvard
University Press, 1952. Out of print.

1684. Parsons, Elsie Worthington (Clews)
        Peguche, canton of Otavalo, province of Imbabura, Ecuador;
a study of Andean Indians. Chicago, University of Chicago Press,
1945. Out of print; ca. $4.00.

1685. Pierson, Donald
        Negroes in Brazil, a study of race contact at Bahia.
Chicago, University of Chicago Press, 1942. Out of print; ca.
$5.00.

1686. Ramos, Arthur
        The Negro in Brazil . . . translated from the Portuguese by
Richard Pattee. Washington, D. C., Associated Publishers, 1939,
$4.25.

1687. Service, Elman R., and Helen S. Service
        Tobatí: Paraguayan town. Chicago, University of Chicago
Press, 1954, $7.00.

1688. Smith, Raymond Thomas
        The Negro family in British Guiana; family structure and
social status in the villages. With a foreword by Meyer Fortes.
London, Routledge & Kegan Paul in association with the Institute
of Social and Economic Research, University College of the

West Indies, Jamaica, 1956. (International Library of Sociology
and Social Reconstruction.) £1/8/-.
U. S. distributor: New York, Humanities Press, $6.00.

1689.   Smith, Thomas Lynn
Brazil; people and institutions. Rev. ed. Baton Rouge,
Louisiana State University Press, 1954, $7.50.

1690.   Smith, Thomas Lynn, and Alexander Marchant, eds.
Brazil, portrait of half a continent. New York, Dryden Press,
1951. Out of print; ca. $6.00.

1691.   Titiev, Mischa
Araucanian culture in transition. Ann Arbor, University of
Michigan Press, 1951. (Michigan. University. Museum of
Anthropology. Occasional contributions, no. 15.) $2.50.

1692.   Tschopik, Harry
The Aymara of Chucuito, Peru. New York, 1951-
(Anthropological papers of the American Museum of Natural
History, v. 44, pt. 2.)
Contents: v. 1, Magic. $3.00.

1693.   Wagley, Charles
Amazon town; a study of man in the tropics. New York,
Macmillan, 1953, $5.00.

1694.   Wagley, Charles, and Marvin Harris
Minorities in the new world; six case studies. New York,
Columbia University Press, 1958, $6.00.

1695.   Wagley, Charles, ed.
Race and class in rural Brazil. Photos. by Pierre Verger.
Paris, UNESCO, 1952. Out of print; ca. $3.00.

1696.   Wagley, Charles, and Eduardo Galvão
The Tenetehara Indians of Brazil, a culture in transition.
New York, Columbia University Press, 1949. (Columbia Uni-
versity Contributions to Anthropology, no. 35.) $3.75.

1697.   Willems, Emilio, and Gioconda Mussolini
Buzios Island: a Caiçara community in southern Brazil.
Locust Valley, N. Y., Augustin, 1952. (Monographs of the
American Ethnological Society, 20.) $2.75.
Distributor: University of Washington Press, Seattle.

d. West Indies

1698.   American Association for the Advancement of Science
Caribbean studies; a symposium, edited by Vera Rubin. 2d
ed. Seattle, University of Washington, 1960, $3.00.

1699.   Beckwith, Martha Warren
        Black roadways; a study of Jamaican folk-life. Chapel Hill,
        The University of North Carolina Press, 1929. Out of print;
        ca. $5.00.

1700.   Clarke, Edith
        My mother who fathered me; a study of the family in three
        selected communities in Jamaica. With a preface by Hugh Foot.
        London, Allen & Unwin, 1957, 18/-.
        U. S. distributor: New York, Humanities Press, $3.75.

1701.   De Young, Maurice
        Man and land in the Haitian economy. Gainesville, University
        of Florida Press, 1958. (Latin American Monographs, no. 3.)
        Out of print; ca. $2.00.

1702.   Henriques, Fernando
        Family and colour in Jamaica. With a preface by Meyer Fortes.
        London, Eyre & Spottiswoode, 1953, 18/-.

1703.   Herskovits, Melville Jean
        Life in a Haitian valley. New York, London, Knopf, 1937.
        Out of print; ca. $5.00.

1704.   Herskovits, Melville Jean, and Frances S. Herskovits
        Trinidad village. New York, Knopf, 1947. Out of print; ca.
        $5.00.

1705.   Hill, Reuben, J. Mayone Stycos, and Kurt W. Back
        The family and population control; a Puerto Rican experiment
        in social change. Chapel Hill, University of North Carolina
        Press, 1959, $8.00.

1706.   Kerr, Madeline
        Personality and conflict in Jamaica. Liverpool, Liverpool
        University Press, 1952, 15/-.

1707.   Landy, David
        Tropical childhood; cultural transmission and learning in a
        rural Puerto Rican village. Chapel Hill, University of North
        Carolina Press, 1959, $6.00.

1708.   Leyburn, James Graham
        The Haitian people. New Haven, Yale University Press; Lon-
        don, H. Milford, Oxford University Press, 1941, $5.00.

1709.   Metraux, Alfred
        Haiti: black peasants and voodoo. Photos. by Pierre Verger
        and Alfred Metraux. Translated from the French by Peter
        Lengyel. 1st American ed. New York, Universe, 1960, $8.50.

1710.   Metraux, Alfred
          Voodoo in Haiti. Translated by Hugo Charteris. London,
        A. Deutsch, 1959, 30/-; New York, Oxford University Press,
        1959, $6.50.

1711.   Mintz, Sidney W., comp.
          Papers in Caribbean anthropology. New Haven, published
        for the Dept. of Anthropology, Yale University, 1960. (Yale
        University. Publications in Anthropology, no. 57-64.) $3.50.

1712.   Nelson, Lowry
          Rural Cuba. Minneapolis, University of Minnesota Press,
        1950, $3.50.

1713.   Steward, Julian Haynes
          The people of Puerto Rico; a study in social anthropology.
        Urbana, University of Illinois Press, 1956. Out of print; ca.
        $10.00.

1714.   Zayas Alvarado, Eustaquio
          Worker in the cane; a Puerto Rican life history, by Sidney
        W. Mintz. New Haven, Yale University Press, 1960. (Caribbean
        Series, 2.) $5.00.
          The life story of Eustaquio Zayas Alvarado as told to Sid-
        ney W. Mintz.

Index to Book List

Bosi, Roberto
  The Lapps, 638
Bott, Elizabeth
  Family and social network, 162
Boule, Marcellin
  Fossil men, 498
Bovill, E. W.
  Golden trade of the Moors, 676
Bowen, Elenore Smith
  Return to laughter, 805
Bowen, Harold
  Islamic society and the west,
  710
Bowers, Alfred W.
  Mandan social and ceremonial
  organization, 1392
Boyd, William C.
  Genetics and the races of man,
  478
  Races and people, 479
Bradford, John
  Ancient landscapes, 407
Braidwood, Robert J.
  The Near East and the founda-
  tions for civilization, 677
  Prehistoric men, 381
Brainerd, George W.
  The ancient Maya, 1517
  Archaeological ceramics of
  Yucatan, 1495
  Maya civilization, 1496
Brand, Donald D.
  Quiroga, 1639
Brandt, Richard B.
  Hopi ethics, 1434
Brelsford, William V.
  Tribes of Northern Rhodesia,
  902
Breuil, Henri
  Beyond the bounds of history,
  382
  Four hundred centuries of cave
  art, 250
  Les hommes de la pierre ancienne,
  383
Brew, John O.
  Archaeology of Alkali Ridge,
  1383
Briggs, Lloyd C.
  Tribes of the Sahara, 678
Britton, Nancy P.
  East of the sun, 1077
Bronsted, Johannes
  The Vikings, 599

Broom, Robert
  South African fossil ape-man,
  the Australopithecinae, 499
  Sterkfontein ape-man Plesi-
  anthropus, 500
  Swartkrans ape-man, Paran-
  thropus crassidens, 501
Brown, G. Gordon
  Anthropology in action, 565
Brown, Roger W.
  Words and things, 440
Bruce, Alexander M.
  Anthropology in action, 565
Bryant, Alfred T.
  The Zulu people, as they were
  before the white man came,
  926
Buck, Sir Peter H.
  Coming of the Maori, 1229
  Vikings of the Pacific, 1230
  Vikings of the sunrise, 1230
Budge, Sir Ernest A. T. W.
  History of Ethiopia, 839
Buitron, Anibal
  The awakening valley, 1668
Bunak, Viktor V.
  Contributions to the physical
  anthropology of the Soviet
  Union, 965
Bunzel, Ruth L.
  Chichicastenango, 1640
  Golden age of American anthro-
  pology, 59
  Pueblo potter, 306
Burgh, Robert F.
  Archaeology of Castle Park,
  1384
Burnham, Robert E.
  Who are the Finns? 600
Burrows, Edwin G.
  An Atoll culture, 1231
  Hawaiian Americans, 1595
Bushnell, Geoffrey H. S.
  Ancient American pottery, 307
  Archaeology of the Santa Elena
  Peninsula, 1543
  Peru, 1544
Busia, Kofi A.
  Position of the chief in . . .
  Ashanti, 806
Butt, Audrey
  Nilotes of the Anglo-Egyptian
  Sudan and Uganda, 840

Clark, Ella E.
  Indian legends of the Pacific
    Northwest, 287
Clark, J. Desmond
  Prehistoric cultures of the Horn
    of Africa, 841
  Prehistory of southern Africa,
    928
  Proceedings of the 3rd Pan
    African Congress on Pre-
    history, 793
  Stone age cultures of Northern
    Rhodesia, 903
Clark, John Graham Douglas
  Archeology and society, 386
  Excavations at Star Carr, 589
  Mesolithic age in Britain, 590
  Mesolithic settlement of north-
    ern Europe, 601
  Prehistoric Europe; the eco-
    nomic basis, 584
Clark, Margaret
  Health in the Mexican-American
    culture, 566
Clark, Sir Wilfrid E. Le Gros
  Antecedents of man, 504
  Essays on growth and form, 554
  Fossil evidence for human evo-
    lution, 505
  Foundations of human evolution,
    506
  History of the primates, 507
Clarke, Bryan C.
  Berber village, 683
Clarke, Edith
  My mother who fathered me, 1700
Clawson, Hamilton P.
  By their works, 253
Cline, Walter B.
  Notes on the people of Siwah and
    El Garah, 684
Codere, Helen
  Fighting with property, 1359
Codrington, Robert H.
  The Melanesians, 1232
Cohen, Jerome B.
  Japan's economy in war and re-
    construction, 1151
Cohen, Marcel
  Les Langues du monde, 465
Coker, G. B. A.
  Family property among the
    Yoruba, 808

Cold Spring Harbor, N. Y. Biologi-
  cal Laboratory
  Origin and evolution of man, 508
  Population genetics, 544
Cole, Fay-Cooper
  Kincaid, 1412
  Peoples of Malaysia, 1079
Cole, Sonia M.
  Early man in East Africa, 842
  Prehistory of East Africa, 843
Collier, John
  The awakening valley, 1668
  Patterns and ceremonials of the
    Indians of the Southwest, 1438
Collinder, Björn
  The Lapps, 639
Collins, Henry B.
  Arctic area, 1332
Colson, Elizabeth
  The Makah Indians, 1360
  Marriage and the family among
    the Plateau Tonga, 904
  Seven tribes of British Central
    Africa, 905
  Social organization of the Gwembe
    Tonga, 906
Comas, Juan
  Bibliografía selectiva de las cul-
    turas indígenas de América,
    1300
  Manual of physical anthropology,
    480
Concise encyclopedia of archaeology,
  387
Condliffe, John B.
  New Zealand in the making, 1233
Conference on Archeological Field
  and Laboratory Techniques, New
  York, 1950
  Essays on archaeological methods,
    409
Conference on Traditional Cultures,
  Ceylon University, 1956
  Some aspects of traditional Sin-
    halese culture, 985
Conklin, Harold C.
  Hanunóo agriculture, 1080
Contenau, Georges
  Everyday life in Babylon and
    Assyria, 685
Cook, Sherburne F.
  Application of quantitative methods
    in archaeology, 420

Dale, Edward E.
    The Indians of the Southwest,
        1441
Daniel, Glyn E.
    A hundred years of archeology,
        388
    The megalith builders of western
        Europe, 591
    The three ages, 414
Dart, Raymond A.
    The osteodontokeratic culture
        of Australopithecus pro-
        metheus, 509
Darwin, Charles R.
    The origin of species, 510
Davies, Cuthbert C.
    Historical atlas of the Indian
        peninsula, 987
Davis, Allison
    Children of bondage, 1597
    Deep south, 1598
Davis, Kingsley
    Population of India and Pakistan,
        988
Day, Lal Behari
    see Lalavihari De
De Bary, William T.
    Sources of Chinese tradition,
        1155
    Sources of Indian tradition, 989
    Sources of Japanese tradition,
        1209
Debo, Angie
    The road to disappearance,
        1427
de Laguna, Frederica
    Chugach prehistory, 1333
    The Eyak Indians of the Copper
        river delta, 1329
    Selected papers from the
        American Anthropologist,
        1888-1920, 47
    Story of a Tlingit community,
        1361
Delavignette, Robert L.
    Freedom and authority in
        French West Africa, 809
Dennis, Norman
    Coal is our life, 622
Dennis, Wayne
    The Hopi child,. 320
De Planhol, Xavier
    see Planhol, Xavier de

Desai, Akshayakumar R.
    Rural sociology in India, 990
De Terra, Helmut
    Man and mammoth in Mexico,
        1503
    Studies on the ice age in India,
        389
Devereux, George
    Reality and dream, 321
De Vos, George
    Oasis and casbah, 738
Dey, Lal Behari
    see Lalavihari De
De Young, John E.
    Village life in modern Thailand,
        1083
De Young, Maurice
    Man and land in the Haitian
        economy, 1701
Diamond, Arthur S.
    Primitive law, 183
Diamond, Stanley
    Culture in history, 51
Diaz del Castillo, Bernal
    Discovery and conquest of
        Mexico, 1504
Dickson, Harold R. P.
    Kuwait and her neighbors, 692
Digby, Adrian
    Ancient American pottery, 307
Di Peso, Charles C.
    The Reeve ruin, 1442
    Sobaipuri Indians of the Upper
        San Pedro River Valley, 1443
    Upper Pima of San Cayetano del
        Tumacacori, 1444
Diringer, David
    The alphabet, 443
Dixon, Roland Burrage
    The building of cultures, 89
Djamour, Judith
    Malay kinship and marriage in
        Singapore, 1084
Dobzhansky, Theodosius G.
    Evolution, genetics, and man,
        483
    Genetics and the origin of
        species, 546
    Heredity, race, and society,
        484
    Radiation, genes, and man, 553
Dockstader, Frederick J.
    Indian art in America, 254

Howard, George D.
  Archeological survey of
    Venezuela, 1567
Howell, Paul P.
  A manual of Nuer law, 192
Howells, William W.
  Early man in the Far East, 512
  The heathens, 211
  Mankind in the making, 518
Hrdlička, Aleš
  Aleutian and Commander islands,
    1338
  Anthropology of Kodiak island,
    1339
  Practical anthropometry, 487
Hsu, Francis L. K.
  Americans and Chinese, 1176
  Aspects of culture and personal-
    ity, 333
  Psychological anthropology, 334
  Religion, science, and human
    crisis, 1177
  Under the ancestor's shadow,
    1178
Hu, Chang-tu
  China, 1179
Hu, Hsien-chin
  Common descent group in China,
    1180
Hudson, Alfred E.
  Kazak social structure, 970
Hughes, Charles C.
  People of cove and woodlot, 1605
Hughes, Everett C.
  Race: individual and collective
    behavior, 133
Human Biology, 16
Human Organization, 17
Human Problems in British Central
  Africa, 25
Human Relations Area Files
  Laos, 1108
  North Borneo, Brunei, Sarawak,
    1109
Hunter, Monica
  see Wilson, Monica (Hunter)
Huntingford, George W. B.
  The Galla of Ethiopia, 859
  The Nandi of Kenya, 860
  Southern Nilo-Hamites, 861
Hurgronje, Christian Snouck
  The Achehnese, 1110

Hutchinson, Harry W.
  Village and plantation life in north-
    eastern Brazil, 1678
Hutton, John Henry
  The Angami Nagas, 1014
  Caste in India, 1015
  Sema Nagas, 1016
Huxley, Francis
  Affable savages, 1554
Huxley, Thomas H.
  Man's place in nature, 519
Hyde, George E.
  Indians of the High Plains, 1400
  Red Cloud's folk, 1401
  A Sioux chronicle, 1402
Ikram, Sheikh M.
  Cultural heritage of Pakistan,
    1017
India's villages, 1054
Ingrams, William H.
  Zanzibar, 862
Interdisciplinary conference, New
  York, 1947
  Culture and personality, 335
International African Institute
  African worlds, 785
  Methods of study of culture con-
    tact in Africa, 366
  Select annotated bibliography of
    tropical Africa, 786
  Social implications of industrializa-
    tion and urbanization in Africa,
    south of the Sahara, 787
International Bibliography of Social
  and Cultural Anthropology, 32
International Journal of American
  Linguistics, 18
International Symposium on Anthro-
  pology, New York, 1952
  Anthropology today, 55
  An appraisal of anthropology to-
    day, 56
Introduction to the civilization of
  India, 984
Inverarity, Robert B.
  Art of the Northwest Coast
    Indians, 263
Izikowitz, Karl G.
  Lamet, 1111
Jacobs, Melville
  Content and style of an oral
    literature, 291

314

REXFORD S. BECKHAM

Wagner, Günter
The Bantu of North Kavirondo, 894
Wallace, Anthony
Culture and society, 355
Wallace, Bruce
Radiation, genes, and man, 553
Wallace, Ernest
The Comanches, 1409
Wallis, Wilson D.
Messiahs, 237
The Micmac Indians of eastern Canada, 1422
Religion in primitive society, 238
Walter, H. V.
Pre-history of the Lagoa Santa region, Minas Gerais, 1580
Warner, William L.
Black civilization, 1288
Democracy in Jonesville, 1625
The living and the dead, 1626
Social class in America, 1627
Social life of a modern community, 1628
Social system of the modern factory, 1629
Social systems of American ethnic groups, 1630
Warriner, Doreen
Land and poverty in the Middle East, 764
Land reform and development in the Middle East, 765
Watson, William
Tribal cohesion in a money economy, 923
Wauchope, Robert
Seminars in archaeology, 429
Weber, Max
Ancient Judaism, 239
From Max Weber: Essays in sociology, 139
Protestant ethic and the spirit of capitalism, 240
Religion of China, 241
Religion of India, 242
Theory of social and economic organization, 140
Weidenreich, Franz
Apes, giants and man, 538
Giant early man from Java and south China, 539

Morphology of Solo man, 540
Shorter anthropological papers, 541
Skull of Sinanthropus pekinensis, 542
Weiner, Joseph S.
The Piltdown forgery, 543
Weinreich, Uriel
Languages in contact, 475
Linguistics today, 464
Wells, Kenneth E.
Thai Buddhism, 1134
Wendorf, Fred
The Midland discovery, 1410
Wenner-Gren Foundation for Anthropological Research, New York
Papers on the physical anthropology of the American Indian, 1306
Wertheim, Willem F.
Indonesian society in transition, 1135
West, Carl
see Withers, Carl
West, Rebecca
Black lamb and grey falcon, 654
West, Robert C.
Cultural geography of the modern Tarascan area, 1662
Westermann, Diedrich
The African today and tomorrow, 797
Geschichte Afrikas, 798
Les peuples et les civilizations de l'Afrique, 780
Westermarck, Edvard A.
Marriage ceremonies in Morocco, 766
Ritual and belief in Morocco, 767
Wit and wisdom in Morocco, 768
Weyer, Edward M.
The Eskimos, 1344
Primitive peoples today, 141
Whatmough, Joshua
The foundations of Roman Italy, 614
Wheeler, Sir R. E. Mortimer
Archaeology from the earth, 433
Early India and Pakistan, 1061
The Indus civilization, 1062
Whetten, Nathan L.
Rural Mexico, 1663